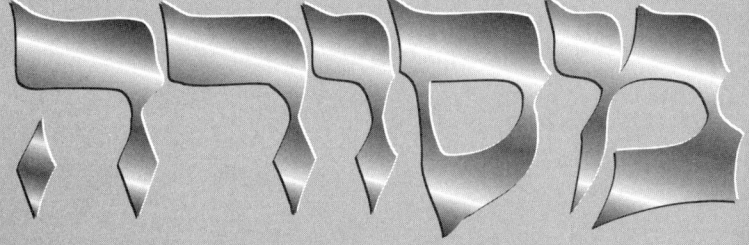

ArtScroll Series®

Rabbi Nosson Scherman / Rabbi Meir Zlotowitz
General Editors

Mountain

Published by
Me'sorah Publications, ltd

Climbers

Inspirational stories of real people overcoming life's challenges

MALKY FEIG

FIRST EDITION
First Impression ... November 2007

Published and Distributed by
MESORAH PUBLICATIONS, LTD.
4401 Second Avenue / Brooklyn, N.Y 11232

Distributed in Europe by
LEHMANNS
Unit E, Viking Business Park
Rolling Mill Road
Jarow, Tyne & Wear, NE32 3DP
England

Distributed in Australia and New Zealand by
GOLDS WORLDS OF JUDAICA
3-13 William Street
Balaclava, Melbourne 3183
Victoria, Australia

Distributed in Israel by
SIFRIATI / A. GITLER — BOOKS
6 Hayarkon Street
Bnei Brak 51127

Distributed in South Africa by
KOLLEL BOOKSHOP
Ivy Common
105 William Road
Norwood 2192, Johannesburg, South Africa

ARTSCROLL SERIES®
MOUNTAIN CLIMBERS
© Copyright 2007, by MESORAH PUBLICATIONS, Ltd.
4401 Second Avenue / Brooklyn, N.Y. 11232 / (718) 921-9000 / www.artscroll.com

---

ALL RIGHTS RESERVED
The text, prefatory and associated textual contents and introductions
— including the typographic layout, cover artwork and ornamental graphics —
have been designed, edited and revised as to content, form and style.

No part of this book may be reproduced
IN ANY FORM, PHOTOCOPYING, OR COMPUTER RETRIEVAL SYSTEMS
— even for personal use without written permission from
the copyright holder, Mesorah Publications Ltd.
except by a reviewer who wishes to quote brief passages
in connection with a review written for inclusion in magazines or newspapers.

THE RIGHTS OF THE COPYRIGHT HOLDER WILL BE STRICTLY ENFORCED.

---

*To contact the author with stories or comments, she can be reached
via e-mail at mountclimbers@neto.bezeqint.net*

ISBN:
ISBN 10: 1-4226-0592-2 / ISBN 13: 978-1-4226-0592-9 (hard cover)
ISBN 10: 1-4226-0593-0 / ISBN 13: 978-1-4226-0593-6 (paperback)

Typography by CompuScribe at ArtScroll Studios, Ltd.
Printed in the United States of America by Noble Book Press Corp.
Bound by Sefercraft, Quality Bookbinders, Ltd., Brooklyn N.Y. 11232

Dedication

When I pictured the cover of this book,
The image of you,
Zeidy,
Came to mind.
The fire in your eyes
Dancing Heavenward,
Your weathered hands
Reaching skyward,
Faithful legs
Forever climbing
upward,
The Ultimate Mountain Climber,
You rose to your challenges
With such equanimity
And grace,

It almost didn't seem
You were struggling,
Blazed a path,
With such vibrancy,
And vigor,
It almost didn't seem
You were climbing,
Your name, **Tovya**,
Captured your essence,
Ki **tov Hashem**.
Neither tiredness,
Nor age,
could get you to falter.
It was
Geloibt der Aibeshter
All the way up
until your very last step.
Zeidy,
You began
The hundredth *kapitel*
The song that was your life,
Mizmor l'soda,
And if I listen,
I can almost hear you
Completing it on High,
Your missive, your secret,
To all of us still climbing,
Ki tov Hashem l'olam chasdo
V'ad dor vador emunaso.

לעילוי נשמת
הרה"ח ר' יהושוע אהרן טובי'ה בן הרה"ח ר' מנחם מנדל
נלבע ב' סיון תשס"ז, ת.נ.צ.ב.ה

Acknowledgments

As a young reader, I generally viewed the acknowledgments section as an unofficial invitation to flip ahead. I was too impatient to get to the heart of the book to wade through a citation of accolades addressed to a list of unfamiliar individuals.

Coming from the other side, I see these acknowledgments as a welcome invitation to flip backward. I am in no rush to surge ahead — the heart of this book, like my own, is thoroughly predictable and familiar to me — and I relish this chance to be able to pay tribute, if only in the most modest way, to the list of dear and cherished individuals who made it happen. This book, after all, and everything that stands behind it, Is a composite of many, many individuals, their love and dedication, patience, honesty, and perseverance. So I indulge, even at the risk of readers skipping ahead ...

To my parents, my strongholds in life, who have outfitted me with the attitude and the tools to see life as a challenge to rise. My earliest memories are of the *maamarei Chazal* hanging over the dinette table, my father's and my mother's spontaneous songs (*Chacham lev yikach mitzvos! kol rega she'adam chosem piv ... zocheh l'or haganuz*) prodding us to reach beyond our limitations and aim for higher, purer planes.

Parents, by virtue of their job description, cannot stand on a pedestal. As children, we see them in their most vulnerable moments (for which, regrettably, we sometimes bear more than a measure of responsibility) and we get the closest glimpse of their frailties. I have seen, and I have absorbed. My admiration knows no bounds.

To my in-laws, whose lives have so enriched mine, and who have demonstrated time and again the power of love and dedication to spur growth in children, even grown children. For the genuine interest, the listening ear, and the gift of your wholehearted confidence in all of our endeavors.

There are few lessons in mountain climbing as potent as watching someone synthesize the often conflicting concepts of uphill and upbeat. Your unaffected ability to appreciate children and fun, your genuine enjoyment in giving, and your talent of intuiting other people's needs leaves me inspired and aspiring.

To my dearest Babi, wise in spirit and young at heart, for giving us such special roots from which to draw strength. For the toys and robes and meat *l'kavod* Yom Tov. For the praise, the pride, and the potato *kugel* (handgrated!), and the determination and devotion with which it sizzles. May you have continued *nachas* from all of us.

To Savta, a seasoned climber, who has scaled much adversity in her life. For the wisdom and the wit, the stories of Siberia, and the unflinching *emunah* you've imparted to the next generation. I'll never forget the way you taught me to hang my linens and sent care packages of your homemade treats all the way from Chaifa. May you have the strength to keep climbing and reaping *nachas* from us.

To my sisters, my lifelines, who have kept me from tumbling backward more times than I can remember. For the black-and-white cookies and the poster projects, for faithfully guarding secrets and running errands, for always being there behind me and in front of me and alongside me, picking up the loose ends. If I were to return all the parts of me that were originally your contribution, there would be frighteningly little left of me.

To my brothers, each of them unique and special, who have a continued influence on me. For the understanding and the unconcealed pride, for remembering me despite your hectic schedules (for birthday calls, emergency succah service, and impromptu visits). Siblings are like bookmarks; they occupy a special place in your life story and they are always there for you, ready to pick up where you left off.

And to my sisters-in-law, each one individually, who have added so much richness and dimension to my life. For the refreshing perspectives, the meaningful conversations, for the personal joy you feel in my success and the heartfelt interest and empathy through the bumps and hills in my life. (And for meals, cakes, basement-hosting, short-term child-care, and the list goes on ....)

To my closest friends whom I owe so much of what I am and aspire to be. Each of you deserves individual mention; it is my hope that you will read between the lines the way you always do. For accompanying me up all my big and little mountains while valiantly trying to scale your own. For sharing and caring and baring your souls and letting me do the same. For your time and devotion, your insight and understanding, your words and your silence. Family is born into, friends are acquired by choice. Your faith in me touches and obligates me.

To a very dear and cherished friend, Gittel Bender. If there is someone who could teach about climbing with grace, it is you, Gittel. May you always feel the accomplishment and joy of touching others with your empathy and generosity of spirit. Just the image of you out there on the mountain, holding on with humor, *tefillah,* and *bitachon,* always gives me the fortitude to go on.

To Rabbi Pinchus Lipschutz and his wife Chani, the united force behind the Yated Neeman. I have rarely, if ever, encountered people who so graciously fuse business with pleasure. Your care and concern for my personal welfare above all other considerations amazes me.

You planted the seed of confidence in my ability long before the name Malky Feig meant anything to me or anyone else. My appreciation is everlasting.

And to Mati and the entire staff at the Yated, who exhibited a superhuman amount of tolerance and patience for my sometimes surrealistic sense of time. Only you will know the near-miracles involved in producing some of these pieces. You have my deepest appreciation.

To Rabbi Nosson Scherman who, despite his overwhelming schedule, always gave me the feeling that my project took first precedence. And to the talented staff at ArtScroll who spared no effort to stamp my work with the unmistakable imprint of excellence for which ArtScroll is famous.

To my editor, Mrs. Judi Dick, who made working on this book an undiluted pleasure. Her personal, around–the-clock dedication, her warmth and unpretentiousness, and her uncommon ability to improve subtle nuances without affecting the essence laid all my preconceptions of editors to rest. You treated every story in this book like a cherished baby. May you derive the *nachas* that is deservedly yours.

To Mendy Herzberg for orchestrating all the different aspects of this book with ease, efficiency, and grace.

To Mrs. Faygie Weinbaum who proofread and corrected the manuscript. Proofreading is one of those skills that is only recognized in its absence. The fact that your work remains deceivingly unapparent is testimony to your uncompromising work.

To Nechama Breningstall for the striking cover design, attractive layout, and pagination. Presentation makes all the difference, and you just proved it. As soon as I saw it, I felt like I was looking at something I recognized and loved.

In my last book, I thanked the readers for their ongoing feedback, the fuel that enabled me to go on. This time, my dear readers, my thanks isn't about feedback or fuel. This book, in its entirety, is yours. It is the account of your lives, your struggles and challenges, your thoughts and feelings and introspection the way you shared them with me. I am indebted to you for opening the window to your innermost selves, for entrusting me with the most precious thing in your possession, your hearts. It is my fervent hope that readers will be as profoundly inspired as I have been.

To my husband, my ongoing support, who deserves infinitely more than a line in the acknowledgments section. This book is only the most insignificant item on the list of things that would never be without you.

To my dear children, precious treasures, who have accompanied this book since its inception. I told you that you would be in the book and here you are. For waiting patiently through long trans-Atlantic phone calls at the most inopportune hours, for forgoing bedtime rituals when deadlines precluded them, for forgiving me when I listened to you with half a mind while the other half searched for a better way to end the paragraph.

For your cooperation and enthusiasm, your innocence and honesty, for the innumerable opportunities you give me to climb and, inversely, to experience the heightened awareness of life's joys from the elevated altitude of parenthood. My blessedness knows no end.

And finally, to He for Whom words are both inadequate and unnecessary to convey my boundless gratitude. For my heart and my soul, my insight and emotion, for the special kindness of intercepting my trail with the trails of so many precious others who have illuminated my life. For giving me the mountains to climb and then holding my hand while I climb them, and for opening my heart to the unsurpassed beauty of the landscape along the way.

Ad heinah azarunu rachamecha v'lo azavunu chasadecha ... v'al titsheinu Hashem Elokeinu lanetzach.

Contents

Introduction 19

מִי־יָגוּר בְּאָהֳלֶךָ ...
Who may sojourn in Your Tent ...

At the Foot of the Mountain 22

הוֹלֵךְ תָּמִים
One who walks in perfect innocence

Over the Hill, but Still Climbing 32
Peering Through the Window 43
Role Reversal 60
Making It Work 73
A Different Mountain to Climb 85

וְדֹבֵר אֱמֶת בִּלְבָבוֹ
And speaks the truth from his heart

Debt End	98
Waving a White Flag	110
Life Insurance	121
A Steal of a Lesson	133
Tools of the Trade	147
Righting a Wrong	158

וְאֶת־יִרְאֵי ה' יְכַבֵּד
But who honors those who fear Hashem

Walking the Tightrope	176
I Lift My Eyes to the Mountains	189
A Child in Pain	201

נִבְזֶה בְּעֵינָיו נִמְאָס
In whose eyes a contemptible person is repulsive

Riding the Roller Coaster	214
Breaking the Pattern	227
Unexpected Roadblock	239
From the Depths	251
Keeping Afloat	263

וְחֶרְפָּה לֹא־נָשָׂא עַל־קְרֹבוֹ
Nor cast disgrace upon his close one

Different Languages of Love	278
Stepping Upward	289
Give-and-Take	302
Keeping the Vessel Intact	314
The Labor of Love	328

עֹשֵׂה אֵלֶּה לֹא יִמּוֹט לְעוֹלָם
The doer of these shall not falter forever

Afterword	346
Glossary	348

מִזְמוֹר לְדָוִד ה' מִי־יָגוּר בְּאָהֳלֶךָ מִי־יִשְׁכֹּן בְּהַר קָדְשֶׁךָ: הוֹלֵךְ תָּמִים וּפֹעֵל צֶדֶק וְדֹבֵר אֱמֶת בִּלְבָבוֹ. לֹא־רָגַל עַל־לְשֹׁנוֹ לֹא־עָשָׂה לְרֵעֵהוּ רָעָה וְחֶרְפָּה לֹא־נָשָׂא עַל־קְרֹבוֹ. נִבְזֶה בְּעֵינָיו נִמְאָס וְאֶת־יִרְאֵי ה' יְכַבֵּד נִשְׁבַּע לְהָרַע וְלֹא יָמִר: כַּסְפּוֹ לֹא־נָתַן בְּנֶשֶׁךְ וְשֹׁחַד עַל־נָקִי לֹא לָקָח עֹשֵׂה־אֵלֶּה לֹא יִמּוֹט לְעוֹלָם.

A psalm by David. Hashem, who may sojourn in Your Tent? Who may dwell on Your Holy Mountain? One who walks in perfect innocence, and does what is right, and speaks the truth from his heart; who has no slander on his tongue, who has done his fellow no evil, nor cast disgrace upon his close one; in whose eyes a contemptible person is repulsive, but who honors those who fear Hashem; who can swear to his detriment without retracting; who lends not his money on interest; nor takes a bribe against the innocent. The doer of these shall not falter forever.

(Tehillim / Psalms 15)

Introduction

Glancing at the price tag of an exclusive sweater, I noticed a cream-colored card dangling from the ticket.

"Dear Customer, Congratulations on your purchase of the finest in knitwear. Please note: knobs and imperfections in the wool are not a defect. They are part of the design, meant to bring out the natural beauty of this handcrafted garment."

Hm, I smiled pensively, *this card ought to be affixed to every newborn baby at birth.*

Knobs and imperfections are not a defect; rather they bring out the natural beauty of this hand-crafted garment.

Human beings crave perfection. Perfect weather and perfect timing. Perfect health and perfect clarity. We like when things run along smooth plateaus, when there is no traffic clogging the highways and byways that lead to our destination. Give me free passage to forge ahead, we say, and I'll show you how far I can go.

We are right, but for one little fallacy.

Life isn't about how far we can go.

Or perhaps it is. It's about the distances we span inside the vast terrain within our souls, the miles we travel across that huge, gaping chasm between mind and heart, pain and acceptance, fear and faith. It's about traversing the uncharted wilderness where jealousy and bitterness grow wild, where rivalry and resentment extend their gnarled roots. And it's about scaling the jagged inclines challenging us to ascend all along the map of our destinies.

Those bumps and knobs that we come up against throughout our days aren't defects or imperfections. They aren't meant to hamper our progress or set us back. They are part of the design, handcrafted and purposely incorporated, to bring out the natural beauty inherent in each and every one of us.

Climbing the mountains of life is what sculpts our personality and shapes our inner self. It's what lifts us to higher planes and offers us a panoramic view of earthly matters. Climbing tightens our grip on the eternal and sharpens our awareness of our precarious footing, of our utter dependence, of our deepest, innermost goals stripped of the extraneous poundage we often lug around.

Life is indeed punctuated by many high roads, yet we, as *Yidden*, believe that adversity is what challenges our free will and spurs us to stretch and grow, that these mountains are what highlight the exalted peaks that can be accessed by the human spirit.

The stories featured in the following pages are true accounts of people like you and me who have scaled, or are endeavoring to scale, a steep hill in their lives. They are sketches of ordinary individuals who have been placed at the foot of the mountain, who have been pitted against the natural odds of anger, resistance, bitterness, and disappointment and have chosen to rise above their inclinations. They are not necessarily, and in fact, necessarily not, stories of life and of death, of tribulations of the tragic scope.

Rather they are of the very stuff that makes up everyday living for the sundry human beings embarking on the arduous climb called life. They are about forgiving and forgoing, overcoming and overlooking, the struggles and ensuing victories that turn ordinary human beings into extraordinary giants.

Because if Heaven is where angels dwell, and earth is the habitat of humans, then mountains are the place where humans can rise so that they transcend even the angels.

מִי־יָגוּר בְּאָהֳלֶךָ
מִי־יִשְׁכֹּן בְּהַר קָדְשֶׁךָ

Who may sojourn in Your Tent? Who may dwell on Your Holy Mountain?

At the Foot of the Mountain

When it comes to saving things, I'm usually not the sentimental type. In a small apartment like ours, with the basic furnishings crowding our three-room dwelling, there really is no space to store old pieces of nostalgia. My schoolbooks have long since been laid to rest, along with the remainders of my childhood collections of apricot pits, *kugelach,* and cards.

There is one piece of yellowing paper, though, gingerly ensconced in an unmarked envelope, that takes exception to the rule. Pressed between my passport and ID card, this scrap of my past remains safely stashed away in the front pocket of my personal file. It is one memento I cannot fathom relinquishing.

Like most little boys living in Yerushalayim nearly 30 years ago, I was the healthy, happy product of an unspoiled generation. We didn't have much in the way of games and gimmicks; our shirts and pants were our brothers' hand-me-downs, and chicken was almost exclusively a Shabbos treat. Still, we lacked for almost nothing as we played cops and robbers with our friends in the courtyard, and relished the savory *salatim* our mothers concocted from the surplus of eggplants they lugged home from the *shuk*.

There was nothing very remarkable about my childhood. I remember happy times, eating dinner around the crowded kitchen table, chatting noisily, chasing around the courtyard with my neighborhood friends. *Cheder* and family were the two focal points in my life, and I relished all the bits and pieces of joy and adventure that make up a young boy's childhood.

This blissful picture came to an abrupt halt when I was nearly 8 years old. It was a day like any other; I had gone to *cheder* in the morning and had returned after dinner. Racing back at day's end, I distinctly remember turning to my friend Nachman and asking him if he would wait while I asked my mother for permission to play at his house. That's the last I remember before my world turned upside down.

I'm not sure how much of the actual accident I actually recall. Over the years, oft-repeated accounts have fused with my foggy memories, so that I don't know to differentiate anymore. All I know is that one minute I was skipping home cheerfully, and the next minute I was knocked flat on the sidewalk amid a haze of pain and the ruckus of frenzied commotion.

At the hospital I was rushed into the operating room where I underwent a long and painstaking surgery on my leg. Ten days later, when I had somewhat recovered, the doctor walked into my room, looking quite pleased.

"Seems as if luck's on your side, Shimon," he winked at me. Then he turned to my father in a more serious tone. "You just never know with these things. Some people seem to suffer a minor injury and sustain irreversible damage, while other patients with multiple fractures heal without serious repercussions. Your son, fortunately, seems to belong to the second category."

"We believe in miracles, " my father whispered. His eyes were glassy with tears.

The doctor proceeded to explain that although it was too early to apply any pressure to the foot, there was nothing more the hospital could offer. He advised me to try to get accustomed to crutches, and to see an orthopedic specialist in another two weeks.

The rosy euphoria didn't last very long.

For the first two weeks, I reveled in all the attention I received. Overnight, I had become a celebrity. My siblings showered me with an open display of love and devotion; my brother gave up his comfortable mattress for me and my sisters decorated the bedroom walls with signs and cards. My friends all came over to visit and took turns trying out my crutches.

The initial novelty had just begun to wear off, when I was suddenly dragged down by the unpleasant reality of what lay ahead of me. One morning, about two weeks after I'd come home, my father walked into my room after Shacharis and sat down on my bed.

"I think it's time to start thinking about going back to *cheder*, Shimmi."

He said it ever so gently, but my heart plummeted to the bottom of my stomach. I had known all along that this moment was hovering around the bend, but I'd been hiding in a cocoon of wishful oblivion.

My face puckered into a tight mask, as I tried to blink away the tears that pricked my eyelids. "How will I get to *cheder*, Abba?"

It wasn't what I really meant to ask, but it was all I could do to swallow the giant lump filling my throat. My inner sense of vulnerability was too fragile to articulate, perhaps even too impalpable for an 8-year-old to be conscious of. The transportation problem was a practical impasse; it seemed like the safest way to keep the future at arm's distance.

My father was understanding, but firm. He allowed me one more day at home, and bright and early the next morning, while all my friends set out on foot, my parents helped me into the taxi that would take me to *cheder*.

Settling back into the day-to-day routine, though, was a small adjustment compared to the next hurdle I had to overcome. My break had not been a simple one, and as soon as we visited the orthopedist in the outpatient clinic, he prescribed physiotherapy twice a week.

Contrary to my expectations, the therapist was a rather pleasant man with an upbeat demeanor. The walls in his room were painted a sunny shade, and the general decor was light and attractive. All that, though, did little to alter the fact that the demands he made of me of me were difficult, if not excruciating. All I wanted was to go home, put the accident behind me, and never ever return there again.

The V.I.P. treatment had dwindled; my crutches, which had been such a sensation, had become standard props; and even the appeal of being driven to and from *cheder* each day had worn off. Now I was left only with a heavy, immobile foot that refused to cooperate, and a regimen of grueling exercises that robbed me of my free time with my friends. I was becoming moody and irritable.

One afternoon, after my fifth or sixth session with the physical therapist, I dragged myself into the house, thoroughly spent. It had been a particularly exhausting session, and I was in a withdrawn mood. The whole family sat around the table eating with gusto, but I sat slumped in my chair, staring apathetically at my soup.

"What's the matter, Shimmi?" my mother asked quietly, "You want me to warm up your portion?"

I shook my head in the negative. I felt too sorry for myself to even talk.

Suddenly, as if a well had burst, the tears came, fast and heavy, dropping straight into my bowl of soup. Horrified, I touched my sleeve to my eyes, but I was powerless against the tide. It was as if a storm had taken control of my emotions.

"I'm not going back to that therapist," I sobbed, "Never! I'm not going back to those stupid exercises; you can cancel the next appointment right now."

My face was wet and swollen, and my sleeve was soaked. Once I had started crying, I couldn't stop. My heart heaved with all the pain and frustration that had been welled up inside for the past few weeks.

My mother quietly continued to serve. My siblings quickly finished up and cleared their plates. An unspoken current of understanding and acceptance enveloped the kitchen. No words were necessary. I pushed my soup to the middle of the table and retreated to my room.

Not a word about therapy was mentioned during the next few days. On Tuesday morning, the day of my appointment, my mother hesitantly broached the subject.

"I told you already," I said, my tone a trifle more defiant than I had intended, "I'm not going back there. I don't have an ounce of strength left for therapy."

"Shimmi'le," my mother tried to coax, "You don't want to stay with your crutches forever. If you don't keep up the therapy, your foot won't ever heal properly."

"I don't care," I shrugged. I was too weary to listen to logic. And anyway, no one had been willing to promise I would ever walk normally again, even after all the arduous work. Why bother trying on the premise of a doubt?

My mother didn't answer me. She stroked my back and then bent down to help me tie my shoes so that I would be ready for the taxi that would take me to *cheder*.

That afternoon, my father sat down next to me after he finished his lunch.

"Is it a good time to talk, Shimmi?"

I stiffened. "If it has anything to do with the therapist," I said, the tears catching in my throat again, "then I don't have to talk. I'm not interested in going."

My father nodded, as if to acknowledge my feelings. He put his arm around me and took me into the dining room, which also doubled as his study. Then he closed the door the way he did when he had important company. I found myself momentarily intrigued by the formality.

Abba drew a pen out of his breast pocket, and pulled a sheet of paper out of his personal drawer. He bent over the paper and drew two stick figures: one at the foot of a mountain, and one at the top.

"Look Shimmi," he pointed to the drawing of the two boys. "There are people who will always stand at the bottom of the mountain, and there are people who will always be at the top. Do you know the difference between these two types of people?"

I shrugged, not sure what direction my father was taking.

"Those who stand at the top are the people who tell themselves:

'Look at yourself. You're strong, you can do it, you have what it takes to make it.'

"The people at the bottom don't look at themselves. They look at the mountain, and they give up. 'Look what a steep mountain this is,' they tell themselves. 'Forget it; it's a waste of time. You're so small, you'll never get up there.'

"And they don't. They stay right at the bottom all their lives. But don't think they're happy there, Shimmi. People who don't try climbing always feel that they've missed out on something."

At that point, I just listened quietly. I was an astute 8-year-old, and I knew my father was trying to tell me something, but I still didn't grasp the connection between his analogy and my situation.

"Shimmi," Abba asked, "Where do you, for instance, think you stand?"

"Me?" I echoed, flustered by the question, "Ummm, I don't know. Me?"

"I'll tell you where, Shimmi," Abba quickly rescued me. He put down the pen and looked directly into my eyes.

"If you decide that you don't have the strength for therapy, that you've finished with the exercises, finished with practicing at home, finished with everything, then you're going to stay right here." He pointed to the stick figure at the foot of the mountain.

"So what should I do?" I protested.

At that moment, I felt a wave of despair wash over me. I felt the enormity of the mountain pressing down on me, crushing my morale, and an involuntary tremor passed through me. *I might really stay at the bottom of the mountain for the rest of my life.*

"You may be right," Abba continued, his voice soft but determined, "The doctors can't promise anything, but there's one thing I can promise you for certain. If you don't continue trying, if you don't continue exercising and climbing, then you will stay in the very same place that you are now."

"But Abba," I whined, "It's so hard, I can't!"

"No, Shimmi," Abba wagged his finger sternly, "don't say that. Say, "Abba, it's so hard, but I can! It's very, very tough, but I'm going to make it."

At the Foot of the Mountain / 27

Abba hugged me close. Even at that young age, I could tell his speech had taken a lot out of him. He had spoken strictly, but I could feel his love for me surging beneath his words.

" 'I'm strong.'" Abba dictated, "Say it after me Shimmi, 'I have the strength, and *b'ezras Hashem* I can do it even though it's hard.'"

"Say it," Abba prodded.

"What," I stammered, "what should I say?"

"Say, 'It's not easy, but I can. I'm strong and with Hashem's help, I will make it.'"

I looked at my father, confused, not sure he was really serious. I felt kind of silly. What did he expect me to do, say the words after him, like some character in a play? Nonetheless, I repeated the script, if a little falteringly, word for word.

"It's not easy, but I can. I'm strong and with Hashem's help, I will make it."

"Good!" my father beamed, "Excellent! And now for homework, Shimmi, I want you to repeat this sentence ten times over the course of the day."

I smiled shyly, a little amused by the idea.

"Out loud, though, Shimmi," Abba reminded me, "and slowly. Don't forget to think about what you're saying."

The next day I went to therapy. Abba came along with me, and stayed in the waiting room. Before I went inside, he patted my shoulder and whispered, "Remember, Shimmi, if it gets hard, you whisper to yourself, 'This is hard, but I can do it, this is hard, but I can do it.'"

That was the first time in my life that I experienced the impact of that one short sentence. Like a stroking hand, it prodded me on and lingered in my ears, giving the push to continue.

There were many times when I declared very emphatically that I wasn't going back to therapy. There were other times when I announced I was quitting *cheder*. I was a little child who longed only to be carefree like everyone else. Instead, I was expected to spend hours and hours practicing my exercises, and watch all my friends race around the yard, while I lagged behind. I was physically drained and tired of always being the odd one out.

Each time, my father pulled out his drawing of the two boys and coaxed me to repeat his motto: "It's hard, but I can do it."

When the therapist suggested that I try and walk to *cheder* all by myself, I was gripped with apprehension. Though I had already progressed to walking without crutches, a half a year of riding to and from *cheder* by taxi had shaken my confidence in my ability to undertake the walk. Just the thought of embarking on the long trek to *cheder* petrified me.

"Not yet," I begged to be exonerated. "I can't do it, I'm not ready."

"Shimmi," my father reminded me in mock reprimand, "What did we make up?"

"That I can, that I will make it," I parroted lamely, entirely unconvinced.

Yet the next day, I set out by myself.

I left the house at 7:15 instead of 7:45, with my parents' parting wishes ringing in my ears. I walked ever so slowly, concentrating all my energy on putting one foot in front of the other. Each time it seemed that I would never get there, or that my foot hurt too much to go on, I found myself murmuring, "It's hard, but I can do it; it isn't easy, but I'm going to make it."

I got to *cheder* at 8 o'clock, sweating and exhausted, but glowing with the mastery of success. I had done it. I was a boy who could, who did, who had climbed the mountain.

Over the years, I've encountered many mountains. Big mountains and little mountains, jagged mountains and steep mountains, mountains that led to more mountains and mountains that leveled off into big open plateaus.

And each time I find my father's words ringing in my ears. "You can. You have the strength. It's difficult, but *b'ezras Hashem*, you can do it."

The words followed me through trying phases in yeshivah, through painful social experiences. They helped me rise above my physical limitations and free myself of negativity when people around me seemed callous or unfeeling.

Each time, an image would suddenly spring to my mind, the image of a boy climbing a mountain, reaching for the top.

"You can, you're strong, strong enough not to get blown away by insult or difficulty."

At the Foot of the Mountain / 29

Thirty years ago, before modern psychology had even begun to make its inroads, my father possessed the perception and foresight to hand a beaten little boy his own handcrafted key to success.

Today, nearly 30 years later, that little boy is married with a wonderful family. He works successfully in the mornings and spends his afternoons learning. Aside from a slight limp, a constant reminder that he belongs to a special league of climbers, you can't tell him apart from any ordinary person his age.

And there is a crumbling sheet of paper that he keeps next to his passport and ID card, a drawing of two stick figures with a mountain in between them. It is the document of his personal identity, his passport to success, the secret that he shares with his children and with anyone who crosses his path.

It isn't easy, but with Hashem's help, we all can.

הוֹלֵךְ תָּמִים

One who walks in perfect innocence

Over the Hill, but Still Climbing

It was an odd scene, to say the least: my father, his face radiant, clasping the hands of a white-bearded man several decades his senior, in a dance of euphoria.

Not that it was strange to see my father dancing. He is generally the most ebullient participant of any *simchah*, be it a wedding, *bris* or *sheva berachos*. To the best of my knowledge, however, there was no occasion marking the calendar on that particular summer evening, nor had my father ever met the elderly stranger before.

The visitor had rung the bell about a quarter of an hour before, an ordinary *tzeddakah* solicitor on an ordinary evening. He had spoken in a hoarse voice at the dining-room table, presumably detailing the financial difficulties of his institution, and my father's occasional questions and comments had punctuated the conversation. It had all been very commonplace.

And then, with no warning, the two were linked in an embrace of joy, stepping in and out to the tune of some impromptu melody.

"*Netzach Yisrael lo yeshaker,*" followed by "*Siman tov u'mazal tov.*" The two were going strong. Despite the man's apparently advanced age, there was strength in his knuckles, vigor in his step. We hovered near the dining-room door, watching the curious spectacle.

"*Kinder,*" my father beckoned for us to come in as the little dance came to a spontaneous end. "*Reb Shloime macht chasunah zein ershter kind* (Reb Shloime is marrying off his oldest child.) "

Ershter kind? The same question bolted through our minds, as we stared in disbelief. Reb Shloime definitely looked as if he had passed the four-score marker.

"Come listen to his story. It's not every day that a Yid has such a tale to tell."

I was born in 1910 in a little town in prewar Poland, to a family of nine children. I was welcomed with special joy. That joy was shadowed soon enough by a cloud of sadness. I had barely reached my second birthday, when my father, who I barely knew, passed away.

Unlike most carefree children of today, my earliest years were devoid of the fun and adventure of childhood. The sharp spear of tragedy punctured my bubble of security over and over again, filling my home and family with inconceivable sorrow.

I often hear people today saying that no generation has suffered the multiple *tzaros* inflicted upon our generation. I must say, it is a comment born of crying ignorance. It is true that we are witness to terrible tragedies today, accidents, illness, emotional and spiritual breakdown. While I was growing up, though, there was all of that and more.

Childhood diseases were rampant; pneumonia, diphtheria, tuberculosis, whooping cough, all these were deadly monsters that sank their merciless fangs into the happiest families and left bleeding holes where there had been rosy cheeks and shining eyes.

Somehow, the fact that we read about these incidents in numbers does something to diminish our keen sense of grief. Yes, we nod knowingly, if a trifle sadly; it was common in those days for children not to survive infanthood.

As if the commonness or the emotional barrier we erect between ourselves and "those days" draws the personal agony out of those nameless little *neshamos* lost to their families. Rarely do we stop to see each of them up close, to stroke their curly hair, or touch their velvety *bekelach,* to wash their little *hentelach negel vasser,* ushering them into a brand new day of promise and opportunity.

Rarely do we pause to imagine the mothers of "those days," mothers like ourselves who beamed with pride as their babies got their first tooth or took their first step, and fervently murmured that they go *"in gutte vegen."* No, we don't usually envision those *brissim,* the fathers' hearts racked with sobs, imploring that *"k'sheim shenichnas l'bris, kein yikaneis l'Torah l'chuppah ul'maasim tovim.* Just as he is brought to his *bris* he should be brought to [a life of] Torah, to the *chuppah* and to [do] good deeds."

If we replace the naked facts with images of our own beloved children, may they live and be well, then it is difficult, brutally difficult to conceive that by the time I was 9, I was the sole survivor of my family.

All my sisters and brothers, adorable infants, mischievous toddlers, pure little *cheder yingelach,* and *yiddishe maidelach,* had been ruthlessly torn away from us in the grips of fever and infection.

My mother, a weak and sickly widow, bereft of eight children, pleaded with Hashem to give her the strength to raise her one remaining son. Her wish was not to be granted. I have a faint memory of her, delirious with fever, talking to me as I sat solemnly near her bed.

"Shloime," she whispered, her frail hand stroking mine, "I lost eight children. Chana lost seven children; the *Ribono shel Olam* wanted me to lose eight. You are the only one left. Promise me you will always be an *ehrlicher Yid.*"

I was only 9 years old at the time, much too young to bear the impact of my mother's words. And yet life had matured me beyond my years. I nodded gravely, holding my mother's hand tightly. I knew that the Angel of Death was hovering in the room; I recognized him only too well.

I didn't want to part with my mother; she was all I had in the whole wide world. Even now, so many, many years later, I still feel a current of love surge in my heart when I think of my mother. My image of her physical countenance is worn and faded by the travails I've been through since, but the warmth of her presence still courses through me when I bring up the memories of our short years together.

Since I had lost the last of my siblings, my mother had smothered me with everything she had. In the way of physical indulgences that hadn't been much, but she had transformed the deep abyss of her grief into a fierce shield of devotion. She had showered all her maternal love on me, her only surviving son.

Now, she too was gone.

I was 9 years old, and alone in the world. Not a father with whom to walk to *shul,* not a brother with whom to say *kaddish,* not a sister to share the heavy burden of my sorrow. My maternal grandparents took me under their wing and provided for my basic needs. Still, though they were kind and loving, even the barest provisions were difficult for them to spare. I had bread and milk, soup at dinnertime, and occasionally an egg.

I had nobody, though, who could infuse those bare meals with the sweetness of a mother's love, nobody who could patch my pants with prayers and tears, nobody who could look into my sad eyes and see that a 9-year-old boy still needed a hug.

Fortunately, I was a bright *talmid* and a fairly uncomplicated child. In *cheder*, I was praised for my diligence and quick grasp, and I learned to find joy in my learning. After my bar mitzvah, I was sent to a larger yeshivah out of town, a common practice in those days.

I blossomed in yeshivah. Finally, I was a *bachur* between *bachurim,* not a poor little orphan growing up without family. In the atmosphere of learning and *mussar,* solid *sedarim* and secure bonds of friendship, my childhood scars began to heal. I began to look forward to building a better future.

I didn't know how long yet I had to wait.

I was a talmid in the yeshivah of Navaradok when World War II broke out. There is no way I can possibly do justice to that dark era in a few deft strokes. Anybody who has survived the war knows that volumes can be written about the daily horrors, the torture and suffering, the *nissim* and *hashgachah*. Yet he who was there needs no words, and he who wasn't there could never read enough words to understand.

With *nissim giluyim,* I made it to the end of the treacherous road. Together with a few *chaveirim,* I clung to the only thing I had: *emunah* that there was some loftier design to all the inhuman suffering, and *bitachon* that a sun would yet dawn on the terrible night.

When that sun finally dawned, there was only a handful of broken *Yidden* to rise for Shacharis.

Rise, though, we did.

Stripped and battered, we trickled toward the detention camps, huddling together for closeness and *chizuk*. For several years, we had shed every vestige of routine and normalcy, and had cleaved only to one goal: survival. Now, we were like prisoners at the end of a long sentence, stumbling numbly toward a rusty locker where our confiscated identities had been tossed an eternity before.

For my few surviving *chaveirim,* the first thing that meant was setting out on a search in the hope of finding remaining family. For me, there was no past to anchor my existence, no hope with which to nurse the little flame in my heart. I couldn't go to sleep with dreams of reunion, with fantasies of finding a familiar face. Nobody, I knew, in the whole wide world, was living with the sole hope of seeing me again. I was 35 years old and all alone in the world.

Fortified with the strength of Navaradok, I steeled myself to go on. If you don't have a *mashkin* in this world, I told myself, then the *Aibeshter* will be your *mashkin*. He is looking for you, waiting for you, yearning to hold you in His embrace. I turned to Him to free me from the anguish of my loneliness.

About two years after the war's end, I was married to a woman who, like myself, had been through the worst horrors. Our *chuppah* was a simple *tallis,* my *kallah's* gown was a borrowed dress sewn of some unadorned white fabric. Yet the music came from the depths of our hearts, from the innermost part of our souls, the first real notes of ecstasy since the outbreak of the war.

I was 38, my wife a few years younger. My life had been severed so many times; my heart fluttered with the notion of finally having a family, of finally bonding the pieces of my life to set up my very own nest.

The first year or two passed in the euphoria of being a couple. We immigrated to America and were occupied overcoming the hurdles of setting up a home on foreign soil. Slowly, however, time gave way to the silent yearning within our hearts, the indescribable longing to cradle an infant in our arms.

Every couple waits for that moment, the moment when their destinies will be fused by a tiny little human being who holds the key to the future. Every *chassan* and *kallah* wishes, hopes, prays, for the blessing to visit their home, to bathe their *mikdash m'at* in the glowing rays of *simchah* and turn them into the parents of a *Yiddishe neshamah*.

How much deeper was that instinct within us, that dream to see the *berachah* of parenthood come true. We were each the sole survivor of our family, two lone flowers so desperate to plant a garden of our own. We had little past to look back to, scant present to hold on to, only the future to look toward with optimism and faith. I was nearly 40 and my wife only slightly younger. Our time was running out.

My wife was a wonderful woman, gentle and soft spoken, who always knew what to say to lift my spirits. The harsh suffering she had endured, however, had left its mark on her body. She suffered terribly from bad circulation and respiratory problems. She was constantly falling ill, and it took months for her to fight the germs that attacked her weakened body.

I tried to ease her plight by working hard to make a living, and offering her words of hope and encouragement. Still, inside, my heart ached for her, for myself, for the silent walls of our home that pleaded to hear the cries of an infant, the ringing laughter of childhood.

It was not to be. After 20 years of valiant suffering, my wife's frail body gave way. I was alone in the world again.

I was 58 years old, just a few years away from the American notion of retirement. The thought threatened to engulf me in despair. I was not a father, let alone a grandfather. I was nearly 60 years old; what did I have to show for my life?

The spirit of Navaradok, though, stirred within me, like a flame that had almost burned out, suddenly rekindled. "*A mentch darf tuhn,*" they would say in Navaradok, "*Der Aibeshter vet shoin oiftuhn.*" (A person's task is to do; Hashem will see to accomplish.) In the world at large, perhaps, 60 years was the age nearing retirement. In *Yiddishkeit*, one never retires.

Infused once again with the drive to continue, I began to seek a *shidduch*. I approached *shadchanim* and told my friends that I was interested in remarrying. I shared my secret hope that I would find a woman who was still of childbearing age. As long as there was still a chance, I couldn't let go of my dream of fathering a child of my own.

My friends tried to be tactful. "You're almost 60, Reb Shloime. It'll be easier for you to understand the mind-set of someone closer to your own age."

I wasn't naive. I knew what they were trying to imply, that most young women had no reason to marry a 60-year-old widower like me. Still, I wasn't deterred. Perhaps, I reasoned, a young widow with several children to support would overlook age for financial security. I was willing to undertake an additional job to enable me to support a family, were I to find a suitable young widow.

Again, my friends were skeptical. "Now? At your age," they tried to dissuade me, "you're going to start raising children and marrying them off?"

I was firm in my decision.

"I'm still a young man," I joked, "I have another 60 years to live until 120."

When my friends saw that I was not to be swayed, they began to look earnestly for a woman who fit my description. I wanted someone who was steadfast in her *Yiddishkeit* and shared my ideals. Thankfully, I was engaged within a relatively short period of time. I found just the woman I had pictured, a kind and modest widow with five young children.

We were married, and I was filled with renewed hope. I worked hard each day trying to juggle two jobs, and returned home exhausted each evening to the lively sounds of bickering and playing, running bathwater and bedtime rituals. It was like music to my ears, the childhood I never had, the children I never had. While many of my contemporaries were winding down, enjoying the peace and quiet of their emptying nests, I relished the sounds of children stirring up a racket in my very own home.

One year later, we were blessed with the priceless gift I had almost despaired of ever having; my wife gave birth to a healthy baby girl.

It is hard to describe the emotions that washed over me as I walked down the hospital corridor, bearing the glad tidings. "I'm a father!" I wanted to shout, "A father to a real live baby girl!"

I watched the regular ebb and flow of doctors and nurses changing shifts, and I wanted to run over and shake them. "Do you know what just happened? I've just become a father!"

It took all my restraint not to break into a boyish skip as I left the maternity ward, and headed out to the brisk spring day. The birds were chirping. My heart was singing. I thought of my parents, my sisters and brothers. The chain would carry on.

"Ad heinah azarunu rachamecha, v'lo azavunu chasedacha, Hashem Elokeinu, v'al titsheinu Hashem Elokeinu lanetzach."

Our second daughter was born about two years later. The older children were thrilled with their two little sisters, and we were a happy family indeed. When I found out that I was to become a father the third time around, my joy knew no bounds. I went to the Satmar Rav, *z'l*, and begged him for a *berachah* that I be *zocheh* to a *ben zachar*.

"And what's wrong with daughters?" the Rebbe smiled, after hearing my tale. *"Zun ken men nisht kleiben; eidemes ken men oiskleiben talmidei chachamim* (One can't choose sons, but one can choose sons-in-law who are *talmidei chachamim*)."

I understood the Rebbe's intent, and was buoyed by his wise perspective. Several months later I welcomed my third healthy daughter into the world.

True to my commitment, I continued to work hard to support our family, and we began to marry off my wife's children. Though not all of them were easy children, I put my heart and soul into raising them, trying to care for them as if they were my own. I knew what it meant to be an orphan, and I found tremendous satisfaction in tending to their needs; it was as if I was coming full circle, giving them the father I never had.

Four years ago, we married off my wife's youngest child. My own daughter was 20, and we began to search for a *shidduch*. I remembered the Satmar Rav's words, and was resolved to choose a serious *ben Torah* for my daughter, true to her deepest aspirations. Things did not go easily. Many of the suggestions that came up did not suit our criteria, and we faced the bitter taste of rejection more than once.

"Don't let it get you down," I encouraged my daughter. "I got married the first time at 38, and look where I am today. *A mentch darf tuhn*," I cited my oft-repeated motto, " *Der Aibeshter vet shoin oiftuhn*."

We continued to brave the stormy waves of *shidduchim*, waiting for the sea to split. I had waited until 60 to hold my first child; I would wait patiently just a little longer until the *Ribono shel Olam* saw fit to send us her destined partner.

Thankfully, one month ago, just a little after my daughter turned 24, our *tefillos* were answered, and she became a *kallah* to a budding *talmid chacham*, as we had both dreamed.

I crossed another bridge in my life for the very first time.

It was through a blur of tears that I gazed at the elderly Yid gracing our dining room table. Reb Shloime had been through so much, had been thrown down to the bottom of the mountain so many times, and yet he had lost none of his vigor, none of his optimism and hope. He was determined as ever "*tzu tuhn*," confident that "*der Aibeshter vet oiftuhn*."

"*B'ezras Hashem*," he said, his eyes shining, "after I marry off my third daughter, I plan to open a yeshivah."

I swallowed a smile. Reb Shloime was 84 years old. He had two more children to marry off, and he still had plans in the offing.

"I always dreamed of opening a yeshivah for *bachurim* with special emotional needs, " he went on. "I have a special soft spot for these children, and I feel that I can accomplish much with them. During the years when I was trying to provide for my family, I simply had no time to devote to my project. Now that I've married off my wife's children, my funds are severely drained, and I'm busy trying to be *mezakeh* generous *Yidden* to help me marry off my own daughters.

"As soon as I have some more time on my hands," he concluded, "I would like to actualize my dream."

He asked my father whether he had ever dealt in *chinuch,* and when my father replied that, in fact, he was a *maggid shiur,* Reb Shloime beamed.

"Good, good," he approved. "It's a *zechus* to be *mechanech* the next generation, to mold each child according to his own personal *derech.*"

"If you ever need an *eitzah* in *chinuch,*" he offered, "you can call me. After all," he sized up my father who was already a grandfather many times over, "you're only a *yungerman'chik;* it's always helpful to talk to someone with a lot of life experience."

My father thankfully took his number, and handed Reb Shloime his wholehearted contribution toward the expenses of the upcoming wedding.

Reb Shloime thanked my father profusely and then, as an afterthought, he added, "If you ever call, don't mention to my wife that I've met you while trying to raise funds. It might cause her unnecessary embarrassment if she knew. I've got to be extra sensitive with my *shalom bayis,*" he winked, "It's a *zivug sheini* (second marriage), you know."

With that, Reb Shloime stood up, pumped my father's hand, and walked to the door, leaving his unforgettable imprint on those of us who were privileged to have witnessed the scene.

Epilogue: Six years ago, at a relative's simchah out of town, my father suddenly spotted a vaguely familiar elderly man being honored

with the reading of the tenaim. In a moment, recognition dawned. The Yid was none other than Reb Shloime, still Baruch Hashem going strong.

My father greeted him emotionally and expressed his happiness at seeing him. Reb Shloime related that he had baruch Hashem merited to become a zaide. When my father asked him if he was related to the chassan, he was quick to respond.

""*K'eelu yoldo!*(As if I gave birth to him).*"*

Then he proceeded to explain that although financial considerations had precluded the possibility of opening the yeshiva of his dreams, he had not given up his ideal. He had begun to learn privately with several bachurim who had difficulties, and he was baruch Hashem immensely successful. Tonight's chassan, he concluded, was one of those bachurim. In appreciation, the baal simchah had paid his ticket so he could reap his rightful nachas.

The last time my father met Reb Shloime was two years ago in Los Angeles. He was well over 90, bli ayin hara, and still full of youthful vibrancy. May he be granted arichas yamim, and may his message continue to inspire us all.

Peering Through the Window

"Hi Mindy," it was Rina on the line. "You must be very busy; I know what it's like to be making a bar mitzvah."

"Oh hi, Rina! How are you?" *Where's that prescription?* "Yes, I guess I *am* pretty busy, *Baruch Hashem.*" *I better remember to call the pulmonologist.* "Not too busy to be talking to you, though. What's doing?"

"That's what I'm calling to know; tell me what I can do for you. I won't forget how you helped me when I was so overwhelmed before Pinchos's bar mitzvah three months ago."

Oh, the bar mitzvah.

"I mean, I'm not very worried about you, Mindy; if anyone has it together, it's you. Maybe I can help you with errands, though? Or a salad for the bar?"

"Thanks so much, Rina; it's so sweet of you to offer," *What time is it? When does the lab close?* "Right now, I feel pretty under control." *At least for the bar mitzvah.* "Maybe I'll need some errands next week. I'll let you know when we get a little closer."

"Please do, Mindy. I'm circling the date on my calendar. Loads of *hatzlachah*. If you need anything else before then, give me a ring."

If you need anything else.

I needed many things before then.

Many, many, things.

Nothing, though, that Rina, or anybody else, could give me.

There are certain moments that remain etched in one's mind forever. No matter how many years pass, no matter how many encounters overlap that piece of history, one can always tap into that moment and recapture it with startling clarity.

The birth of one's first child is one such moment. Life may wind along many unforeseen bends, successive children may be born, *simchos* and hardships may wax and wane; still, one can never forget the rapture of that beautiful, almost sublime moment.

Poems have been written describing the velvety softness, the silken newness, the almost fragrant purity of these newborn treasures. When it is one's own first miracle, those adjectives are compounded by a sense of enormity, by the heady, tingling awe of receiving the gift of parenthood.

We were a couple like any other, jittery with nervous excitement as we walked through those swinging doors that would usher in that magical moment. I went through my first labor, while my husband fervently recited *Tehillim*, stopping intermittently to support and encourage me.

If I close my eyes, I can still feel the chill of the air conditioning a little too cold, still see the hanging fluorescent fixtures, the big clock on the wall. And the scale.

Every time I felt my stamina waning, I stole a glance at the baby scale standing ready, in the corner. It gave me the fortitude I needed. In just another short while, there would be another human being in the room, a little, screaming, wriggling infant that would make us into a family.

I remember discussing the name with Akiva. If it was a boy, we had both agreed we would call him Shragi after Akiva's grandfather who had been *niftar* recently. Although, technically, the choice belonged to me, I knew what the name meant to Akiva.

Hashem had showered us with his blessings, and I was brimming with gratitude. The least I could do was to start our family on the cornerstone of love and *vatranus*.

Indeed, it was a boy. A lovely, little newborn bundle, six pounds, seven ounces, swaddled in sterile hospital whites. Akiva was jubilant. He held him up proudly, *reishis arisoseichem*, and my eyes filled with tears. *Baruch shehecheyanu la'zman hazeh*. We were actually the parents of a tiny baby boy.

I spent a while in recovery while Akiva made the phone calls. A few hours later, I held the baby in my arms to nurse him for the first time.

Like every new mother, I marveled at the perfection of his minuscule features, his hair and eyebrows, his tiny nose and perfectly formed ears. The lines on his palms, his fingers and toes, eyelashes and nails, everything was there in perfect symmetry. I was overwhelmed with appreciation. Such a little body with everything inside.

Suddenly, as I beheld his adorable face, I was struck by the oddity that his lips seemed blue tinged. When Akiva came into the room soon afterward, I shared my observation with him. For a moment we both hovered worriedly over the baby; then we laughed together at our overanxious first-time-parent phobias.

"I'll ask the nurse about it when she comes in," I said, just to allay our fears. I was sure she would chuckle and tell me something about the circulation regulating during the first few hours.

Instead, the nurse looked at the baby gravely. She marked something down on his chart, and asked me to put him back into the little Lucite bassinet. She smiled tensely and said she needed to take him back immediately for testing. I felt my heart drop.

I looked at Akiva. His eyes anxiously followed the nurse's deft movements. At that moment, we didn't need words. We were both thinking the same thing. *Don't tell me there's something wrong with the baby. It can't be; he looks so perfect.*

By the time Friday came around, we knew the truth. There was something very wrong with our picture-perfect baby, although the doctors had not made their final diagnosis. It seemed he had been born with a rare syndrome that affected his lungs and respiratory system, among other things. His breathing was labored and was now aided by an oxygen tent. He was still undergoing extensive testing to determine the exact nature of his illness and its implications.

Akiva and I made an immediate decision not to share the diagnosis with anyone other than our parents. As far as friends and family, Akiva and I preferred to keep the baby's condition under wraps. We wanted to be a normal family, to continue to enjoy the regular give-and-take of social life.

We also wanted little Shragi to have a normal childhood, or as normal as possible under the circumstances. We didn't want him to be the subject of pitying glances and overprotective indulgence. We knew that keeping everyone blissfully unaware would give Shragi the best chance of interacting naturally with his environment.

Our decision wasn't ironclad; if the need arose, then we would share our burden with whomever we needed to (and indeed, as the years passed, we did disclose the facts to a few people to whom we felt close). Of course we also knew that when the time came for *shidduchim*, we would be completely forthcoming. Generally, though, we felt most comfortable keeping the knowledge to ourselves.

According to hospital policy, I had been released 24 hours after the birth. The baby, however, remained in the NICU, (Neonatal Intensive Care Unit), attached to intravenous and oxygen. We told concerned friends and relatives that the baby had swallowed fluid doing the birth, and had to be monitored before he could be brought home.

Thus began the harrowing trips back and forth to the hospital. I would spend the day there and Akiva would take over for the night. Friends, who didn't even know the emotional aspect of the load we were carrying, would ask me how I was doing it.

"You're barely a few days after birth; how are you handling all of this?"

The answer I gave them was, unwittingly, the line that would keep us going for the next 12 years.

"I'm not handling *all of this*. I'm trying to handle one day at a time, one hour at a time, one minute at a time. Anything is possible for a minute."

Indeed, both Akiva and I forced ourselves to blot the future out of our minds. Hashem was giving us this *nisayon* one day at a time, and with it, He was giving us strength to handle each day as it came.

Akiva told me a beautiful *mashal* of a king who had commanded his subject to transfer an imposing mountain of bricks to a vacant building site. The subject merely looked at the mountain, and wrung his hands in despair.

"How in the world am I going to move this mountain? It's impossible. I may as well give up right now."

To which the king replied, "I don't want you to move the mountain. All I ask is that you lift one brick every day and carry it to the lot."

The first brick was planning the *shalom zachor*. We had loads of family and Akiva had a big crowd of *chaveirim*. I had stocked up the freezer over the past few months in anticipation of our *simchah*. Now everything would come to good use.

Even as we spoke in the lobby in front of the NICU, the doctors came by to brief us on the baby's situation.

At four days old, our little son was not an innocent, carefree soul. He was being pumped with large doses of antibiotics and was struggling with every breath. Unlike most lighthearted first-time parents, we, too, were struggling.

Still, we were determined not to let our worry eclipse the atmosphere at the *simchah*. Akiva greeted over a hundred guests in our small dining room that Friday night. My sisters-in-law called me *Motza'ei Shabbos* to tell me what an especially lively affair it had been.

"How long do you expect they'll still keep the baby?" people constantly questioned us.

"They said to give it a few weeks; they don't like taking chances with newborns."

"*Oy*, it's not easy. At least it's nothing worse, though. I'm sure you see plenty of that in the NICU."

We did. Right inside the crib of the child we knew and loved most dearly.

When we came home, the whole neighborhood celebrated. We got cakes and *kugels* and gifts and flowers. And a whole bunch of visitors.

Unbeknownst to our well-wishers, the baby was still hooked to oxygen. We had learned how to operate the machine, how to connect the tube and adjust the flow. It was a hassle, disconnecting the baby every time we took him out of our room to show him off.

"Oh he's adorable. Look at those perfect features. *Bli ayin hara*. And he looks like a good baby too."

"*Baruch Hashem*, he is, *bli ayin hara*."

"The ones who give you the hardest time at the beginning are the easiest afterward. Take it from me."

It was ironic how many times this, and similar, exchanges took place.

Before we knew it, Akiva and I had become experienced paramedics. We learned how to operate the oxygen, which medicines had to be diffused in the nebulizer and which had to be sprayed nasally. Our kitchen cabinet soon became cluttered with Shragi's paraphernalia.

Even though we had learned the ropes fairly quickly, things never seemed to settle into a smooth routine. Shragi's lungs were inflamed and infected; his body was full of mucus and toxins that predisposed him to all kinds of germs.

We were always at the doctor, and not infrequently in the hospital. Shragi was prone to high fever and all kinds of infections. When I thought of all the antibiotics that were in his tiny system, I couldn't help but shudder.

"Think of it this way, Mrs. Katz," the pulmonologist tried to console me when I shared my anxieties, "You're lucky we *have* all this stuff. You wouldn't want to see his system without it."

Looks were so deceiving. Shragi had the most cherubic little face. He flashed a winning smile and cooed good-naturedly. He was developing nicely, learning to lift his head and grab toys with his hand. His racking cough was the only external clue to what was going on inside his body.

Friends would come by to visit and they would exchange notes.

"Oh, let me see, what kind of carriage did you get? I see you got the navy model. Don't ask what I went through until I decided on mine."

I tried to seem equally interested in these trivial details. It wasn't as if I felt superior or self-absorbed. I really *was* interested. The immediacy of Shragi's everyday needs, however, automatically made everything else fade in comparison.

I wasn't jealous or bitter. I simply ached to experience one day of motherhood, blissfully free of serious concerns. What did it feel like, I wondered, to stroll around with your baby, not hurrying to get to the doctor, not hassling to measure antibiotics, not worrying about fever and coughs. It seemed like a fairy-tale existence.

Even as I entered the hospital for the birth of my second child, my thoughts were focused on Shragi. It was the first time we had ever left him in someone else's care.

"You think my mother will remember when he needs the cortisone and when he needs the nebulizer?" I asked Akiva.

"Don't worry, Mindy," Akiva smiled his reassuring smile. "A grandmother is the closest you can get to a mother, and besides, you wrote everything down."

I supposed he was right. Exhaling the tension of the day, I finally allowed myself to concentrate on what was happening. My heart was pounding with anticipation. Although we were awaiting our second child, in a sense it had the element of a first birth. We were finally about to experience what it meant to have a normal, healthy baby.

"I can't imagine only having to nurse, burp, hold, and change diapers," I joked to Akiva. "It sounds too easy to be true."

Nothing prepared us for the eventuality that was to be.

Within minutes after Eli's birth, a grim-faced doctor broke the news. Eli had been born with the same syndrome Shragi had.

I felt the room spinning around in circles. It seemed like a nightmare. Was this really happening all over again?

For the first time since Shragi's birth, I felt like breaking down. How were we going to handle this; how? For the past two years, we had tackled Shragi's medical crises as they had come, never thinking ahead, never speculating or worrying. We had gotten through each day, always hoping for better times.

This time, the thought of the future seemed to pin us under a hopeless weight. We knew the road that lay ahead of us only too well: oxygen, antibiotics, steroids, doctors, nebulizers, surgeries, and more antibiotics.

How could it be? How would we be able to go through it all, to watch another baby struggle with every breath, to put another beautiful infant through the harrowing rounds of testing, to hear another innocent child cough that bone-jarring cough all the time?

I looked at Akiva for support. His face looked like a mirror of my feelings, pallid shock, crushing despair. *It must be a mistake*, his features said; *the Ribono shel Olam doesn't give anyone more than he can handle.*

For a moment, we had nothing to say to each other. I felt the depth of Akiva's pain as keenly as he felt mine. There were no illusions to escape to, no hopes to take shelter in. Only the staggering reality closing in on us.

Incredibly, the blackout lasted only a long moment. Slowly, one at a time, the lights inside us flickered back on.

The Ribono shel Olam doesn't give anyone more than he can handle. The very same thought that, only moments before, had constituted proof of the impossibility of the situation, now bounced back with an echo of encouragement.

We definitely weren't capable of coping with a *nisayon* of such magnitude on our own. If Hashem had sent us the challenge a second time around, though, then He would fortify us with everything we needed to make it possible.

Looking back over the past two years, there had been so many hurdles we had never thought we had the strength to overcome. We had experienced remarkable *Siyata diShmaya* with Shragi, and now Hashem would grant us that same special treatment with our new baby.

As soon as I had recovered enough to get off the bed, Akiva and I went to see the baby. Just like his older brother, he was beautiful. He didn't have that puckered, splotchy look many newborns sport a few hours after birth. His features were delicate and sculpted, tiny, flat ears, rosebud lips and a little pug nose, just like Shragi's.

An almost painful current of love shot through me. He was such a gentle little thing. I bent over to stroke his silky cheeks, to put my finger into his tightly clenched fist. Akiva looked on through a film of tears.

As paradoxical as it sounds, I felt a strange sense of happiness wash over me, happiness for the little *neshama'le* lying so angelically in his crib, happiness that we were chosen to be his parents. *You have so much ahead of you, zisse tzaddik; at least you have parents who love you so very, very dearly.*

Akiva and I couldn't tear ourselves away from his crib. Although we had loved Shragi from the start, too, we formed an instant attachment to little Eli, a bond that had taken us longer to cultivate the first time around.

Perhaps it was our fierce desire to cushion him against the pain we knew was to come, perhaps it was our deep passion for Shragi manifesting itself in our affection for his brother in flesh and in spirit. Perhaps there was also something of the reassurance that we were as best prepared to help him as parents could possibly be.

Again, we kept Eli's condition as ambiguous and as low key as we could, telling only my parents the truth. Relatives and neighbors knew the baby would have to stay in the hospital for a while, but we reassured them it was nothing to worry about.

Some friends innocently asked if it was the same complication that Shragi had been hospitalized for as a newborn; others commented that they knew others whose babies also had to stay for the same reason. Akiva and I exuded such calm, nobody would have guessed there was really something serious seething beneath the current.

Shragi was such an adorable toddler; nobody viewed him as a sick child. He ran around and giggled with other kids and got into trouble. Friends and neighbors treated him naturally, the way anyone would treat a normal 2-year-old. We wanted little Eli to be treated the same way.

Miraculously, Akiva and I basked in each other's unwavering support. It was as if we had signed a mutual agreement that we would each go beyond the constraints of our own pain in order to make the other one's burden more bearable.

Though it wasn't easy taking care of Shragi while I tried to shuttle back and forth to the baby, I took care to greet Akiva with a smile and a hot coffee when he came in from his shift.

Likewise, I would come home after an exhausting day in the hospital to find my favorite chocolate and a heartwarming note. We weren't competing about who was working harder. We were trying to make it easier for each other.

By the time little Eli had had his *bris*, we were pros at doing what had to be done. In other homes, there was the routine of bathtime, suppertime, and storytime; in our house, we had physiotherapy-time and medicine-time and nebulizing-time. Akiva would take care of Shragi while I fed the baby, then I would take care of Shragi while he kept Eli occupied. Akiva and I often wondered jokingly what other people did with all that extra time.

Despite all the everyday measures that we took in order to prevent toxic buildup inside the kids' systems, we inevitably landed at the doctor's office at least once a week. There was always some infection cropping up, some germ causing fever, some complication that called for more antibiotics or hospitalization.

Taking our Shabbos-afternoon walk, or visiting the zoo on Chol HaMoed, we often pondered the irony of appearances. To anybody in the world, we looked like the perfect picture of bliss. A young couple, trim and well dressed, strolling along with a chattering toddler and an adorable baby gurgling contentedly in the carriage.

Indeed, even our closest friends and family were taken by our upbeat attitude. No one dreamed that beneath the placid surface of our uncomplicated little family, lay an entire subterrain of rugged territory.

Akiva and I both loved having guests and my sisters-in-law were always inviting themselves over for Shabbos or Yom Tov meals. Akiva was a gracious host and friends and family looked to him for advice and support.

"It's so relaxing in your house," a friend would admire. "I guess it's different than having five kids and working."

I would smile inwardly. "It certainly *is* different than having five kids and working," I'd concede.

"I don't know about relaxing, though," I'd chuckle to Akiva later on when I recounted the conversation as we each measured out antibiotics for one of the kids. There was a certain little pleasure in keeping our suffering from the world, a certain element of normalcy. At least as far as anyone else was concerned, we were a happy, normal, even enviable, family.

Ironically, even amid our hardships, we *did* feel like an enviable family. We were grateful for our deep understanding of each other, for the special relationship we shared. We were infinitely thankful that our children had so many advantages; they were happy, functioning, adorable-looking kids. And we felt privileged for the intimate *kesher* that our *nisayon* had forged between Hashem and ourselves.

When Shragi and Eli were joined by a little baby sister, nobody fully appreciated the depth of our gratitude. Rivky was the cutest little baby, reminding everybody of Shragi as an infant. To us, she was a first, a first girl and a first healthy baby. No oxygen and medication, no NICU and no doctors. Just the normal, routine needs of a normal, routine baby. It was a novelty to us.

The boys were growing, and with them, the challenges we faced. Though Akiva was still learning in *kollel*, he was strongly considering some sort of job to supplement our income. Though he was exceptionally talented, however, circumstances made it impossible for him to undertake any traditional work schedule.

We were perpetually on the run with appointments and often had to be in the hospital. Our life was a constant flux of unpredictability. There was no telling when we would have to leave for the hospital on a moment's notice, or when the doctor would schedule an unforeseen surgery. Some days had our family on the road for hours on end, with only the briefest stop to snatch something to eat.

We learned to live on two fronts. On one front, we were cleaning and cooking and carpooling like anybody else in the neighborhood. We celebrated the births of children and attended other's *simchos*. I was busy cooking and baking for Yom Tov and Akiva was studying *Hilchos Shabbos* in *kollel*. Our kids were going to school, fighting, playing, and doing homework at home.

On the other front, we were constantly on the vigil, ready for the next command. While the two older boys played, we listened anxiously to their hacking coughs; while they slept, we hovered wakefully, watching their restless tossing. It was so hard to see their innocent existence constantly punctuated by rude reminders of their ill health.

Eli chronically suffered from terrible headaches, a side effect of his condition. Though we gave him pain relief when it got really bad, there was nothing to do for him on a constant basis.

"Do you want to stay home today, Eli?" I remember asking him one day when I noticed his eyelids drooping in pain.

"Why?" he asked.

"Because I see your head really hurts," I replied.

" I feel like this every day," he countered, so casually, I could have cried. "Why should I stay home?"

I felt my heart contract. His head hurt every day. He had fever almost every day. He coughed all the time. His nonchalance unnerved me.

To Akiva and me, these symptoms were like spears. The constant coughing in our house wasn't just a sound in the background. It was a tearing, ripping gash in our souls. It was a palpable reinforcement of the radiologist's assertion that he had never seen a child capable of walking into his office with such infected, inflamed lungs. It was the piercing sound of medicated bodies struggling to breathe.

During the day, I found myself forging ahead, doing what I had to, joking, disciplining, serving, settling fights. Before bedtime, we would settle into the den for our nightly routine, and then we would put the kids to sleep.

By the time I hit the pillow, I should have been finished. I was. So was Akiva. Sleep, however, always seemed to elude us. All we could hear, as we struggled to fall asleep, was the groaning of the mattresses in the other room, testimony to two innocent children who couldn't even lapse into a comfortable sleep at the end of their pain-filled day.

I would often get out of bed and go into the kids' room to plant a kiss on their furrowed foreheads. Then I would grab my *Tehillim* as the tears slid down my cheeks into the worn pages. *Please, Hashem, help my kinderlach. You see their pain like no one else does. Send a cure to alleviate them already.*

Somehow, the words always soothed me, always reminded me that Hashem was watching over my treasures, was suffering along with their pain and giving them the inner strength to deal with their difficulties. The timeless *pesukim* always had a therapeutic effect. *Hashem ro'i, lo echsar.* I didn't have to worry; Hashem was holding us, hugging us, helping us.

Tefillah became our stronghold in the face of our physical and emotional tribulations. All throughout the day, we kept strong and cheerful, focusing very pragmatically on what had to be done next. *Davening* became our timeout, our opportunity to express our innermost feelings and reach out for the *Aibeshter's* support.

I would reach for my *siddur* with the urgency of someone grabbing a painkiller to soothe a bad headache. *Melech, ozer, u'moshia, u'magen*, I would relish every word, savor every syllable. Each phrase was so acutely meaningful to me, every paragraph so calming and reassuring. *Atah gibor l'olam Hashem*, I'd acknowledge and entreat at the same time, *someich noflim, v'rofei cholim. Mi chamocha Baal Gevuros, u'mi domeh Lach?*

While I *davened*, I was on another planet, on an island where only *Hakadosh Baruch Hu* and me existed. Holding my *siddur* close, I gave vent to my anguish, to my tension, to my physical exhaustion, to my anxieties about the future.

With Hashem, there were no fronts and no defenses. I broke down and cried like a little child, sobbing freely about every little and big thing weighing down on me. It was as if — no, not as if; I *had* been granted a half-hour audience with Someone Who had the power to solve all my problems.

I found *davening* to be like exercise. No matter how dispirited I was when I started out, no matter how low and disconnected I felt before I opened my *siddur*, the act of *davening* always infused me with strength. The words cleansed my heart, the tears drained my tension. By the time I sang *Aleinu*, I always felt uplifted and energized. *Hu Elokeinu, ein od, emes Malkeinu, efes zulaso.*

As I'd fervently kiss my *siddur*, I'd linger a moment before I returned to the rigorous demands of my schedule. I was like a child swinging from a monkey bar, reluctant to leave go, petrified of being suspended midair. I'd find myself wistfully putting down my *siddur*, reminding myself that the next *Shemoneh Esrei* was only a bar away.

And the *Ribono shel Olam* would be holding me until I got to the next bar.

In a real sense, though, I never did leave go. All through the day, I found myself touching base with the *Ribono shel Olam*, asking Him, telling Him, consulting with Him.

I asked Him to make the red light turn green so we could get to the appointment on time; I asked Him to bring Eli's fever down so we wouldn't have to be admitted to the hospital. It was as if I had an ongoing direct line. Hashem had given us extraordinary circumstances and with it, He had given us His private number. It was the only way we got through any crisis.

The crises came in all shapes and sizes. There were the crushing moments, moments when the top men in the field admitted that there wasn't much more they could do for us, moments when tests showed regression after long and taxing attempts to effect improvement.

Then there were the heartbreaking moments, moments when Eli cried that he didn't want even one more spoon of yucky medicine, moments when Shragi asked why the younger kids always outran him in races while he panted for breath.

There were times when we had to listen on the sidelines, fighting our tears, like the time Eli told his little sister Rivky. "This Rosh Hashanah, I'm going to *daven* so hard that Hashem shouldn't make me sick anymore. I don't know why, I'm always getting sick."

Though the kids knew that they had to take medicine to strengthen their lungs and that they sometimes had to be hospitalized to treat infections, we had never formally sat them down and labeled their condition. They were both young and spirited, full of ambition and youthful optimism. All the experts we consulted felt it was healthiest for them to perceive themselves as normal children.

Incredibly, despite their chronic pain and discomfort, both Shragi and Eli *did* lead normal lives. They both loved school and did their homework like every other child. They both had loads of friends, went swimming, took part in plays and choirs, and did their share of jobs in the house. Akiva and I demanded the same performance of them that we demanded of the rest of our children.

At the same time, we made a conscious effort to cultivate a happy atmosphere in our home. Both of us being naturally upbeat, we always had music playing, always had a song going, always had a joke to share. We made time for lots of fun activities, baking together, doing craft projects, making our family album.

Occasionally we also tried to get away. During the summertime, we would go on a family trip for two or three days, leaving everything but the most essential paraphernalia behind. Those trips were a literal breath of fresh air. They rejuvenated our spirits, gave all of us the break we needed from medical routines, and fused us as a loving, happy family.

Looking back at progressive snapshots of our family on vacation, first four, then five, then six precious faces, pretty outfits, smiling parents, I'm confronted again by the stark deception of external impressions. If there's one thing I've learned from our personal experience, it's that there is no telling what lies beneath anyone's family picture. *Anyone's.*

Akiva would take the boys to *shul* in their Shabbos suits and crisp white shirts. They looked so sharp and handsome, rich velvet *yarmulkes*, atop freshly washed hair, *peyos* tucked neatly behind their ears. As they walked, Shragi and Eli would recount what they had learned that week in *cheder*. It was a *nachas* to listen to them. They were both top students who loved their learning.

When they got to *shul* one Shabbos, Shragi asked Akiva if he could make a *Mi shebeirach*.

"Remember Avramy?" he asked.

Of course Akiva remembered. Avramy was a 3-year-old boy whom we had met in the pediatric ward the week before. He was grappling with a terminal illness. Shragi had been touched by the fragile little boy. His sensitive soul ached to do something for his newest friend. Akiva was moved by his request.

Relaying Shragi's request to the *gabbai*, Akiva discreetly bent over and whispered Shragi's own name into the gabbai's ear to be mentioned for a *refuah shleimah*.

And then, Akiva, the mortal *av rachum,* bit his trembling lip, as he stood to a side trying to stanch the tears blurring his vision.

Avinu av harachaman, he silently implored, *Please look at my innocent little yingele, intervening so sincerely for a friend even sicker than he is. He's Your yingele too. Send him the refuah shleimah he needs.*

All these memories, clippings of the past 13 years, snapshots, tears, conversations, flitted through my mind on that Monday morning last week when Rina called me about the bar mitzvah.

What do you know, Rina, I mused reflectively, as I ran my finger along the buttons on the cordless phone. *You think I'm the carefree woman that you see, shul friend, neighbor, energetic mother of six, preparing for her oldest son's bar mitzvah.*

Indeed, this would be our first bar mitzvah. Indeed, we were busy with a caterer and a musician; our home was humming with the festivities of invitations and errands. Shragi looked like a picture of *nachas* in his new hat and suit. He would have a beautiful bar mitzvah, and we would all look our elegant best, *b'ezras Hashem*.

There was so much more, though, on our hearts and minds.

Shragi was our *bechor*, our precious son who had turned us into parents and had turned us into the *Ribono shel Olam's* clinging children. He was our little boy with whom we had been through so much, and he was our giant from whom we had learned so much.

And now our dear Shragi would be undergoing surgery one month before his bar mitzvah to suction out his lungs and remove some of the badly inflamed tissue. What couldn't be accomplished by all the antibiotics, steroids, and countless hours of physiotherapy had to be achieved by the inevitable: surgery.

Akiva and I would take turns being there with him. And then we'd go home and get busy with all the nitty-gritty details that make a bar mitzvah celebration complete.

Because ever since that day almost 13 years ago, that's what our life has been all about; a synthesis of the very significant and the very insignificant, a picture focused on the major, and yet not absent of all the little joys that come with the frills of life.

We haven't become impassive to mundane living; we've just come to see it the way it looks from our perspective up on the incline.

Up there, where the mountain gets steep, there is something clear and invigorating about the air. There is something quiet and elevated that one doesn't always get to hear in the din below.

And that something is the whispered connection between oneself and one's purpose, between oneself and one's Creator.

As Shragi practices his *derashah* and I whip up a cheesecake for the *kiddush*, my heart is engaged in those whispers. As Akiva picks up the *tefillin* and then drives with Shragi to the hospital in Manhattan, his heart is engaged in those whispers.

I close my eyes and picture the allegory that I know only too well, the scene of a child being admitted for surgery.

As the parents walk through the hospital doors with their child, the child takes in the austere surroundings. He sees the brisk gait of doctors and nurses, hears the clanging of metal carts, smells the antiseptic odor.

"I'm afraid, Tatty," he whispers, "I want to go back home."

The parents squeeze his little palm reassuringly.

"Yes, it's frightening, mein kind, but we're with you. We're not going to leave you alone."

The child swallows and nods bravely, calmed by the security of his parents' presence. They are given a room. The anesthesiologist walks in. There are consent forms to sign.

The child looks up, pale and afraid.

The mother smiles encouragingly.

"It sounds so scary, mein teier kind, but you're going to be all right. Tatty and Mommy are with you."

The child is given a hospital gown to change into. And a sterile cap. He has to leave his familiar clothing behind. He looks at his parents, panic stricken.

They lovingly take his hand, and accompany him to the second floor. They hold his hand and walk until the swinging doors. Then they cannot hold his hand anymore. They must part.

The child gulps. He shuffles into the operating theater in his sheer gown and slippers, his whole body suddenly convulsed with chills. Cold hands show him to the table. He stumbles up. His palms feel clammy. His heart thuds wildly. He lies down. He cannot swallow.

Suddenly, he looks up, and a small smile spreads on his wan face. Up there, above the operating table, is a little oblong window. And through that window, he sees the faces he knows and loves most, the comforting faces of his parents smiling down to him.

Sometimes He holds our hands, and sometimes He seems to leave go. But He is always looking down from that little window.

Avinu Malkeinu, I implore, *Chamol aleinu;* we are Yours. *V'al ola-*

leinu; Shragi and Eli are Yours. The rest of our *kinderlach* are Yours. All of *Klal Yisrael* are Yours.

Avinu Malkeinu, shelach refuah shleimah l'cholei amecha.

You have brought us all until this point; just keep holding our hands. Keep holding our hands and smiling down through that window, because it's the only way we can keep climbing.

The only way we can keep looking up without falling down.

Role Reversal

If climbing is measured in terms of change, then I've done an awful lot of climbing in my life. Interestingly, however, my toughest climbs were not necessarily about swinging my weight over a precarious precipice, or leaving go of my foothold in order to leap. The hardest ascent was the tedious inching inside the confines of my very own soul once I had reached a plateau.

We emigrated from Iran to the United States when I was a few months old. I grew up in a family where Judaism was somewhat like a winter sun; it emanated the light, but not the warmth. We kept Shabbat at the most basic level; no driving, no lights, no telephone. We had the TV on a timer, though, somewhat of a depiction of our observance at large. The life was inconsonant with the style; there was the shell without the inner beauty, the mechanics devoid of the feeling.

Somewhere during my high school years, I crossed the median between traditional, liberal Judaism to a committed Torah life. The high school I attended, founded as a *kiruv* effort, gave me a glimpse of the dimension I was missing. Our teachers introduced us to the heart of Judaism, the warm vibrancy pulsing beneath the framework of mitzvos and halachos. They gave us the opportunity to interact with families who represented and lived these ideals. I was hooked.

I attended Neve Yerushalayim, where I lapped up the inspiration like a thirst-crazed desert nomad hitting an oasis. I couldn't get enough of the learning, *Chumash, Navi, Parashah, Medrash, Hashkafah*. I loved the intellectual stimulation, the spiritual elevation, the joy of discovering a world of wisdom that resonated with the deepest whispers of my soul.

The subject that particularly strummed at my heartstrings was *tefillah*. Uttering the words of *Pesukei d'Zimrah*, of *Uva l'Tzion*, of *Hallel*, I felt a palpable sense of connection. It was the joy of fulfilling my truest needs, of satisfying my innermost desire. With the *Kosel* only a bus ride away, I utilized every opportunity to stand in front of the worn stones and pour the innermost whispers of my heart into my *tefillah*.

Every time I reached the plaza, squinted up at the ancient sand-colored stones against the intense blue sky, I felt an acute sense of tenderness, an almost breathtaking wave of yearning overwhelmed me. It was the ecstasy of coming home.

There was no brisk business going on, no politics blaring in the background, no shallow socializing. Only the cool, reassuring stone, and the bright, warm sun and the rhythm of the eternal murmurs, almost like the even breathing of the Wall itself.

I savored those trips like a child savors time alone with his mother. I felt so attached, so in tune, so very close to the place where the *Shechinah* forever rests.

And then the year was over.

Coming home was like reentering a fluorescent-lit house after being in the sun-bathed outdoors. For those first disorienting weeks, I could only blink in a daze. The stagnant air, the dusky darkness, the humdrum monotony, all stood in such stark contrast to the dazzling holiness I had felt in Yerushalayim.

I didn't want to leave go of that holiness. I enrolled in a post-seminary learning program and got busy looking for a job. Soon after, one of my mentors approached me with a *shidduch* proposal: Michoel Schwartz. The name was not a new one. Though the boy I had known had been called Mike, I assumed they were one and the same.

Mike had attended the same school I had, and though officially, boys and girls occupied two different floors, we had met up with one another on occasion. In fact, back in ninth grade we both had even acted in the school play! I remembered Mike as being witty and entertaining, traits I wasn't particularly drawn to at this point in my life.

My teacher heard me out, but insisted that Michoel was a complete changeover from the Mike I had known as a freshman. He had finished school and had gone on to yeshivah in Eretz Yisrael, where he had become as *frum* and committed as myself. He was a star learner and had aspirations of building a *yeshivishe* home.

I was willing to give it a try.

Michoel spoke about yeshivah, the impact his *rebbeim* had had on him, and the kind of home he dreamed of building. I shared my *Neve* experience, my love of learning and prayer, and my hopes of following the example of my mentors.

We were engaged in two months. Coming from similar backgrounds and having both experienced a reawakening to *Yiddishkeit*, we shared a strong understanding of each other.

We were married a short while later.

Michoel commuted to work, spent the mornings at his job and the rest of the day at the place he loved most, in front of the *shtender*. I had a job teaching at a local school, and kept busy discovering the joys of housekeeping. We were happy and fulfilled, reveling in the bliss of a new marriage. We waited in eager anticipation to join the growing community of budding families.

At first, the months passed almost imperceptibly. Of course, Michoel and I each secretly fondled the sweet dream of becoming parents. It was still a shadow in the background, though, a dream not yet strained by the tension of anxiety.

When a few more months passed with no news, our unspoken thoughts turned into worried conversations. Why weren't things going the way they seemed to go for everybody else? We had seen enough young couples turn into parents over the last few months; judging by the amount of carriages and strollers we saw, the appearance of babies seemed so natural, so effortless.

We decided to wait another while before we pursued any medical leads. In the meantime, we both reviewed every detail of our *shemiras hamitzvos* and tried to pinpoint areas we could strengthen. We also intensified our *davening*. We both knew that although the field of infertility had made great advances, the underlying reasons had not changed much since the times of the *Avos*.

Hakadosh Baruch Hu mis'aveh l'sfilasan shel tzaddikim (Hashem longs for the prayers of the righteous). *Tefillah* was not the last resort when all else failed. *Tefillah* was the first and most potent avenue to pursue. *Tefillah* was pulling the strings with the Top Brass.

When another half a year passed and there was still no harbinger on the horizon, we consulted with our *moreh derech* and were told that *tefillos* notwithstanding, some *hishtadlus* was in order.

There is something about the world of medicine that labels ambiguous anxieties, files them, and graphs them on a hard grid. Although nothing had actually changed, we had crossed the invisible line from vaguely impatient newlyweds to officially infertile couple.

Up until then, it was as if we had been nonchalantly standing around a lobby of newlyweds waiting for our names to be called out for parenthood. All at once we realized that the chatting had died down and the crowd had thinned, dispersed with strollers and infant seats.

Only a solid wooden door faced us now from the end of the hall, a door sporting a forbidding brass plaque. Was that our name the receptionist was calling?

I began to lead the double life anybody who has been there knows. On the outside I was functioning normally, attending *shiurim*, dancing at weddings, shopping, tutoring, volunteering. Only I was privy to the other side of the picture, the appointments at the oddest hours, the bloodtests and ultrasounds and injections.

I had always known that having children was a drain on one's time, one's energy, and one's budget. What I hadn't known was that *not* having children could be an equal strain on all those resources.

Friends would often ask me to go out with them, naturally assuming that my schedule was free or at least flexible. After all, I didn't need to get a babysitter, and I had no one to run fetch from kindergarten at any given time. I would be asked to bake the cake for the party or set up for the dinner. Wasn't I the perfect candidate? I had no homework to oversee, no itchy fingers dipping into the batter.

I'd find myself fumbling awkwardly for excuses. *Mothers had it so simple,* I'd think; *all they had to say was that the baby was teething or that they had an appointment with the older one, and they were off the hook.*

Not that I was bitter or envious. I loved my friends' kids and appreciated when they included me in their experiences. I found it hard, though, walking the lonely trail alongside the hectic highway of their lives. Purportedly, we were traveling the same route, *kollel*, working, housekeeping, shopping, and *chessed*. That's where it ended, though. While they were struggling with colicky infants and moody toddlers, I was up against rigorous treatment and repeated dashed hopes.

After we had gone through two failed rounds of treatment, we both felt we needed a break. Medicine had such an insidious way of bogging one down, of drawing one into the deceptive spiral of cause and effect and making one feel hopeless. We both felt that a trip to Eretz Yisrael would restore our perspectives and rejuvenate our spirits.

Indeed, as soon as we descended the movable metal staircase into the brilliant Israeli sun, we were awash with optimism. We were coming back home to Eretz Yisrael, to the land of *kedushah* and purity, the land that transcended the natural order of the world.

We felt refreshed and invigorated. Our first stop was the *Kosel*, where I lovingly embraced the stones I had parted with several years earlier. An overwhelming sense of closeness overtook me. It was like rocking in the clasp of a dear friend one hadn't seen for a long time, impervious to the surrounding onlookers, oblivious to the passing of time.

Finally, after an eternity of standing and stroking the stones, I opened my *siddur* and gave vent to my innermost emotions. I had so much to catch up on. Though I *davened* every day in New York, there was a certain sense of intimacy I felt standing in my familiar niche beneath the shrubbery jutting from the Wall.

I felt as if I could stand there forever. Michoel, too, was completely immersed in his *tefillah* on the other side of the *mechitzah*. After a good two hours *davening*, Michoel signaled that he thought it was time to go. I shuffled backward in the waning sun, feeling cleansed and uplifted.

Our next two weeks were packed to capacity. We traveled the length and breadth of Eretz Yisrael, visiting every *kever* we knew of, meeting with countless *gedolim* and *Rabbanim*. We had audiences with several *Rebbes* and *mekubalim*, all of whom gave us their warmest blessings.

Although we *davened* at the *kevarim* in Miron, Tzefas and Teveriah, and picked up numerous *eitzos* and *segulos* along the way, my biggest boon was still being able to *daven* at the *Kosel*. I cherished every moment there, praying, entreating, beseeching that we be endowed with the gift of parenthood soon.

When our two weeks were over, we both felt a deep sense of peace and fulfillment. We had refueled spiritually and felt ready to go back and face our *nisayon* again.

During the initial few weeks home, we were still heady with the ecstasy of our trip. As soon as we had gotten settled into routine, though, we started making phone calls about resuming treatment once again.

Incredibly, our efforts proved unnecessary. By the time we walked into the doctor's office for our appointment, we were already the bearers of good news. Without any intervention at all in the physical realm, our prayers had been answered.

It's hard to describe the succeeding months, the all-consuming excitement, the anticipation, the feelings of gratitude and elation that quite literally intoxicated our beings.

When our son was born, we felt as if the Heavens had parted to send him to us. The maternity ward ceased to exist. The doctors and nurses and hospital routine receded into the background. It was only *Hashem* and us and the baby, ensconced in a cocoon of closeness and rapture. We were sure the world had stopped.

Our parents were on a high. The entire community participated in our *simchah*, calling, congratulating, showering us with gifts. Our home was suddenly transformed from the staid, orderly home of a working couple to a cheerful disarray of gift boxes, baby paraphernalia, and a constant stream of visitors.

I still get the chills when I remember the first time I took the baby out in his carriage. It was as if the world had been staged for the occasion. I could barely suppress my excitement as I gingerly placed him on the brand-new pad and tucked a diaper into the bag. I was actually taking my baby for a walk.

My baby for a walk.

Those were the most delicious words I had ever tasted.

Though I had shared in so many of my friends' births, nothing had prepared me for the fierce swirl of affection, for the overwhelming sense of joy and completeness that Moishy brought into our lives.

And nothing had prepared me for the colic.

Though I tended to his needs like a doting mother hen, Moishy screamed around the clock. He would pull up his little legs, pucker up his tiny face, and wail incessantly, leaving Michoel and me helpless to do anything. We took turns holding him, pacing the apartment with him, giving him bottles of gripe water and chamomile tea, anything that promised to soothe him. To no avail.

I turned to other young mothers for advice. The suggestions were conflicting and confusing. Don't nurse him before three hours; nurse him whenever he cries. Just hold him and cuddle him; let him cry, there's nothing else you can do.

Many times I just wanted to join Moishy and cry in utter frustration. I was tired and sleep deprived and Michoel wasn't home most of the time. I felt like a total non-manager, barely getting to the essentials, never mind getting to read something or attend a *shiur.*

Then I would bite my lip and admonish myself. I had *davened* so hard for this, had spent years hoping and dreaming of holding a baby; how could I be tearful and overwhelmed?

One instance in particular, stands out in my memory. It was Rosh Hashanah, between Shacharis and Mussaf, the high point of my day. As I got ready to recite *lamnatzei'ach*, I felt a twinge. *Tekias shofar* had always been an uplifting experience for me. The impact of the shofar blasts usually provided inspiration way into the year. On the days preceding Rosh Hashanah, I would prepare a list of the various thoughts and feelings on which I wanted to concentrate.

This year, between Moishy screaming and trying to prepare the basics for Yom Tov, I hadn't gotten to do much mental preparation. Standing right by the *mechitzah*, I tried to capitalize on the moment and focus inward. I didn't want to forfeit the priceless opportunity.

The *gabbai klapped* on the *bimah* and the *baal toke'ia* intoned the *berachos*. There was a palpable sense of *din* as the first blast pierced the pin-drop silence, tempered by feelings of *rachamim* evoked by the *shofar's* plaintive cry.

I buried my face in my hands, engulfed in the holiness of the moment. Suddenly Moishy's screams burst through my introspection. Dropping my *kavannos* midthought, I quickly scooped him up, rocking him frantically. His lusty cries only escalated. Left with no choice, I walked out of the *shul*, battling my tears.

My heart was in a turmoil. Intellectually, I knew that my role was the holiest role I could fill, that caring for a child was no less of an exalted task than concentrating on *tekios*. I also knew that last year, as I had stood in the very same place, I had been entreating for just this.

Still, I felt a sense of loss and disappointment. My abridged *davening* had hardly been the inspirational experience it had always been, and the hurried *tekios* I heard from my husband right before the meal barely afforded me the time or composure to concentrate properly.

Looking back, that encounter was my real introduction to motherhood. Although today I am grateful beyond words, elated to see Moishy on Michoel's shoulders on Simchas Torah, thrilled to have a reason to attend Uncle Moishy concerts and Chol HaMoed events, for that first year, it took all my coping skills just to keep Moishy's needs met and the house running smoothly. I had no time to dream about cultivating my own needs.

As Moishy grew older and settled down, I was able to pursue my spiritual interests a little more, attending a weekly *shiur* and subbing occasionally at schools. If we had thought that having a first baby was a one-time ticket to parenthood, circumstances proved otherwise.

By the time Moishy was fully trained and out of the crib, we began to feel anxious again. Although nothing in the world could compare to the intensity of waiting the first time around, having a child had changed the quality of our yearning.

My maternal wellsprings had been tapped, and they could not be stilled. Besides, Moishy himself so badly wanted a sibling. He was one of the only ones in his kindergarten class without a baby under him and constantly badgered us to bring home a baby for him.

I taught him the concept of *tefillah*, and we *davened* together. As I baked challah with him, I'd say the *berachah* and put aside a piece of dough and he'd join me in my prayers that another child join our family soon.

We went through rough times, but our prayers were answered again. Our little baby girl, Racheli, made us into a real family. Moishy was a proud older brother, puttering around her crib and rocking her carriage. From the start, the two were the best of friends. I felt my mother's heart overflowing at the banks.

When I looked at the two of them, our cute little *cheder* boy and our charming infant, I was filled with gratitude and awe. Ours wasn't a home where the joys of having children were taken for granted. Every first tooth, every first step, every milestone invited such utter excitement. Every *parashah* sheet, every *siddur* party was another thrilling ribbon bedecking the priceless gift of parenthood.

It was a gift we had to beg for each time anew. Racheli, too, enjoyed a prolonged day in the sun, occupying the coveted position of baby for a few years before she was joined by a sister. Michoel compared it to the timeless cup of tears that had to be filled to the overflowing each time before the *geulah* dawned.

When our baby Ruti was a few months old, we won tickets to Eretz Yisrael at a Chinese auction. I was elated. Although the kids' airfare wouldn't be covered, I knew what I wanted to do. We had spent the past few summers in a bungalow colony. Now, with Moishy 10 and Racheli 5, I thought they were old enough to appreciate a summer in Eretz Yisrael.

Seeing my enthusiasm, Michoel endorsed the plan. I got to work, feverishly planning our itinerary. Michoel only had two weeks off in the summer, so we would have to cram all our plans into that time. I felt like a toddler trying to pack the world into an undersized shopping bag. I wanted this to be the trip of a lifetime; if we couldn't live in Eretz Yisrael, at least we could try to absorb all the *kedushah* we could on our short trip.

We would spend the first few days in the Old City so we could be at the *Kosel* for Shacharis, Minchah, and Maariv. Then there were about a dozen *tzaddikim* I wanted my children to see. There was Tzefas and Miron, the *kever* of Reb Meir Baal Haness, the Rambam , and of course the *kever* of the Shelah Hakadosh.

I felt the tingle of excitement just mapping it all out. On the way back to Yerushalayim, we could stop at the Arizal's *mikveh,* and at the *kever* of Chanah and her seven sons. That would leave us with a few more days in Yerushalayim, visiting friends and family, perhaps even stopping by at Neve and sitting in on some classes. I reserved the whole last day for an unforgettable few hours at the *Kosel.*

When Michoel caught a glimpse of my itinerary, he smiled.

"Looks like an amazing itinerary, Chanah;" he said. "Where are you planning to leave the kids?"

My eyebrows arched questioningly.

"I know you want to get the most out of this trip, but we can't forget that this is the kids' summer vacation. I think we have to make some adjustments here."

Although I infinitely trusted Michoel, I couldn't help feeling an inner tug of resistance. *The kids will have a great time; how many kids are lucky enough to go on such a trip?* Worse came to worst, I reasoned, if it proved to be too much for them, we would cancel some of the plans at the last minute.

Landing in Eretz Yisrael awakened some charged memories. Eleven years earlier we had been a couple unencumbered by strollers and diaper bags, weighed down instead by the heaviness inside our hearts. This time, we each held a child's hand while I pushed the stroller ahead of me. Our hearts were full, laden with gratitude and pride.

As soon as we had deposited our luggage and had the kids washed and fed, I forged straight ahead,

"Let's go, kids," I called, my voice trembling with emotion, "Remember all those stories about the *Beis HaMikdash*? Well, now we're going to stand in front of a real wall that surrounded the *Beis HaMikdash!*"

The kids, catching my infectious attitude, bounced up and down in excitement. I settled them on chairs and wistfully approached the Wall I had missed for over a decade.

True to my itinerary, we spent the next two days in and out of cars, on and off busses. Though it was, indeed, a bit heavy on the kids, they cooperated. I felt like I was soaring on some higher plane, imbibing the *kedushah* of Eretz Yisrael, pouring out my heart in *tefillah* at the holiest places in the world.

Toward the end of the week, Michoel hesitantly told me he'd made plans to take the kids camel riding. Seeing my crestfallen face, he quickly reassured me that I could keep my original plans if I wanted to and he would take the kids. Somehow, that didn't sit quite right with me. Reluctantly, I gave up my itinerary and joined the trip.

The kids had the time of their lives. They were seated in age order from the littlest to the biggest, and even Ruti, who was only 10 months old, giggled hysterically each time the camel got up or down, shifting the two older ones forward. I melted at the sight. Pulling out my camera, I recorded the shots for posterity and then had someone else take a picture as Michoel and I posed with the kids. It was a memorable experience. Still, the whole time, I felt this gnawing, niggling feeling at the bottom of my heart. We were finally in Eretz Yisrael after so many years. We had so few precious days to spend here. Was this what we had come for?

I went to bed that night, feeling frustrated and upset. Michoel told me he planned to go take the kids swimming and rowing. I kept quiet. The days were slipping through our fingers and we weren't getting to half of what I had planned. When would we ever do this again? We could always go swimming and rowing in New York.

The night before our last day in Eretz Yisrael, Michoel helped me pack, while we reminisced about our trip.

"It's too late for whatever we didn't do," I sighed in resignation, "but at least tomorrow will be the highlight of our trip."

I sat down on the couch, exhausted, smiling as I envisioned the next day.

I couldn't wait to spend the entire day at the *Kosel*, *davening*, saying *Tehillim*, just absorbing the sound of all those *tefillos*, basking in the presence of the *Shechinah*. I wanted to achieve a level of closeness to Hashem, a lasting feeling that would accompany me homeward. Who knew how long it would take until I would be here again?

My husband zipped the second suitcase shut.

"I heard there's a new park nearby; I thought that the kids might really enjoy it." Seeing my obvious disappointment, he quickly reassured me.

"Of course we'll visit the *Kosel* before we leave, but I think a few hours is way too much for the kids. Maybe we should spend the morning there and save the afternoon for the park."

I didn't share what I was feeling, but I went to sleep choking back my tears. A park? There were so many parks back home. I wouldn't even be able to enjoy it, thinking of the experience I had forfeited. Why, I had looked forward to the day at the *Kosel* from the moment we had arrived.

Indeed, I tried to make the most of my time at the *Kosel* the next morning. Before I had a chance to really part with the stones, it was time to go. The kids were squealing with excitement. They scrambled into the taxi that would take us to the park, talking and giggling as I watched the beautiful scenery whisk past us.

Goodbye, my dear *Kosel*, I thought emotionally; Goodbye, Old City, goodbye all you trees and mountains and stones. I had a huge lump in my throat by the time we reached the park.

Oblivious to my roiling emotions, my kids tumbled out of the car, running ahead of us to the colorful playground equipment. They climbed on the monkey bars and slid down the slides, laughing, cheering, and singing, reminiscing about their favorite places in Eretz Yisrael.

And as I watched their merry abandon, listened to their tinkling laughter and whoops of joy, it was suddenly as if I was seeing them for the first time. Looking at their radiant faces, I remembered how we had longed to hold a baby in our arms on our last trip to Eretz Yisrael 11 years earlier. In my mind, I relived the many hardships we had been through before each of them was born.

And suddenly, I was struck by the glaring irony of my mistake. The purpose of our trip last time had been to storm the Heavens for these priceless treasures. We had begged, hoped, implored that we wouldn't be able to do those very things we had been able to do then.

Here we were, our dream fulfilled, yet I was somehow still looking for spirituality measured in tears and prayers. I looked at Moishy, wispy brown *peyos*, *tzitzis* flying. Racheli was panting right behind him, perpetual smile flashing on her face. And there was little Ruti, chubby hands grabbing the yellow bar, determined to get up the sliding pond.

These were my gems, my destiny, my prayers. These were my *ruchniyus*, my *tafkid*, my *ratzon Hashem*.

Opening my trusty *Tehillim*, I turned the pages to the psalms of *Hallel*, my whole heart aflame with the joy of my discovery. I felt a decade of inner conflict roll off my chest as I sang the words, thanking Hashem for the past and for the present, for my wonderful husband and family, and most of all for the stunning clarity of my soul's revelation.

Motherhood *was* holiness. Not prayer and not learning, not shul-going or shofar blowing, but the simple nurturing of my family's physical needs were *my* spiritual fulfillment.

Moshivi akeres habayis eim habanim s'meichah, Hallelukah.

He (Hashem) transforms the barren women of the house into a joyful mother of children, Hallelukah!

Making It Work

I sat down in the waiting room at the pediatrician's office, holding my newborn bundle. Something about the way I refolded her blanket and fluffed up her beret must have given it away.

"First baby?" the woman sitting next to me smiled.

I nodded, smiling back.

"Welcome to the club", she chuckled. "Take it from an experienced mother; it gets easier. May you have lots of *nachas*."

"How old is your oldest?" I asked, after we had been sitting in comfortable silence for another few minutes. I was curious if I had surmised right.

"Oh, he's 11 already," she replied, instinctively hugging the freckled little boy next to her.

I smiled again, this time to myself. Suspicion confirmed. She was probably just about the same age I was. I had, indeed, just had my first baby, but it had been a long road.

I appreciated her wishes, though. I could use them.

Throughout high school and seminary, we had been constantly prepared for our roles as Jewish wives and mothers. It was an unspoken convention that we would graduate, take jobs, and, sooner or later, find *shidduchim*. Never did I entertain the thought that "later" could mean more than a decade. A decade fraught with *tefillos*, anxiety, hope, rejection, and disappointment.

If you've ever spent an hour waiting at an appointed spot to make a bus or meet a friend (without a cell phone!), you know something about the anxiety of waiting. You keep checking your watch, scanning the horizon, biting your lips in mounting impatience.

Greater than the impatience, even, is the feeling of futility, the frustration of being suspended in limbo. There are a million things you could be doing with your time and yet you can't go back home and you can't go ahead with your plans.

Waiting at my personal bus stop, when I started noticing that the crowd was obviously thinning, I began to feel that edge of uneasiness worming its way into my consciousness. If I knew how long I had to wait, my mind reasoned, I'd pace myself, throw myself into something else for the time being. Not knowing left me stalling for time. One more date, maybe this time, one more summer, one more year of teaching.

It was right then and there that I decided to change my attitude. I wasn't waiting at the bus stop at all. I was *on* the bus. A different bus, perhaps, than most of my peers, a different bus, perhaps, than the one I'd envisioned myself riding at this stage of my life, but nevertheless, a moving, progressing vehicle.

When I'd been 19, I had once had the opportunity to attend a Bikur Cholim *melaveh malkah* where Rabbi Josh Silbermintz, *z'l*, spoke. I listened carefully to his inspiring words about making every person count. As Rabbi Silbermintz made his way through the crowd after the speech, he noticed me and gestured that he wanted to tell me something.

"I want you to know that I especially noticed two or three people in the crowd and you were one of them. There is a striking quality about your face. I can tell you have extraordinary *kochos*. I only hope you won't be too busy to use them."

I blushed, feeling awkward and complimented at the same time. What had Rabbi Silbermintz seen in me that had compelled him to single me out? To this day, I have no idea.

All I know is that his words were the remedy preceding the affliction. They accompanied me like a heavenly calling, demanding, encouraging, consoling me, and prodding me to do the most I could do with my time over the ensuing years.

And I did. I became a dedicated Bikur Cholim volunteer, heading various committees for over seven years. I got involved in *kiruv* and tutored over the phone. I also made a firm commitment to join a weekly *shiur*.

It was this *shiur* that introduced me to some of my dearest friends, singles like myself who were living in basement apartments and jokingly called themselves the Boro Park Underground. Though I was living at home with my family, our plight was the same.

We understood one another without words. We were able to laugh and cry, smile and sigh together. While most of my contemporaries were busy with growing families, car pools, pediatricians, and supper, I was able to share my interests and ambitions with girls on my own turf.

Being part of the weekly *shiur* also gave me a chance to cultivate relationships with married women. Although technically, I lived with my parents in Boro Park and didn't need invitations, I greatly appreciated being invited out sometimes. It gave me a chance to observe family interaction, and gave me a break from the pressure I sometimes felt at home. I knew I was weighing heavily on my parents' hearts and it put a strain on our relationship.

My friends in the same boat (or on the same bus) often complained that birthday celebrations had turned into morbid markers of their escalating age. I, however, never stopped celebrating my birthdays.

Though I was anxious to get married, I never viewed myself as a human being on hold. The *Ribono shel Olam* returned my *neshamah* each day with a purpose in mind, and single or married, that behooved me to grow. My birthdays gave me a chance to reflect back on the past year and assess my self-improvement, my mastery of *middos*, my contribution to *Kiddush Shem Shamayim*.

Like every older single, of course I had my moments of crisis, days when I felt disheartened, even pained. My colleagues at work would kibbitz, "*Nu,* so when are you getting your M.R.S. degree?" and I would respond in kind, "As soon as I graduate, I guess." Despite my attempt at lightheartedness, though, comments like these, blatant insinuations that I was somehow responsible for my status, hurt me deeply.

Friends and relatives would berate me for refusing another date, or question my premise for not considering a particular *shidduch*. Though I knew they were driven by the desire to see me join their ranks, the barely concealed accusations struck my most vulnerable spot. Hadn't anyone learned about the outcome of Peninah's well-meaning gibes?

Pondering my own pain, I couldn't help but pray that these well-meaning critics be spared. The pain of a shattered soul is more potent than most people realize. Especially when that pain is unnecessarily exacerbated by unsolicited comments.

When my sister, six years my junior, got engaged, I braced myself for the wedding. Two of my friends who had gone through the same experience called me to offer their support. One of them prepared me for a difficult ordeal, assuring me that I would survive. The second one wished me a great time, encouraging me to try and enjoy myself.

I was surprised at how helpful her advice proved to be. The knowledge that I was doing my utmost gave me a terrific sense of serenity. There was nothing more I could do; being miserable wasn't part of *chovos hahishtadlus*. I danced joyously at that wedding and was even joined by a few of my close friends who made an effort to attend.

Tefillah played an important role in my life. Though I made a point of keeping a cheerful facade, there were times when I let the tears spill freely, beseeching Hashem to hear my pleas and send me my *basherte* partner.

An aunt of mine once bought me a beautiful *Tehillim* as a token of her empathy, and it became my cherished companion. I found my feelings mirrored in the words of David HaMelech and drew insight and encouragement from the *pesukim*.

All throughout my ordeal, there was one thing I knew. The *Ribono shel Olam* had been my first *shadchan*. He had set aside a partner for me before I was even created, and that partner was somewhere to be found.

Hakol b'chezkas sumin ad sheHakadosh Baruch Hu meir es eineihem (All [human beings] are considered blind until *Hakadosh Baruch Hu* opens their eyes). When the right time came, Hashem would remove the obstacles and I would find my husband without a hint of delay.

Hakadosh Baruch Hu runs His world with precision unfathomable to the human mind. There is a reason for every minute of waiting, a purpose behind every rejection. Sometimes, in retrospect, we get a glimpse of what we conceive as an explanation.

When my time came, I was privileged to such a glimpse. My husband and I hailed from different backgrounds; I was as American as you could get, while he was of traditional, no-nonsense, British schooling. I was an emotional, intuitive thinker while logic and discipline dominated his personality. Had either of us been introduced to each other earlier on, we would never have given it a long shot.

At 30, I was willing to give it a try. I had matured enough to respect differences; life had taught me not to underestimate integrity, maturity, and strong Torah commitments; traits I saw in him from the outset. My husband, too, was ready to compromise on the mind-set familiar to him in lieu of my favorable qualities.

The moment had come, not a minute too early, not a minute too late.

When I called Aunt Dina in my euphoria, I mentioned how much I had treasured her *Tehillim* throughout the arduous climb.

"Don't close the *Tehillim* now, Miriam," my aunt exhorted me. "You need the *tefillos* now more than ever before."

If her words had the sound of a beaten cliche, they held all the wisdom in the world. The *Ribono shel Olam* had, indeed, walked me to the top of the path. I was dizzy with gratitude, lost in a halo of happiness. Right there, though, right at the peak of my joy, stood the foot of the next mountain.

In my fantasy of marriage, the ebullient rings of mazal tov had always constituted the last page of the single's saga. *The elusive moment had arrived. They drank l'chaim and it became official. Mazal Tov!*

The end.

And they lived happily ever after.

Sheva berachos was enough to explode the myth. If marriage was an adjustment at 20, then it was an overhauling at 30. A massive overhauling.

We had each spent the last 10 years of our lives, growing, molding, climbing on our own. We had adopted ideas and ideals, had cemented our views on life. And we had each developed commitments and bonds.

Making It Work / 77

My husband had been learning in yeshivah for years, and wasn't accustomed to running his *sedarim* around someone else's schedule. He had his systems of doing things and his beliefs of how things should run. On the domestic front, he held his mother in the highest esteem and had never really had much contact with any other woman.

I myself had been involved in a host of activities and had a very close circle of friends. As an older girl, I had often promised myself I would never snub my single friends once I was lucky enough to marry. I wouldn't disappear into the clouds together with my husband like some of my newlywed friends, leaving my single soulmates to wait in isolation down below.

How much time, I used to wonder, did it take to call a friend and let her know you were thinking of her? How much effort did it require to make contact once a day, or at least once a week?

I learned. It wasn't a question of time and it wasn't a question of effort. It was a question of loyalty, of proving that one was deeply and wholeheartedly faithful to one's spouse.

I don't think I ever would have understood this, had someone explained it to me earlier on. What was the problem? Husband came first and friends came second. Crisis resolved.

The best of theories, though, are refuted by life. My husband was the youngest of five boys and had rarely interacted with anyone of the female species other than his mother. His years of singlehood had given him plenty of time to observe her.

My mother-in-law was disciplined to the extreme and had little need for a social life. She never thought of using the telephone barring emergencies or social formalities. The concept of casual schmoozing was foreign and frivolous to her.

My friends were all working and their free time coincided with my husband's. For me to be on the phone then for any reason less than pressing would have been a blatant insult to him, an open sign of disregard. Why would I need to talk to other people if I had him?

Though I had prayed for just this adjustment for many pain-filled years, I found myself feeling cut off and stifled. I had left an excellent job so I could move to Lakewood, and had seriously downsized my involvement with *kiruv* and *askanus* in order to make room for my new role as a wife. All at once, I felt strangely isolated and unfulfilled.

I had spent the last decade of my life cultivating my independence, reinforcing the notion that productivity rather than status measured my self-worth. I had worked so hard to be active, to branch out and pursue my interests, develop my talents. Now I was being asked to make a U-turn, undo my mind-set, and neatly fold away everything that had made my lonely existence bearable.

Aside from reprogramming my attitude was the simple difficulty of giving up my freedom after operating singly for so many years. As committed as I had ever been to my parents and employers, I had still been basically my own boss. I had woken up at the hour that suited me, spent my free time the way I wanted, went to sleep when I felt ready to call it a day.

I had made my own decisions based on my individual needs and sense of judgment, pursued the challenges that spoke to my soul. I had never been forced to work my schedule around someone else's, to share my car, to miss a *shiur*.

My husband respected my interests, but he couldn't understand why I would still feel a need to pursue them. His mother had never worked out of the home; she had been a practical, wholesome, full-time wife and mother. Couldn't I be the same?

It was a tall order. I had grown up in an easygoing American household with two working parents. People were allowed to slouch when they ate and rest if they felt tired. Meals were basically informal, as was the general decorum. We were as far from standing on ceremony as you could get.

My husband, on the other hand, was accustomed to rigid, uncompromising standards. In his parents' home, proper etiquette was expected at mealtime and resting during the daytime was unheard of. Early to bed and early to rise was the motto.

While my idea of love was warmth expressed by words and gestures, his concept of solidarity was defined by punctuality and dependability. While I loved music and art he dismissed them both as a waste of time and money.

I had grown up in a house where *chessed* had taken first priority. My mother volunteered for several organizations and my father was involved in community work. My husband's family placed an emphasis on *halachah* and *kashrus*. Many of the foods I had grown up eating were completely unacceptable to him.

Integrity, maturity, and commitment had seemed like such admirable traits when I had seen them in him as a *chassan*. In real life, these same qualities seemed a trifle forbidding.

I found myself feeling trapped, caught between my desire to be a good wife, and my need to feel validated and fulfilled. I missed my social life, my involvement in *klal* work. Even technically, I felt restricted. Any time I took the car anywhere, I felt pressured to return home on time; if my boss ever asked me to stay late at work, I felt intimidated to ask my husband.

I was too vulnerable, though, to take anyone into confidence. My marriage was so fragile; I had gotten a late start. I was afraid that outside advice might unnecessarily rock the precarious boat.

While I had been single, I had often joked that I was stocking up on advice and *chizuk* and storing them for the future. Driving to and from work during those difficult days, I had listened to countless *shiurim* and tapes on *shalom bayis* and *chinuch habanim*. Now I found myself drawing on those resources.

During one of those speeches, I had heard that the ultimate level of *ahavas Hashem* could be achieved by simulating the harmony between a husband and wife. Then and there, I had decided that I would work the other way around. If I had no marriage to model after, then I would concentrate on my *ahavas Hashem* first. Then, when the time came, I would try to foster those same tools in my home.

At that point, I had reviewed the words of *ve'ahavta* with *Rashi*. *B'chol levavcha — b'shnei yitzrechha* (with both inclinations); *u'vchol nafshecha — afilu notel es nafshecha* (even if He were to take your life); *u'vchol meodecha — b'chol mamoncha ... b'chol middah u'middah shehu modeid lach* (with all your possessions, and with each and every measure that He metes out to you).

Love wasn't something you fell into. It was something you worked on with every fiber of your being, with every cent in your possession, with every ounce of acceptance and trust. Love wasn't something that conquered your heart; it was something your heart had to conquer.

I knew I could easily focus on our differences. I could draw up a list of everything I had wanted in a husband and hadn't gotten, of everything I thought I deserved and wasn't receiving. I knew that if I wanted to, I could present a pretty good case.

The question was whether I wanted to present a case or whether I wanted to preserve my marriage.

I wanted the latter.

Again, I strengthened myself in my belief that *Hakadosh Baruch Hu* Himself had been my *shadchan*. He had chosen the perfect husband for my ultimate growth and had orchestrated events just so that we would meet at the destined moment and fuse our futures.

I knew that my assignment had changed. I had spent 10 years trying to find the elusive answer to the algebraic equation of my life. Now the challenge had been turned inside out. The solution was there in black and white. I would have to figure out the variables that would make the equation work.

In the meantime, however, I felt I needed to talk to someone. My husband constantly measured me against his mother, comparing the way I cooked, shopped, and kept house to the way she had done it. I felt inadequate and unappreciated.

In my heart of hearts, I knew I was comparing him too. I was comparing him to the husband of my dreams, the man who would smile and sing and compliment, the man who would discuss his feelings, listen to mine, and learn *Mesilas Yesharim* with me. Though I didn't voice these emotions, my disappointment definitely affected our interaction.

I was tempted to turn to my friends, but I held back. I knew that their natural devotion for me wouldn't allow them to see things objectively. At that point, though I wouldn't have minded some good old pity, I knew that wasn't what I needed. I needed the objective wisdom of someone who could guide me constructively.

I sought out an older mentor of mine, who had received positive reports about my *chassan* for me before I had gotten engaged.

I knew she would be predisposed to see him in a good light and would be able to help me focus on his strong points.

I came out of our discussion fortified with *chizuk*. The thrust of her advice was refreshingly simple: focus on building. Building yourself, building your husband, building your home.

"When one renovates," she illustrated, "one often crowds into less than ideal accommodations for a while. One is willing to bear an unusual amount of mess and noise for an outcome that will be bigger and better than that which one presently has.

"When you forgo, Miriam, think of where it will eventually lead you. If you can see something positive ahead, then persist, even if it entails temporary discomfort. Things like putting out place mats or using a different type of shoe polish are small prices to pay for the preservation of one's home and family.

"If you feel as if you are destroying a part of yourself, however, beware. Try and present your needs to your husband in a non-confrontational way. Don't knock him or try to get him to admit that you're right. Remember that your goal is to build. It isn't about proving either one right or wrong.

"Try to find interests you can cultivate without encroaching on his time or respect. Even if you feel he isn't as understanding as you would like, as long as he doesn't openly object, you are doing him a favor by building a happy, fulfilled wife.

"And just a reminder of something you surely know. We all have our imperfections. When we remember that we surely have qualities and habits that provoke our spouse, it makes it a lot easier to tolerate *his* faults. If we want to be understood and appreciated despite our shortcomings, the first step is to accept our spouse's failings."

I listened carefully, taking in every word. She gave me her warmest wishes along with a few more tidbits of practical advice. She also reminded me that no one married a complete person, and that with time, respect, and acceptance, people could definitely change. I felt my sagging spirits lift as I went home, determined to build.

As a metaphor, building has an idealistic ring, an echo of achievement and promise. Watch any construction site, though, and you'll know. Demolition is easy. Construction is hard work. Sweating hard work.

I came home fueled with motivation and good will. I would make a nice dinner, make it just the way his mother made it, using the *hechsherim* he was *makpid* on. Why, I was ready to do anything at all to make it work.

My idealism was somewhat deflated when my husband came home and asked how I had checked the strawberries, and if I had gotten to make the monthly payments that afternoon. Though I felt my good mood dissipating like a mountain of suds under a gush of water, I kept my smile on my face.

Trying as hard as I could not to sound defensive, I told him I had checked the strawberries according to Rav Falk's *sefer* and that I had been busy this afternoon, but I would gladly prepare the bills in the evening.

I was surprised to see how well my response went over. Though he may not have been gushing with compliments, he nodded understandingly, and got ready for supper.

When the children started coming, I had to redouble my efforts. I learned to take short vacations on my own or with the kids instead of seething with resentment that I wasn't getting my much-needed break. My husband disliked vacations for the disruptions they constituted, but was perfectly willing to stay home and fend for himself occasionally so that I could recharge.

I've also made a simple investment recently, which has made a marked change in my life. I bought a second cell phone that nobody has access to other than my husband. He can always reach me if he needs to and I can always touch base to tell him I will be out longer than expected, or that I've made a change of plans.

It's amazing what a simple little technical step can do for a relationship. I am free to go wherever I have to without my husband feeling tense that my boss called or that he won't have the car back in time. *Shalom bayis* and mobility for $20 a month; an honest bargain, in my opinion.

I've learned to appreciate the little windows that open along the way, subtle gestures many women take for granted, but that mean a great deal to me. When I notice a bud of sensitivity where I have planted acceptance, when I see a shoot of understanding where I've worked the soil with silence, my heart expands.

No, my husband will never write a poem, or analyze psychology, or get excited over a baby's gibberish.

Those were never the criteria, though, set by the Torah for building a *mikdash me'at*.

I've waited long enough to build my home to appreciate the solidity of its foundation, the uprightness of its walls, the supreme *kedushah* generated by the efforts to maintain its existence. I've waited long enough to know the sweetness of something cultivated with patience.

There are still struggles. Struggles to see eye to eye on raising children, struggles to keep things running as efficiently as possible, struggles to find and respect the many positive aspects I often overlook.

Believe me, the pages of my Aunt Dina's *Tehillim* are worn with use.

With patience and forbearance, though, and an inordinate amount of prayer, I can see an edifice going up. We have, *baruch Hashem*, been blessed with adorable, healthy children who have brought love and laughter into our lives. More than that, however, they are the living testimony to the fact that when either of the partners puts their heart and soul into building a palace out of the existing beams, the Third Partner comes through.

A Different Mountain to Climb

If you looked at me, you would never see a mountain climber. You would see a thin, young, well-dressed woman with a wonderful marriage and six healthy children, *Baruch Hashem*. You would see a clean, tastefully decorated home, and a husband who makes a nice living, setting aside time each day for learning.

Looks can be deceiving, they really can.

Not that I'm complaining; I'm eternally grateful for the bountiful *berachos* in my life, and I sincerely *daven* that they continue. Sometimes, though, when I watch the young idealistic seminary girls in my neighborhood set out to school, I am overcome by a yearning to go back in time and join them.

I don't miss the term papers. Or the tests. I miss the way the discussions fit neatly under one topic or another, categorized evenly under independent headings. The way the lessons, like the text they were so skillfully carved out of, were imprinted in stark black on white.

Torah was about giving up material pleasures for a life of spiritual bliss, *emunah* was about clinging to Him through the vicissitudes of life, *shalom* was about *vatranus* and *shemiras halashon*. I don't even have to go back to seminary; 12 years later, I can still rattle it off in my dreams.

Life, though, is not about school and not about dreams. Life has a funny way of mixing and matching the titles so that no one situation really fits any one lesson in the notebook. It took me some years to learn that. Some years and more than some tears. I'm not through the lesson yet.

I grew up in the typical *yeshivishe* environment. Sorry for the colloquialism; there's just no way I can describe my upbringing without resorting to the local vernacular. My father is a well-known *mashpia rucheni*, my mother the archetypical *eishes chayil*. Our house was the kind that bespoke a natural, unpretentious simplicity that I always took for granted.

Deprivation was as far from my childhood as affluence was. Our home was happy and lively, saturated with Torah values. My mother never sacrificed for Torah. In fact, I never heard the concept until I entered high school. We simply lived on a budget that befit a large family of a *talmid chacham* who brought in a far-too-inadequate salary.

Our house was simply furnished, sporting all the necessities yet missing all the frills. Our clothing came from what we used to call The Cousins' Boutique or Mom's Basement, also know as hand-me-downs. We girls earned our summers in camp by serving as part-time mothers' helpers for staff members, and tutored all through high school so we could attend reputable seminaries in Eretz Yisrael.

All this was done without fanfare or ceremony. No speeches were made, no awards were given; it was part of the atmosphere we breathed in my parents' home. Interestingly, we never resented it. On the contrary; we were downright proud to belong to the elite. We celebrated my brothers' *siyumim* with homemade *bulkelach,* and took tremendous pride in my father's love of learning and selfless devotion to his *talmidim.*

My older brothers proudly followed in my father's ways. They didn't merely learn; they were steeped in their learning. *Bein hazmanim* in our home was like running a yeshivah on the premises. The meals invariably turned into a lively Gemara *shiur,* and long after we *bentched,* there would be *sefarim* piled high on the otherwise cleared-off table.

My sisters' husbands, likewise, fit right in. Hailing from similar backgrounds, they understood that my parents couldn't help them very much in the way of monetary support, and instead enjoyed their unstinting admiration. There was little pressure where material concerns went. *Simchos* were kept simple and heimish, and the second generation faithfully perpetuated The Cousins' Boutique, albeit a trifle updated since our times.

Then came my turn for *shidduchim.* Fresh out of seminary, and surrounded by sisters and sisters-in-law who were living role models of the lessons I had absorbed, I knew one thing: I wanted a serious, full-time learner.

The phone calls came as expected. The best boy in Lakewood, the *masmid* of Mir, the *illui* of Ponevezh. The *rosh yeshivah's* nephew, the *mashgiach's* grandson, the *maggid shiur's* son.

As *shidduchim* go, many suggestions dissolved before they even evolved. Anyone who has had sons and sons in law in the yeshivah world knows how difficult they can make *shidduch* hunting. It's hard enough for two parents to do their research, but when five investigators scrutinize the case, it's an almost impossibility.

This one heard from the roommate that the boy was an incurable slob, the next one knew from his *chavrusa* that he had difficulty sticking to *sedarim*. The older one *davened* with the father, who came across as very imposing, and the younger one knew the younger brother who had some emotional issues.

"That's it," my father declared one day, "There's a new policy in effect. No negation without recommendation. We appreciate everyone's input, we really do. If you have nothing better though, to offer, please don't be so hasty to veto."

My brother-in-law, Rafael Aryeh, was the first to catch the ball. "You know; did anyone suggest the Stern boy from Switzerland? He may not be the son of the *rosh yeshivah*, but I know him personally; he's a *tachshit* of a *bachur*."

My father perked up at the suggestion. He trusted Rafael Aryeh's discernment, and subsequently heard rave reports about the boy. His *middos* were exemplary, he had a *seder* with the *rosh yeshivah*, and was unusually settled and mature for his age.

And finally, although my parents had never put money on the priority list, the fact that the boy's father was well off and was prepared to offer financial support was definitely a peg in favor of the *shidduch*.

I remember standing expectantly near the dining-room table, nervously folding the cover of the telephone book as my father completed his conversation with the *Rosh Yeshivah*. I could see the glint of excitement in his eyes.

"The *Rosh Yeshivah* didn't have sufficient words of praise for the *bachur*: A *masmid atzum* with *goldene middos*. *Muchshar l'gadlus*."

(A strong *masmid* with exemplary character traits. Destined for greatness).

Two weeks later, I stood in the same spot in the dining room, flushed with excitement, against the backdrop of clinking *l'chaim* glasses and an explosion of flashing cameras. My *chassan's* parents stood by beaming, and the *chassan* himself was smiling shyly under the spotlight. My heart expanded as the men joined hands and drew the *chassan* into the circle. A swell of pride washed over me, mixed with feelings of joy and gratitude. This was all I'd prayed for.

The engagement period whisked past me in a blur. There was so much to do, shopping to take care of, appointments to make, errands to arrange. I tried to take heed and remember the words of a wise seminary teacher. "In their eagerness to prepare for the wedding, many girls forget to prepare for the marriage."

Though I was busy trying to juggle teaching and shopping, I made time to listen to *hashkafah* tapes on the subject. A friend lent me a beautiful collection of letters and articles specifically addressed to the *kallah,* and I found myself approaching the physical preparations with a newfound dimension of joy and mission. I was setting out to build a *mikdash m'at.*

We were married five months later. The first few months passed in that slightly artificial sweetness of early marriage. I enjoyed experimenting with the recipes in the cookbook, and my meals were always ready and set out when my husband came in from *kollel*. It was a challenge, starting a new teaching job and trying to prove myself in my capacity as a wife and housewife.

My husband was everything I could have wanted in a spouse. He was sensitive, considerate, and undemanding, always complimenting my cooking and housekeeping prowess. He loved listening to my ideas for teaching and had great insight when it came to handling my students. He was an easy guest at my parents' house and fit right in with my brothers and brothers-in-law.

I found myself earnestly thanking Hashem for having given me such a wonderful partner in life. Where was all the arduous mountain climbing they'd repeatedly referred to on the tapes? Where was all the giving in and giving up that marriage was supposed to consist of? Oh, sure I was giving; I was preparing meals and sandwiches; I was bringing in a salary and lending a listening ear. It was so effortless, though. So un-difficult, if there was such a word. Had I missed something, perhaps?

I hadn't missed a thing. Like many young wives, I simply hadn't unrolled enough of the fabric to perceive the entirety of the design.

There is no song comprised of only alto notes; there is no hill with only a descent; there is no marriage that is solely easy gratification.

None.

Back then, though, I was almost deluded by the soft harmony breezing through our little apartment. I was a wife, a good wife, I had a great husband, and we had a beautiful marriage.

And then came the crash.

It was about a year after our wedding, one pleasant spring evening, when my husband came in after Maariv. I had just finished baking and was delighted to serve him a thick slice of fresh cinnamon yeast cake, still warm out of the oven. He usually sat down with a *sefer* before I joined him for our nightly schmooze, but tonight he seemed unusually pensive.

He stood near the table, staring at the cake, while he smoothed his thumb and forefinger over his mustache and beard again and again. I recognized the pose. He often looked that way when he was trying to make some sort of calculation, or when he was concentrating intensely on his learning.

"What's the matter, Nassan?" I probed, making a show of picking something up off the floor while I waited for his response. I didn't want to push.

"Huh? What?" he asked. I waited silently for him to fill me in. I knew he had heard me. He was just preoccupied with whatever it was that he was mulling over.

"Are you in the mood of talking, or would you rather not?" I asked, trying to temper my curiosity.

"Yes" he said, shaking himself out of his stupor, "yes, I actually wanted t,o talk."

Our conversations usually flowed freely, the kind of informal chats that began spontaneously and ended when the clock and good sense dictated that we call it a day. This time was different. Something about Nassan's brooding expression and stilted response made me experience that jittery formality I had felt when we first met.

I brought myself some cake and sat down. The air was thick with something; I couldn't make out if it was my suspense or his nervousness.

"I wrote up a resume today," Nassan started, straining to sound nonchalant.

"A resume?" I stuttered. "What for?"

"Well, I saw a vacancy for a mortgage broker in Klein's Realty."

"What?" I watched the circles on the crocheted lace tablecloth get bigger and smaller in dizzying succession. What had he said? *A vacancy for a mortgage broker.*

"I know we never spoke about this, but I really feel that if I want to be candid with myself ..."

What was he saying? Candid? Since when did Nassan use such highfalutin language?

"... a few months ago, but ..."

My mind was reeling. I had been so bowled over by the initial punch that I had missed the first few carefully rehearsed sentences of Nassan's speech.

It was just as well. Nothing he could have said, as cleverly as he would have worded it, could have cushioned the impact of his intent.

"Wh — what did you say?"

"I don't have to go into it full time yet, but I really feel I need to take the first step."

"One minute, Nassan," I said slowly. I felt like a dangling stuffed doll that had just been given a good spin.

"You're talking about going out to work?"

"Yeah, I guess," said Nassan, painstakingly picking the streussel off his cake. He opened his mouth to say something and then thought better of it.

"But why, Nassan?"

I couldn't believe we were having this conversation. It seemed unreal. Make-believe. Nassan was silent.

"I'm earning a decent salary from my teaching, and your father is so willing to help out. We're even managing to put money in savings every month."

"It's not the money, Yehudis."

"So what is it then?"

My voice rose an octave.

"We don't even have a family yet. Why in the world should you leave *kollel* if you don't have to?"

I knew it was childish, but the first thing I envisioned was my family. My parents. My brothers. Rafael Aryeh. What would they say when they heard that their gem of a *chassan* was going out to work barely a year after his wedding?

"I haven't come to this decision impulsively. Believe me, I've thought about it very seriously and I've spoken to my *Rebbeim* at length. This is what I need to do at this point."

I was dumbfounded, speechless. I just sat there, staring at the tablecloth, mindlessly twisting a loose loop that had raveled, feeling as if the design of my life had disintegrated.

How had this happened? I had *davened* so hard for a *ben Torah*, a real *masmid*, someone who would devote his life to Torah learning. I knew the sacrifices involved, and I had been ready to live the life. I had been so geared to climb the mountain, to sweat and strain, to scrimp and save, to be part of the group of *ameilim baTorah*. And now there would be no mountain.

No mountain, but what a climb!

I don't recall too much of the actual conversation. There was a lot of silence; that much I remember. A lot of painful, stunned silence and a lot of tears. I finally cleared the table and Nassan tried to clear the air. Unsuccessfully. We turned in for the night.

I don't know if either of us slept.

The next few days passed in a mental fog. It was vacation time and I didn't have the structure of my job to propel me through the routine. Instead, throughout the day, my mind played and replayed the fateful conversation with ruthless relentlessness.

Again and again I was cutting that cake, humming to myself, happy, motivated, at the top of the world. Then, I was setting it on a plate, unconsciously preoccupied with a thread of benign thoughts.

And then, suddenly, the whole film would shift into slow motion and Nassan would be talking with excruciating deliberateness.

"*I wrote up a resume today.*"

There was no way to fast-forward those ominous words.

At that point, the scene would go black and a million thoughts and emotions, too rowdy to discipline into any sort of sequence, would storm my mind. Unfairness. Anger. Disbelief. Denial. Fury. Jealousy. Guilt. Disappointment.

Crushing disappointment.

I should have thought of this when I originally heard that Nassan's father was a successful businessman.

I actually did. Why didn't I voice my opinion then?

Because everyone else had seemed so sure.

So why hadn't the shadchan told us?

Told us what?

My mind spun around in frenzied circles, blaming, rehashing, accusing, desperately trying to find some scapegoat upon whom I could vent my spinning whirlpool of emotions.

I couldn't tell my parents. Not now, when I was in such turmoil. They were too emotionally involved to be able to offer objective support and advice. I needed to unload my feelings without having to censor them, without having to play the diplomatic double part so familiar to married children caught between their loyalties.

Lines from speeches I had heard, lessons I had learned, floated through my mind. Lines about the wife's role, about the power of the woman to effect changes in her husband. I had always listened to these ideas with half an ear, smugly assuming they weren't being addressed to me. I *knew* what the wife's role was. I wouldn't have to effect changes; I would marry a committed *ben Torah*.

Suddenly, I didn't know where I stood, didn't know what was expected of me. I felt like a student who had studied all the material for the wrong test. I picked up the phone and dialed Rebbetzin Greenzweig, a trusted teacher with whom I had forged a personal bond during my seminary year. She listened empathetically, barely saying a word. I could tell that she understood my pain.

"Yehudis," she said. "Sometimes we long to give a *korban* to Hashem; we so badly want to offer a sacrifice that will honor and please Him. We take inventory of our stock and we choose what we think is the nicest, most fitting offering. But Hashem says, *'Adam, ki yakriv mikem.'*

"You really want to make Me happy? You really want to bring honor to My Name? Then do what I ask you to do. Serve Me the way I tell you to serve Me. What I want from you is not necessarily what you deem fitting, but that which is hardest for y*ou;* those innermost desires that are part and parcel of your soul; those dreams and aspirations that are cut of your very heart."

I listened quietly. I was sure I had heard this before. Then, however, we had been discussing *korbanos*. Now we were talking about my life.

"*Adam, ki yakriv*," Rebbetzin Greenzweig emphasized. "Adam Harishon was the first, and for a while the only, one in the world. His motives to bring a *korban* were purely self-inspired, not born of social expectations, not spurred on by environmental pressures.

"I know you, Yehudis, and I know how much it means to you that your husband learn full time. Your father is in *chinuch,* your brothers and brothers-in-law learn. Your cousins are married to *b'nei* Torah, your friends' husbands are all *kollel yungerleit*. You would have loved to follow the well-trodden path, to dress simply and accept hand-me-downs, to work from dawn to dusk, as long as your husband remained in the *koslei beis hamidrash.*

"The *Aibeshter* is calling on you to hand Him your life's dream and accept instead, your life's work. Like Adam, you're going to have to close your eyes to what the world admires and truly be *makriv mikem*.

"Your assignment may have changed, Yehudis, but the root is the same. It's a *korban laHashem,* building a *bayis shel Torah* in the way that the *Aibeshter* mapped out for you."

She let her words sink in. It was a big dose for one time. I would need time to internalize what she had said. I would need a lifetime to *eternalize* it.

Relinquishing a dream is no easy feat. Nassan began his job. It took every bit of effort, and then some more, to set my disappointment and resentment aside, and treat my husband with the respect and appreciation that had come so naturally before. Every morning, I firmly made up my mind that I would greet Nassan happily and take genuine interest in what he was doing.

When he came in from work, however, my resolve invariably crumbled. Instead of the warm greeting I had promised, my welcome came out sounding distant and strained. I knew that this wasn't what Hashem wanted of me; that exuding condescension and negativity was a lot more contrary to a Torah life than working in an office. Still, I couldn't get myself to translate my intellectual acceptance into complete emotional submission.

Nothing had really changed. He was the same considerate husband; he still *davened* with *kavannah* and had creative ideas and insights to offer. Still, I couldn't let go of the lifelong portrait I had painted of my husband. The teachers in the teachers' room were all juggling their obligations as *kollel* wives, my friends all referred to the yeshivah's *sedarim* as if they were the universal agenda, my family planned events to coincide with *bein hazmanim*. Only I, Yehudis, was left out, standing all alone at the foot of an unfamiliar, very forbidding, mountain.

I knew what I had to do. I had to throw away my old map, the one I knew with my eyes closed, the one I had sketched so lovingly over the past 10 years, the one that wouldn't get me where I needed to go.

Chachmas nashim bansah beisah; a wise woman could lay the cornerstone of her home. All the *sefarim* implied that a wife could help fashion her husband's desires, could turn her home into a tent of Torah by encouraging him to set aside time for learning and showing appreciation for his growth.

First, however, I knew, I would have to *be* a wise woman. I would have to put aside my personal desires, whether they were altruistic or egotistic, and treat my husband with the respect he deserved. Unconditionally. His growth would come later. First I had to provide the water and the sunshine.

I searched for illumination and I found it. Listening to a *shiur* for women by a well-known Torah luminary, I heard what I knew since time immemorial, but what I needed so badly to hear again.

"Of all places in the world," the speaker thundered, "the Torah was given in the *midbar*. Not in Madison Square Garden and not in the Javitz Center. Not in Ponevezh and not in Mir. Not in Lakewood, and not in Bnei Brak. In the *midbar*, the wilderness. Because the midbar is *hefker*, and Torah is *hefker*.

"Torah wasn't set aside for any one sector of *klal Yisrael*. It wasn't given to the *kollel yungerleit* and it wasn't reserved for those with *kishronos*. It wasn't given to the rich and it wasn't given to the poor.

"Being in or out of *kollel* is not the criteria for a *ben Torah*. Torah is the inside of a person, his preoccupation, his thoughts, his desires. Torah is the way he lives his life and the way he views this world. Any and every *Yid* can have a *chelek* in Torah and Torah can be a *chelek* of any *Yid*."

I was consoled.

Indeed, it's been a rough climb, it really has been. And it isn't over. We have *baruch Hashem* built a family, brought precious *neshamos* into this world together. And in our own way, we have laid the foundation for a *bayis shel Torah*.

No, my *tefillos* haven't changed my destiny, but my destiny has changed my *tefillos*. They are so much richer and so much humbler than they once were. I am not praying for *kavod*, for status and self-gratification. I am pleading with Hashem to endow my family with the most precious gift there is.

When in davening I pray *ve'haarev na*, I beseech Hashem with every fiber in my being that my husband and children experience the sweetness of His Torah over and above any other. When I say *v'sein chelkeinu b'sorasecha*, I don't just mumble the words. I beg, plead, implore that Hashem give my family their rightful *chelek* in His Torah.

And when Nassan comes home from the office after a long day and runs off to give a *daf yomi shiur*, when he dances with the kids because Moishy finished *Mesechta Berachos*, or expends the entire profits of a hard-earned deal on helping struggling *talmidei chachamim*, I know my *tefillos* have been heard.

My *tefillos* have been heard and my *korban* has been accepted.

A Different Mountain to Climb / 95

וְדֹבֵר אֱמֶת
בִּלְבָבוֹ.

... and speaks the truth
from his heart.

Debt End

The phrase "Love thy neighbor", had always sounded to me like a heavy-handed rendition of the Torah's bidding to love each and every *Yid*. Neighbors, when I was growing up, were as removed from my struggle to love and live with in peace as the next person on line in the supermarket.

I grew up in a one-family house with a sprawling lawn on a fairly quiet street. We generally sufficed with polite greetings and friendly inquiries, occasional Friday-night visits, participation in each other's *simchos,* and neighborhood *tzeddakah* solicitations.

So it was with some wonder and skepticism that I would read accounts of strife and misunderstanding between neighbors. *I guess I just don't relate to that kind of thing,* I thought; *it must take two very testy individuals to turn an adjoining address into a reason for discord.*

When I moved to Eretz Yisrael soon after my wedding, I was introduced to a new dimension of living; communal living. Instead of walking up a paved driveway and then entering a nice big front hall that ushered you into your private quarters, you virtually turned off the street into the lobby of an apartment building, usually bumping straight into some other occupant of the building.

Surprisingly enough, however, I took fairly well to the adjustment. I was generally a warm and open person and I took it in stride when the neighbors knocked with various excuses, anxious to get a glimpse of the new American young couple. Though I was awkward with the language, I chuckled at my own mistakes and made use of the universal human dialect, smiles, interested nods, loving gestures to the little ones. Slowly I got to know the inhabitants of the building.

Not having found a steady job, I had plenty of time on my hands. Homesick for my own siblings, and eager to give, I invited my neighbors' kids into my apartment and offered to have them play while I did my housework.

The kids were only too happy to cash in on the offer. Though I didn't have an assortment of toys in my house, I let them color and cut and they loved to help me bake. Innately Israeli, they had no qualms about asking me for cake or for anything else in my house, for that matter.

I was grateful for their openness. It helped break the ice with my neighbors and created a natural flow of give-and-take between us. I felt comfortable borrowing items I had run out of, and in turn I'd offer to take their kids with me to the supermarket. There was no tit for tat; we each contributed in the way that was most natural. By the time my oldest son was born, he had a bunch of cooing, cuddling friends just waiting to play with him.

It was at about that time that we began to hear sounds of renovations going on in the vacant apartment next door. Sawdust and cement filled the elevator and the shrill rattling of a drill splitting through stone reverberated through the building. I wondered who the new neighbors would be.

One Thursday morning, several weeks later, the moving truck arrived. All morning, I kept hearing the swing and the slam of the elevator door, and the sound of heavy cartons scraping across the floor. At about noontime, I went out to see if there was any way I could help.

Supervising the activity, I met a tall bespectacled woman wearing a colorful tichel. Pulling at her hand and swinging playfully was a little girl of about 4 or 5, with warm brown eyes and two pigtails bobbing at her sides. I smiled a greeting.

"We're so happy to have new neighbors," I said genuinely. "What's your name?" I turned to the little girl.

"What's your name?" the mother prodded, looking expectantly at her daughter. "Huh?"

"Chaya'la Baum," said the little girl, smiling shyly.

"Her name is Chaya Baila," the mother clarified, "but many people call her Chaya'la."

Mrs. Baum looked like an intelligent woman, fine, but not shy. I don't know if it was her straight posture or her even gaze, but something about her conveyed unmistakable strength of character.

"Can I make you supper tonight?" I offered spontaneously.

"We're so busy, we actually haven't thought about supper. You know how it is."

I nodded.

"We could have done the moving over two days, but we're not the type that likes to schlep things. Like my husband says, 'The longer it takes, the longer you're in limbo.' Better to work hard and get it over with. We're not afraid of hard work," she winked.

She spoke dramatically, and had the command of a teacher.

"Then count on me for supper," I said, getting back to my original offer. "And if Chaya'la wants, she can come over to play with my little son. He's only 3 months old," I said, turning to Chaya'la, "but he loves being on the floor near kids."

"What's your name?" squinted Mrs. Baum, "I don't think you mentioned it."

"Oh that's right, I'm sorry," I said, feeling flustered, "Goldy. Goldy Blau."

"Yehudit Baum," she introduced herself formally, shaking my hand. "*Na'im meod* (it's been a pleasure)."

The elevator door opened, and a man, whom I surmised was her husband, exited. Even in his shirttails, he looked distinguished. I smiled politely and went back into my apartment, thinking about what to make for supper. *I wonder if there are any other children*, I mused. Mrs. Baum didn't look like the type to leave children unsupervised downstairs. On the other hand, she didn't look young enough for Chaya'la to be her oldest. *Oh well*, I figured, *time will tell.*

As it turned out, I didn't have to wait too long. About 10 minutes later, as I took the baby out of his crib to feed him, I heard a knock on the door. There stood Chaya'la, her brown eyes glittering under long lashes, just waiting to be ushered in.

'Bati l'sacheik (I came to play)," she informed me cheerfully. "*Zeh hatinok shelachem* (is this your baby)?"

I smiled, lowering the baby, so she could see him at eye level. "Come in," I told her. "He has to eat now, so I'll give you a paper to color. As soon as we're done, he'll be very excited to get to know you."

"That's it?" she asked, "Only one baby in your family?"

Children, I thought amused. *They had no social graces dictating their lives. Yet they possessed the sweetness that adults lacked, to temper their directness.*

"Yup, so far we have one little Yosse'le. But he keeps us pretty busy."

"If you want, I could be his big sister," she offered, following me down the hall. "We both don't have any sisters or brothers, so we could keep each other company."

So Chaya'la was an only child.

I didn't realize just how seriously she had intended her proposition. If Yossi had enjoyed a rotating carousel of adopted sisters and brothers until now, he now had a permanent playmate on the premises. Chaya'la would be over as soon as she had deposited her lunchbox at home, and her mother would know to come knock at our door as soon as her food was ready.

"Here you are, Miss Blau," she would greet Chaya'la in mock dismay. "In case you've forgotten where you live, I've brought you your lunch." She would then uncover the plate, holding the day's fare, which included a host of homemade surprises.

"The bought pizza doesn't come to this," Mrs. Baum would hold the plate for me to examine. "I have an excellent recipe for the dough, and I have some secret ingredients that I put into the sauce. Chaya'la gets the real stuff," she chuckled proudly.

"Wow," I'd admire, "You really put a lot into your meals. Maybe I'll take the recipe from you."

"*K'dai*; it's worth trying," Mrs. Baum would recommend, and though I had my own recipe for pizza, I'd find myself dutifully copying down the exact instructions as she demonstratively outlined each step.

Though she had only one 4½ year-old daughter, Mrs. Baum always seemed busy and fulfilled. She attended an art workshop, sewed all of Chaya'la's dresses, and spent a lot of time cooking and baking in the kitchen. I noticed that they always hosted a lot of guests for their Shabbos meals — *bachurim,* seminary girls and *baalei teshuvah* couples — and were generally involved in *kiruv.* Now and then, I knocked on their door to borrow things, and Mrs. Baum was always proud to show me some project or another that she was in the middle of at the time.

When Yossi was joined by a little sister, I found myself treating Chaya'la as I would a real oldest. "Chaya'la, can you bring me the diaper for the baby?" I'd ask, and she would know just which drawer to open in order to fetch it. She kept Yossi occupied while I fed little Ahuvi, and then joined us as we set the table for lunch.

"Oh no, I'm out of milk," I would fret, "my husband's going to be home any minute, and I don't see myself getting out now with the two little ones. Chaya'la," I'd resort to her naturally, "can you ask your mother if she has a bag of milk to spare?"

Chaya'la was only too happy to run these little errands.

"Aren't there any other neighbors?" my husband would ask, when he'd bump into Chaya'la time and time again every time he opened the door. "I don't mind her coming occasionally, but it seems as if she lives here."

He was right. For better and for worse, she spent the bulk of her waking hours as part of our family. There were times when she really proved to be a help, keeping the little ones entertained. At other times, like all 6-year-olds, she was bothersome and demanding, taking my time and energy when all I wanted was some space and privacy. Especially trying was when she knocked on the door two hours before Shabbos, while I was bustling around, trying to tie the last loose ends together.

I tried to be fair. I knew it was a package deal. If I wanted her help, then I had to contend with her when she was a nuisance. Besides, I thought of it as an opportunity to do *chessed*. Though Rabbi and Mrs. Baum invested everything they had to give Chaya'la the happiest, most well-adjusted childhood, they couldn't give her the fun and adventure of a family. Those were such integral things to a little child growing up.

Indeed, the Baums were devoted, conscientious parents. I'd often see Mrs. Baum sitting with Chaya'la on the porch in the evenings, reading her stories and teaching her *Pirkei Avos*. She bought her books and tapes, always educational, and would spend time writing meaningful inscriptions that a 6½ year-old could internalize and understand. Very often, she'd come to show me these gifts before she wrapped them.

I found Mrs. Baum intriguing. She was a woman of principle; everything from her tightly tied scarf to her manner of speech bespoke purposefulness. Yet she had an unmistakable flair for creativity. She cultivated a little garden of spices on her porch, and enjoyed hanging up whimsical signs on the door to her home. "Entrance fee: smile," or "Lashon Hara free zone" were some samples.

From the bits and pieces of her past that she shared with me, I gathered that she was very much a self-made person. She had lost her parents very young, and her husband's parents were elderly and living abroad.

"I was in my late 30s when Chaya'la was born," she often recounted, "and believe me, I had no one to teach me. My husband and I figured it all out on our own; I gave her her first bath with my husband instructing me right out of Dr. Spock's book."

I expressed my genuine admiration, and commented what a wonderful *chinuch* they were giving Chaya'la. "She is extra sensitive and very mature," I complimented. "May you have a lot of *nachas* from her."

The first barb came a few months later, like a lightning bolt on a clear day. It was gone by the time it flashed.

"Chaya'la," I asked her, late one afternoon, as she pulled up the stool to watch me prepare French toast. "Can you ask your mother if she has four slices of bread? I see I'm short."

Chaya'la came back a few minutes later, smiling awkwardly.

"Do you have the bread?" I asked, a little dismayed. Yossi had just accidentally smashed an egg on the floor, and Ahuvi was frantically tugging at my skirt. I had just been over a bout with the flu and felt irritable and overwhelmed.

"My mother said to tell you that the grocery is open," she said, looking uncomfortably at Ahuvi.

The grocery is open.

I dropped the bread into the bowl of beaten eggs as if I'd been stung. I knew the grocery was open. It was 5 o'clock in the afternoon. I felt a bitter taste rising inside me, an acrid mixture of anger and hurt and shame.

Feeling foolish in front of the kids, I wiped the tears from my eyes. *Big deal*, I told myself, *so I'll make something else. I bet you Chaya'la misunderstood her mother.* But it took an extra effort to muster my patience and listen attentively to Chaya'la's ongoing commentary as I tried in vain to placate Ahuvi and think of an alternative supper.

By the next week, I had forgotten the incident. Not that I had completely forgotten. Something inside me steered me downstairs, rather than next door, when I needed two squares of baking chocolate to complete a recipe. Otherwise, though, our relationship remained unchanged. Mrs. Baum smilingly held the elevator door open for me as I tried to maneuver the kids inside, and I, in turn, thanked her, and wished her a good morning. I could almost have chalked the incident up to my imagination.

It was wintertime, and the weather outside was cold and uninviting. Even in the house, I found myself bundling up against the elements. The stone floors and walls were damp and cold, and I thought wistfully of our warm, carpeted home back in America. I had been fighting to ward off an obstinate cough and sinus infection, and felt like a windblown aircraft weaving in and out of heavy gray clouds with only the briefest interludes of clear sky.

I tried making meals that would take the chill out of our bones.

I deliberately put up supper early, so the vapors would warm up the kitchen and make our home smell pleasant and cozy.

Split-pea soup, I thought to myself one morning, when the cloudy skies heralded yet another dreary day. Though I had never appreciated it much as a child, I now dreamed of a good, thick, split-pea soup bubbling on the stove. Foraging through my dwindling supplies, I noted with disappointment that I was out of split peas. *Hm*, I thought, poised in front of the open refrigerator, *what now?*

Looking out at the thin drizzle, I vetoed the idea of venturing outside. Scooping the baby onto my hip, I knocked hesitantly on the Baums' door. I smiled as I surveyed Chaya'la's drawing of a smiling sun bursting through the clouds. "Behind every cloud hides a smiling sun," Mrs. Baum had captioned underneath in black marker.

I heard the muffled sounds of some tape being shut, and then the turn of the lock. "Hi Bentzion," Mrs. Baum tweaked the baby on the cheek. "That's a pretty velour he's wearing."

"Thank you," I replied, suddenly nervous about making my request. *Too late*, I thought, *can't chicken out now*. "Um, I was wondering; do you by any chance have a cup of split peas to lend?"

I saw a shadow pass over Mrs. Baum's brows, and then that resolute look settled in her eyes.

"Listen," she said, closing the door behind me, "I think we need to put a stop to this."

The baby squirmed in my arms, and I wished I had a mother's arms to squirm in myself.

"I'm sorry, but this can't go on. We're living on a tight budget just like you are, and I think all this borrowing is absolutely inexcusable."

I was stunned into silence.

"When Chaya'la was a baby, I would bundle her up against the fiercest Yerushalayim snowstorms to go out and buy bread. Why was someone else's time and energy any less valuable than my own? If a person is organized enough, he should never have to borrow. You stock up on the basics, and you do without anything extra until you can get out yourself."

I nodded mutely. I felt my stabbed ego throbbing through every pore on my face, the tears pricking just beneath the surface of my eyes.

"Look," she showed me, going into her kitchen to fetch a can of powdered milk. "I keep this on hand all the time, so that in case I ever run out of milk, I'd have what to fall back on. A person has to be prepared." She stopped to catch her breath.

"And what about all the items you've borrowed and forgotten to return? If it were a one-time incident, I'd find it within myself to look away. But this seems to be an ongoing problem.

"Before Rosh Hashanah, you borrowed a half a cup of honey, and never returned it. And there were some other items too. *I do everything I can to be self-reliant, even when it means scrimping on the basics. Every penny adds up, and when you're talking about someone else's money, even one penny is *gezel*."

I knew I had to say something, but I felt my mouth twitching uncontrollably. I fussed distractedly with the baby's collar, my tears blotting his pudgy little face into a streaky blur. A thousand defenses rushed to my mind, one overlapping the other, forming a messy collage of indignation.

What of all the crayons and papers, the potato chips and ices and candies, the cakes and cookies and presents that I had given Chaya'la over the years? What of the hours she had spent over at my house, the trips I had included her on, the party I had made for her birthday?

What of the fact that I had just pulled out of a bad case of the flu, that my baby was badly congested and my older ones were sick? Wasn't Mrs. Baum very occupied with *kiruv* and *chessed*? Wouldn't she have gladly spared a half a cup of honey and a bag of split peas toward one of her causes?

I tried in vain to articulate my feelings, but the words crumpled up in a heap at the bottom of my throat. I felt the insult well up inside, constricting the passageway for explanation.

"I'm telling you all of this, not because I want to hurt you, but because I want to make you aware of your pitfall. I'm sure you never meant to do anything wrong, but you have to take stock and make a change."

I thanked her feebly and turned around to leave.

"If you really need the split peas, maybe you want to leave the baby here while you get them," she offered magnanimously.

Split peas? Split peas were planets away, obscured somewhere far, far behind some thick gray cloud. A cloud that was hanging menacingly low right now, threatening to vent a torrent of humiliated drops. I, shaking my head in the negative, closed the door quickly behind me.

Burying my head in my baby's soft velour, I sucked in all the hurt for one startled moment, and then let the downpour come. I was too wounded to even sort out my feelings. All I knew was that I felt a choking knot deep at the bottom of my heart, a piercing stab that oozed with fresh tears every time I tried to take a deep breath and compose myself.

I walked into the kitchen and apathetically eyed the carrots and the celery dumped on the counter, waiting to be made into soup. The apartment felt cold and drafty. I changed Bentzion's pamper, mechanically tucking him under the blanket, and closing the shutters. Drained of my tears, I was suddenly filled with an aloof kind of anger.

Whom did she think she was, holier than thou, preaching to me as if I was her wayward student? Couldn't she have gently told me that I owed her some honey and some other things, and that she'd really appreciate if I returned them before I borrowed something else?

Didn't she realize how all out I went for Chaya'la all the time? Silly sensitive me, I had always made it sound like lilacs and roses, as if Chaya'la's constant presence was the biggest blessing ever created since the beginning of mankind. I should have told her the truth, the way she had told it to me.

I opened the window to the clothesline, deftly removing the clothespins from the dry laundry, energized by the thoughts charging through my mind. The phone rang. It took everything I had to focus on the conversation without spilling my own misery. I knew I was too hurt to see things objectively, that I would only be pouring fuel on my internal fire if I pulled someone else into my seething emotions.

Chaya'la knocked on my door that afternoon. I forced a smile. After all, she didn't have to be the scapegoat for her mother's insensitivity. She asked me if she could have the portion of pudding that was left in the refrigerator. I nodded, giving her a spoon, valiantly trying to separate my feelings of resentment from the genuine mitzvah of *chessed* to a blameless little girl.

I felt like a hero. *Hane'elavim v'einam olvim, shomim cherpasam v'einam meishivim* ... The words kept ringing in my ears, lifting me on the wings of self-righteous gratification. Though I had poured out my hurt to my husband, I had resisted my impulse to share my outrage with my other neighbors and friends. And I hadn't given Chaya'la the cold shoulder I had been so sorely tempted to show her.

Later that evening, to the sound of soothing music in a cleaned-up kitchen, I was suddenly struck by a disconcerting thought. Perhaps I was not as pitifully innocent as I had wanted to believe. I had worked so hard on admirably handling my emotions that I had mentally turned myself into the faultless victim before I had really even read the charges drawn against me.

I had always been more of a free spirit, living and giving generously, looking almost contemptuously at measure-for-measure rigidity. If a neighbor requested three eggs, I'd instinctively offer four; if I was asked to cook soup for a family, I'd automatically include noodles or *kneidlach*. I wasn't the type that knew the price of cucumbers down to the penny, or noticed exactly how many cookies I had left in the canister.

It wasn't a matter of having or not having the means. It was a mentality, a way of life. I just never believed that those little pennies determined anyone's fate in this world. And my picture of Hashem had somehow always been in consonance with this mind-set: *Av rachum v'chanun, notzer chessed l'alafim*.

For the first time in my life, I was suddenly pitted against a glaring shortcoming that I had never seen. What about the other of the Thirteen *Middos*, the thought suddenly dawned, *nosei avon vafesha, v'chataah, vnakei lo yenakei*?

This world was calculated down to the last detail, and there were no trivialities when it came to other people. All the *chessed* in the world couldn't cancel an outstanding debt, however small;

generosity and sensitivity, however commendable, didn't exempt someone from seeing to his arrears.

Kiruv and *chessed,* those were each person's private considerations, between himself and His Creator. Perhaps giving to neighbors could and should, indeed, be included among one's charitable acts. That, however, was a deliberation restricted to the one on the giving end. If one wanted to give, he would be rewarded from Above. When it came to taking, though, one had to be scrupulous, regardless of one's own standards.

Despite the chill, I found myself sweating profusely. It took all my exertion to wrench myself from the comfortable spot I had unconsciously carved on top of my laurels and honestly plant myself in front of a window to Mrs. Baum's soul.

She wasn't mean or ungrateful or petty. She was a person who, very unlike myself, lived a precisely calculated existence. Her every step was dictated by logic, by *mussar,* by the very straight lines of halachic right or wrong. I may have differed strongly on her opinion of self-sufficiency; I believed that Jews could and should borrow from one another, but that didn't matter. No ideals in the world could absolve anyone from the stringency of *gezel*. And admittedly, no one else I knew in the world would have had the courage to tell that to me straight to my face.

The next morning, I drew up a list of the items I owed Mrs. Baum. Then, I went down to the rest of my neighbors and asked them if they remembered anything I hadn't returned. Surprisingly, there was quite a list: a scoop of detergent, five garbage bags, half a cup of oil. The kind of things that wouldn't make anyone poor, but could pay someone's ticket all the way back to this world, if he ascended without returning them.

I shuddered to think how many such items must have fallen by the wayside in the past. Small, negligible things like pens and looseleaf papers, quarters and dimes, borrowed in a pinch, and then forgotten in the whirlwind of time. Try as I might, I couldn't possibly gather those feathers scattered in the wind of the past.

Instead, I would make an effort to rectify the past with a commitment for the future. I took out a marble composition notebook and put it into my kitchen drawer. No flyaway notes and wipe off memo pads for me. I wouldn't allow a borrowed item over my threshold without entering it into my notebook.

And one day, when I summoned the courage, I would have to repay the hardest debt of all. I would have to thank Mrs. Baum for serving as the painful catalyst behind this metamorphosis in my life. What was that sign she had hanging on her door on that fateful day?

Behind every cloud hides a smiling sun.

Waving a White Flag

There are certain things you don't learn in Chumash or *halachah*, or *lehavdil*, in chemistry or math. There are some lessons you just don't pick up in school or yeshivah, even college. Those truths have to be learned in life, from life, for life. And though experience is the greatest teacher, you need to be pretty tuned in to those red marks accenting your days, to take heed and make reforms.

I was a catch of a girl, if I may say so, ambitious, talented, and industrious. I pulled straight A's, graduated with honors, and attended a reputable seminary. While still in seminary, I earned my B.A. in special education and went on to pursue a master's degree. By the time I entered the job market, I was a sought-after applicant. I accepted a fifth-grade teaching position in the morning, and took an office job in the afternoon.

I ran a packed schedule. I woke up early in the morning, *davened*, ate something, and helped my mother straighten up the house. By 8 o'clock I was walking briskly to my morning job, blouse crisply ironed, hair freshly blown.

I loved my job. I threw myself into the preparation and infused my lessons with verve and creativity that kept my fifth-grade students on their toes. Though I was exhausted by the time I finished the morning, I found the 10-minute walk to my afternoon job invigorating.

I remember my co-teacher, a young mother, offering me a ride. "It must be tiring, running straight into a second job. At least let me give you a lift."

"Oh, I love it," I remember responding. "The work gives me energy. Save the ride for when I'm 90."

If there was a glint of amusement in her eyes, then I missed it. I guess the combination of youth and success breeds a certain smugness that glosses over these fine points.

I was married before Pesach and finished the school year. We spent the summer packing to go to Eretz Yisrael. Along with the queasy feeling that came with the thought of leaving everything familiar to settle in a new country, I remember feeling a rising sense of anticipation. I was excited to meet the challenges of living in Eretz Yisrael, of setting up our own nest and fending for ourselves.

My sister-in-law, who lived in Yerushalayim, set up a job interview for me even before I arrived. The morning after we landed, I was dressed and ready at 9 o'clock, waiting at the bus stop to the Mattersdorf neighborhood where I was supposed to meet the principal of Shearim, a school for special needs children.

No one would have guessed that my tiny apartment was strewn with cardboard boxes and open suitcases, that I'd pressed my blouse on the creaky kitchen table for lack of an ironing board. I looked perfectly composed, standing there at the bus stop holding my pocketbook with the Israeli bills and coins my husband had gotten at the money exchange after *davening*.

The interview went over well. In typical Israeli fashion, I was hired without pretense or protocol. Before I left the office, the *menahelet*, Mrs. Weitz, suggested that I come to Shearim the next day to meet my supervisor, Shlomit, and get a feeling of the place.

Waving a White Flag / 111

Oh, I remember thinking, slightly taken aback, if I have a supervisor, then I guess I have a job.

Thus began my whirlwind of juggling a full-time job, domestic duties, and the challenges of cultivating a new marriage. I tried to be everything everywhere. I got up early to prepare breakfast for my husband, ran out to my job, and came home just in time to set out a spread for lunch.

I felt an inner pressure to be perfect. My husband had grown up in a large family where things had always run like a clock. My mother-in-law was one of those superwomen who ran an immaculate home and a full-time job. His married sisters were all hardworking mothers who handled jobs and families with aplomb. I was determined to measure up.

I was pretty successful, though I actually found myself quite busy juggling all my tasks. Aside from three meals a day, *sponga*, laundry, and a six-day-a-week job, there always seemed to be technicalities to iron out in the various Israeli offices and ministries.

"Why don't you ask your husband to do these things?" my neighbor asked me when she saw me running breathlessly to the bus stop five minutes after I had come home from work. "I never step into these offices; it's my husband's department."

I was appalled at the thought. "My husband has very tight *sedarim*. Why *shouldn't* I be the one to take care of these things. It's not like I have to schlep with a bunch of children or something."

When Dassy was born, it became more of a challenge to keep up my standards. Though I had never been extremely early to bed, I had always gone to sleep at a reasonable hour. I loved getting up at 6:30, refreshed and ready to tackle a new day.

With a baby, I wasn't my own boss anymore. Dassy was often fussy until 1 or 2 o'clock in the morning, and when my alarm clock rang at 6 o'clock, I felt pretty cranky. Feeding and dressing a baby, packing her diapers and bottles, and leaving those extra few minutes to get to the baby-sitter made a marked difference in my schedule.

Gone were the days when I could take a relaxed shower and put rollers into my sheitel before work. It was rush, rush, rush, just getting the beds made, my husband's breakfast ready, and a salad cut up for lunch.

When I came home from work, I never knew what to do first. Dassy had to be fed, lunch had to finished and set out, and frankly, I myself felt ready for a nap. There was no time, however, for indulgences. I was determined to play the part of the ideal wife, smiling and ready, house neat, with a delicious meal on the table.

My stomach would be a knot of tension as I whipped out the place mats and banged down the cultery, dumped the spiral macaroni into the colander, tossed some breadcrumbs in the frying pan and scooped up a counter full of peels into the garbage can. I quickly piled the pots in the sink and wiped the counter, Dassy's mounting cries tugging at the last threads of my composure.

When my husband came through the door to a tidy house, a smiling baby, and lunch on the table, I had the feeling of having achieved the impossible. *Whew*, I thought, mentally wiping the sweat off my brow, *a man would never conceive what went on here in the past 20 minutes.*

We'd spend lunch catching up on the morning, discussing my progress with the kids at Shearim, his own yeshivah news, and the baby's latest antics. Then Nachman would stretch, look at his watch, and take a *bentcher*. Getting up from the table, he'd run to fetch a *sefer*, quickly don his hat and button his jacket, and ask, almost as an afterthought, "You need anything?"

For some reason, that question, or perhaps the way he asked it, always invited a wave of resentment. Did I need anything? I sure did. I desperately needed to stock up in the supermarket, and I needed to do *sponga*. I needed to put up a challah dough for Nachman's *siyum* the next week, and I needed to iron the pile of shirts that was waiting on the line. I needed to go to *Misrad Hapnim* to extend our visas and I needed to get some sleep. Badly.

He was halfway out the door, though, and he had a *chavrusa* waiting for him. What did I want? I didn't know myself. I didn't quite expect him to stay home and help me. After all, the reason I was working in the first place was to enable him to learn. And besides, there was no justification for it; I only had one baby and I had always been a coper.

Perhaps it was Nachman's nonchalance that annoyed me; the way he seemingly expected to come home and find everything under control, his shirts pressed, the cabinets neatly stocked. If I ever complained that I had nothing to serve company, he would innocently comment, "Just take some cake out of the freezer." As if the freezer baked cakes!

Though I was definitely managing, I had to admit that I was finding motherhood a challenge. Nobody had warned me that one baby was enough to put the most well-laid plans to rest, not to mention the most well-planned rest, to lay. Dassy crawled all over the wet puddles as I tried to do *sponga*, and tugged impatiently at my skirt as I ironed.

There was a constant collision of desires. *I* wanted to roll out yeast cake and prepare an elaborate supper for a new neighbor; *she* wanted to go outside and frolic in the sand. *I* was collapsing from fatigue, dreaming about a nap; *she* was bursting with energy, clamoring for action and fun.

How does everyone else do it, I wondered in frustration; *I'm not the first woman to ever have a child and work. How do all mothers juggle their responsibilities without feeling so frazzled and overtired?*

When I caught sight of my neighbor's cleaning lady, or of another neighbor's husband taking her kids to the babysitter; when I glimpsed women picking up some frozen ready food at dinnertime, my sense of inadequacy abated.

Oh, I thought, as if I'd uncovered some cleverly concealed fraud, *she has a cleaning lady; no wonder*. Or, *she warms up fast food for dinner; that's the trick*.

I worked six days a week, but I didn't have any help. I wouldn't dream of hiring an *ozeret* or buying ready-made food; our *kollel* budget didn't allow for such luxuries. Besides, these short-term services seemed like a ridiculous waste of money to me. I'd sooner spend my hard-earned salary on things that lasted. My husband wasn't available much either. I guess that explained it.

Mendy joined our family rather soon, and Yossi followed hot on his heels. If Dassy's birth had been an adjustment, now I really experienced the multiple demands of juggling work and family. Caring for a newborn and two little ones, trying to keep the house running smoothly, and going back to a full-time job was draining, to say the least.

With parents and in-laws overseas, I didn't even have the convenience of an occasional Shabbos or Yom Tov off. I'd wake up at the crack of dawn Friday morning, put up a challah dough and get to work cooking the rest of the food. By the time the kids got up, the house was filled with the delicious smells of *erev Shabbos,* and the sinks were stacked high with pots and bowls.

Though my husband genuinely tried to help out, his schedule wasn't very accommodating. He left early, before the kids were even up, and by the time he returned home in the evenings, the hassle of baths and supper was basically over. During lunchtime, he'd feed the two older ones lunch while I took care of the baby, but he was always in a rush to make the bus back to yeshivah.

I felt an inner tug of war. On the one hand, I desperately wanted to be the ultimate *eishes chayil,* admirably handling job and family without ever imposing or demanding anything. On the other hand, I felt the mounting inner pressure of my many responsibilities.

I couldn't make peace between my ambivalent feelings, the urge to be open and realistic, and the compulsion to preserve the mirage of the superwoman who could handle anything. Women less enterprising than I was seemed to manage families of 10 or 12, without falling apart. What would my husband think of me, feeling overtired and overwhelmed by three children?

Some days, I ached to express my needs, to propose something; I didn't even know quite what. Perhaps that my husband leave later or come home earlier, or that I cut down my work hours or take some household help. Anything, so I would be able to get a nap when I needed one or to get the house straightened up.

I'd formulate my feelings as I fed the baby or served my husband his lunch. Annoyingly, I'd feel the words die in my throat as our casual conversation wound to a close. I would walk my husband wistfully to the door, wishing he could read my thoughts, as he bade me a good day and threw the kids a kiss. Then, as the door closed behind him, I'd feel the sting of tears in my eyes, the bitter blur of failure and disappointment making a streaky mush of my vision.

It wasn't that my husband was inconsiderate or unapproachable. He simply didn't have a clue. On the outside, things seemed to be running just fine. I was doing well at work, the meals were ready for him when he came home, and the kids appeared taken care of. The ship seemed to be sailing smoothly; how was he to know that I felt like I was sinking, if I wasn't honest enough or brave enough to put out the white flag?

I couldn't let go of my self-imposed standards. If only to prove my competency, I'd promise to bake a cake for Dassy's birthday party or undertake to cut out special flashcards for my students at home. I wanted to be that flawless wife, mother, and teacher, there for everybody all the time.

So I would bake the cake on Sunday, and get raving reports from my students' mother on Monday. Then, when I'd open the refrigerator on Wednesday in a moment of exhaustion, and find the fish from Shabbos still waiting for salvation, the futility of my perpetual panting came crashing down on me. I felt like crying out of sheer helplessness. How was I supposed to swing it all without falling apart?

There was one thing I didn't know.

I was never supposed to.

And so I fell apart.

Valiantly as I tried to fight it, I was feeling tired and irritable most of the time. I conked out in the evenings and woke up barely feeling refreshed. The morning rituals seemed to take everything out of me. By the time I got to work, all I felt like doing was sitting down on a chair and nodding off to sleep.

At work, I somehow pushed through the morning. As I got off the bus, though, and walked up the steep incline to the baby-sitter, I felt as if I couldn't propel my body one more step. I willed my feet to keep going, willed my arms to push the stroller home and yank it up the two flights to my apartment. By the time I got through door, I was finished.

The two older ones were home before I knew it. I felt my head spinning as Dassy and Mendy bickered and whined against the backdrop of the baby's incessant screaming. *This isn't normal*, I panicked; *I'm so tired, there must be something wrong with me.*

I was relieved when my husband came in to save the day. He helped out with serving while I changed and fed the baby. After he left, I could barely muster the energy to clear off the table from lunch and drag myself outside with the kids.

I would sit on the park bench, glossy eyed with fatigue, yawning repeatedly as I held the baby and watched the older ones play. I felt so unlike my usual energetic self, so removed from the loud squeals and animated chatter filling the park.

"Maybe you should go for some blood work," my husband suggested one evening. "I'm really concerned. Maybe you have mono or something."

I grabbed at the lead. When the tests came back inconclusive, my friend suggested an alternative practitioner who had experience dealing with mono and chronic fatigue. I returned from the visit, armed with tinctures and drops that were supposed to detoxify my system and slowly build up my strength.

Though I took them religiously and stayed off yeast and sugar the way a natural nutritionist had advised me, I saw no relief. My husband temporarily dropped his afternoon *chavrusa* so that I would be able to take a nap. We made several other concessions as well. I gave up most of my teaching hours, got my neighbor's cleaning lady for a few hours a week, and hired a baby-sitter for the afternoons.

Just getting through the day was like wading through waist-deep water. The simplest tasks seemed forbidding. I'd get the kids off in the morning through drooping eyelids, and sometimes I couldn't do even that. As soon as they were out of the house, I'd collapse into bed and the morning would dissolve into blessed nothingness.

I received as much conflicting advice as I'd ever heard. Rest up; exercise more. Cut out carbohydrates; stay off fat. Keep working at any cost; quit your job. The more people I consulted, the more opinions I heard. My husband's *chavrusa* kept encouraging us to be patient, assuring my husband that he'd been through the same ordeal and it would eventually pass.

Miraculously, I did start feeling a change after about three months. I didn't know if it was the kinesiologist or the diet, the vitamins or the rest, but I began to feel an obvious improvement. I had more energy and was able to tackle supper and bedtime without feeling wiped out. Slowly, as my vitality came back, I resumed doing chores I had dropped during the period of crisis.

I was gratified. My husband was thrilled to have his good old wife back again. The homey smells of freshly cooked food once again permeated our house, and I enjoyed my children the way I hadn't enjoyed them in months.

I finally felt as if I had my act together again. I woke up feeling invigorated, and sent the kids off calmly and happily. During my mornings home, I got to do some housework and cooking, leaving the heavy cleaning for the *ozeret* on Wednesdays. On the days that I worked, an afternoon baby-sitter enabled me to get a nap and straighten up the house. By the time the kids were back, I felt ready to tackle supper and bedtime.

The waters were still.

The swimming test was yet to come.

"Maybe we can stop the cleaning lady," my husband proposed one evening after supper. "*Baruch Hashem*, you seem to be over the crisis, and it's been a big drain on the budget."

I felt myself tighten involuntarily. If I had thought that my husband had come to terms with household help, it had only been a temporary truce. Though he had been a good sport about it in light of the circumstances, he viewed it as a necessary evil, a momentary compromise. His mother had always done without hired help, and for that matter, so had mine.

I swallowed hard. Feelings of anxiety and panic wrestled with my overpowering impulse to acquiesce to his request. My palms were sweating.

"Let me think about it," I heard myself say. Only I knew what courage it took to voice that tiny bit of hesitation. I gave myself a mental ovation.

Later that evening, while I folded laundry at the clean kitchen table, I tried to sort through the mess of my disjointed thoughts and emotions. Was it my imagination that I felt that familiar sense of heaviness settling over me? Or did it have something to do with my husband's insinuation that it was time to go back to full-force functioning?

I knew that I had taken vitamins and had monitored my diet. I had gone for biofeedback and had read books on deep relaxation techniques. Deep down, though, in that spot where every person can find the real truth if he is brave enough to look, I knew that my illness and the ensuing recovery had a startlingly simple element to it.

Every motor needed to rest sometimes. If it didn't, it stalled. Broke down. At which point it needed repairing.

I had undergone that breaking point. I had run my motor ragged, and my body had finally rebelled. It was time to make some repairs.

Being sick had been a crisis, a real, legitimate reason to disoblige me of my self-imposed standards. It had been my body's way of forcing me to yield, to lower my expectations and accept help.

Now I had to learn to do the same thing when I was well. Perhaps not in the same dose, but in the same vein. I would have to remove that martyr's mask and expose my physical and emotional limitations, to myself and to everyone else. And the first person I would have to be open and honest with was my husband.

It was so much more tempting to go along with his notion of me as the super-mom who could swing it all on my own. I was innately a hard driver; it went against every fiber of my grain to assert myself and say that there was something I needed, something I couldn't do.

I knew, though, that the key to my improvement was the knowledge that I wasn't perfect. And along with that knowledge came the recognition that I couldn't always receive shining approval for everything I did. I would have to risk the lowered regard of people around me, even the very closest ones, in order to give them the best that I could give them.

I looked around at my tidy kitchen, at the piles of clean laundry, at the recent family picture tacked to the refrigerator door. I didn't want to wait for the ultimate collapse again, in order to get my life into line. Indeed, I felt so much better these days. Wasn't that the perfect reason to keep up my revised lifestyle? Didn't my family deserve, above all, an energetic, smiling, calm mother?

My husband walked in from night *seder*. I felt my stomach lurch. The first step was behind me. The hardest part was still ahead.

Inner change is one of the most difficult things to effect. It takes brutal honesty, grueling work, and unremitting vigilance. It is a step forward and two steps backward each time, especially when one still secretly struggles to relinquish one's respect of one's point of departure.

It's taken every bit of awareness and willpower, but I've enacted major reforms in my life. I've made household help a priority above almost everything else, and I've learned to cut the rest of my duties down to size.

So many of us unwittingly pay for productivity with sleep and sanity, love and acceptance, fun and happiness. We pay, and our families pay. And in this distorted world of ours, it's called being efficient.

It's incredible what a struggle it can be to battle that perverted value system. When that perfectionist inside me starts making me feel inferior, I remind myself: coping means choosing. And I choose my family's health and happiness over any income, cake, or admiration in the world.

Life, especially mothering, is all about trade-offs. One woman chooses to compromise cleaning in favor of baking; another downsizes her meals in lieu of starched laundry.

One prefers to earn less and spend less, another decides to work more and hire more help. One tells bedtime stories, and one changes linen every week. One bakes miniatures cookies, and one cuts out puzzles for miniature people.

But there is no doing everything.

I've learned it the hard way, but I've learned. A mother's role is about selflessness and the ultimate selflessness is surrender. Surrender of one's plans and surrender of one's standards. Surrender of one's monetary calculations and surrender of one's need to feel self-sufficient.

So if you notice a white flag blowing in the wind, that's my ship you see. It may be a sign of surrender, but to me, it's my banner of victory.

Life Insurance

"Hello, this is Sarah from Eagle Insurance, can I please speak to Miriam?"

"Speaking,"

"Good morning, Miriam, I wanted to wish you hearty congratulations on the birth of your baby daughter!"

"Thank you,"

"Can I ask you what the baby's name is?"

"Her name is Sima."

"Oh, what a pretty name. I hope you and Sima are both feeling fine. Is she your first?"

If you were on the receiving end of this phone call, and you're like me, at this point you'd probably be thinking: *Lady, let's cut the baloney. You're in this for one thing: my money. So please tell me what you want so I can tell you that I'm absolutely and unequivocally uninterested.*

Not everybody, though, thinks the way I do. I've learned that on the job.

I started working fresh out of *sheva berachos*, bursting with ambition and idealistic energy. "Look at the *Hashgachah*," I gushed to my husband of three weeks, when my good friend, Chaya Esther, called from New York. "Here we were, so worried about finding a job out of town, and then this."

I was a born and bred New Yorker who had spent her last two years out of school earning a paltry sum teaching English. I had been happy enough to find a job in a good high school, surrounded by a staff with Torah values, doing something I liked.

When I had gotten engaged to Binyamin, though, I knew that I would have to switch gears. Binyamin had aspirations of immersing himself into his learning full time, an ideal that I both shared and admired. Though our parents greatly encouraged his ambition, neither side had any means to speak of to be able to help us materialize our dream.

For us, *kollel* wouldn't be something we would be receiving together with our trousseau, a self-understood part of the package. If we wanted to seriously pursue a *kollel* lifestyle, it would mean cutting a lot of corners and looking for some source of steady income.

With those considerations in mind, Binyamin's Rosh Yeshivah encouraged him to enroll in an out-of-town *kollel*. Rent would be substantially more affordable than in one of the central metropolises. The only matter of concern was where I would be able to find a job. I had no contacts in the community, and didn't even have an idea of a field I would be able to work in.

The first week passed in a whirlwind, what with unpacking, stocking the house, and getting acquainted with the unfamiliar neighborhood. Gracious neighbors sent in salads and cakes and offered to show us around the shopping areas.

Binyamin started the *z'man,* and I embarked on my career as a full-time homemaker. Neither of us mentioned anything about a job. Binyamin would bring home the classified ads and we'd religiously comb through the employment section every morning after breakfast. Otherwise, we were both quite occupied acclimating to married life in general and to life out of town in particular.

It was about two weeks into this routine that I got a call from my friend Chaya Esther.

"Hi, Sori!" she greeted me excitedly, "I've got regards from you."

"You've got regards *from me*?" I was bewildered. Who, in these unfamiliar parts, could have given Chaya Esther regards?

She chuckled, obviously enjoying the suspense she had created. "Believe it or not, I've got spies all the way out there."

Chaya Esther and I had been night-activity counselors together. I guess she hadn't outgrown her whim for breakouts.

"You forgot that my sister-in-law grew up out of town."

"You mean your oldest brother's wife? Don't they live in Lakewood now?"

"I see you're pretty behind with the news. They started off in Lakewood, but they've moved at least five years ago. My sister-in-law said she saw you in the supermarket."

"Really?"

"She said you made a very good impression."

I blushed self-consciously. I guess I felt a little violated, being reported on when I'd assumed I was on foreign territory. Besides, I'd never realized one made an impression, let alone a good one, while wheeling a shopping cart.

"I thought those days were over," I joked. "What kind of proposition did your sister-in-law have in mind?"

"Well, actually, she asked me if I thought you were the right candidate to work for their company."

I was caught off guard. I had only been asking in jest. Chaya Esther sounded serious now.

"What kind of company do they have?"

"Well, my brother manages Eagle Insurance for his father-in-law. I don't know if you ever heard of it, but it's an international insurance company that offers home-, life- and fire-insurance policies at really affordable rates."

"Sounds good. Not that I know the first thing about insurance. What kind of job are you talking about?"

"Well, that's the thing. They're looking for someone in the sales department, telemarketing, customer service, that type of thing. Personally, I thought you would be great. You have excellent social graces, and I'm sure you'll pick up the business jargon in no time."

"Thank you, thank you," I said in mock formality. "It was worth moving out of town just to hear what an old-time friend thought of me. What are the working conditions like? I mean, I'm acting as if I'm the one deciding, instead of the other way around."

"Well, actually, if you're interested, I think you stand a good chance of getting the job. Of course, they'd call you for an interview, but generally speaking, my word goes a pretty long way with my brother.

"As far as the office goes, I understand it's a very pleasant working atmosphere. *Frum* women only, a few blocks away from where you live."

"Great," I declared, "Couldn't sound better. How do I proceed from here?"

"I guess they'll call you down for an interview. I'm sure you'll do wonderfully. And now that we've got the business behind us, could we go on to the pleasure? How are you settling in there?"

Chaya Esther and I launched into a discussion on the finer points of homemaking, and she brushed me up on some New York news. After 15 minutes of schmoozing, I hung up, impatient to let my husband in on the latest developments.

The office at Eagle Insurance looked just the way I had envisioned it. The room was one big area partitioned off into tiny cubicles. About half a dozen women sat busily at their desks manning phones or punching data into the computers. The quick rhythm of computer keys clacking created the backdrop for the persistent ringing of phones and the intermittent bleep of the fax machine. A busy office in the middle of the day.

I was ushered into the manager's office. He asked me some general questions and then outlined what he was looking for in an insurance agent. His demeanor was courteous, yet formal. After a few minutes, he politely dismissed me and promised the secretary would be in touch with me.

I was pleased with the interview. As I walked home, I imagined myself sitting in one of those cubicles at Eagle Insurance. Though I had never really made business phone calls before, I had a way with people and had always done well on the phone. While I understood that the starting salary wouldn't be anything grand, the hours were good, and there was lots of potential for growth. This might be just the job I'd been hoping for.

It didn't take a week before I was hired. My husband was thrilled at the turn of events, and our parents showered us with their warmest wishes. My boss dropped off a thick manila envelope stuffed with reading material to get me initiated. There were sample policies, business forms, management procedures, and plenty of technical information. I spent the next few days conscientiously studying the material. I was to start working the next week.

If I was worried about my lack of business acumen, I needn't have been concerned. I quickly learned the particulars of the company, and my aptitude for language helped me integrate the insurance terms fairly easily. Perhaps I would have done well, though, to take a course in psychology before I entered the world of telemarketing. As it was, I fell into it headlong, blindly unaware of the pitfalls.

Customer service had sounded so benign before I'd been hired. The words evoked an image of a brass plaque hanging over a glass partition where a no-nonsense middle-aged clerk greeted you in an automated, almost boring, drawl, "Customer service, may I help you?"

I guess my imaging capacity suffered from some serious limitations. I was either uncreative or very naive, but aside from the brass plaque, customer service in the 21st-century bore not the foggiest resemblance to either the no-nonsense clerk or the boring drawl in my fantasy.

If marketing today was a crafty tool capitalizing on the modern consumer's inadequacies, then *telemarketing* took the tactic one step further. The personal element was an underhanded assault on the crumbling social mores of the era we live in. If the salesperson sounded charming and caring, he or she stood a good chance of keeping the connection long enough to throw the bait.

If I didn't realize any of this before I began, I was in for a rude awakening. Though Eagle Insurance was a company owned and run by *frum* Jews, the customer base was nondiscriminatory. What that meant, for me personally, was that I would be dealing with people from all walks of life, albeit via the telephone.

As I sat down to begin my campaign promoting the latest life-insurance plan offered by Eagle, Debby, the sales representative sitting in the next desk, modeled a phone call for me. It sounded something like the thrust in the beginning of this article.

"Do the customers really go in for all that phony interest?" I asked her, incredulous. "I mean, I'm all for courtesy, but isn't the motive here embarrassingly transparent?"

"Well, yes and no," answered Debby confidently. "*You* might feel phony, but you'd be surprised how many people take the bait. Telemarketing is not successful on account of people like you and me who say, 'I'm sorry, I'm not interested' and go on to cook their suppers." Debby laughed amiably and continued.

"Of course you'll get the inevitable phone slammers who'll hang up, no matter what you say. A personal greeting, though, will soften anyone lacking the slightest resolve. And once you've built that initial rapport, you have that much more chance of selling your pitch."

That was my first psychology lesson. As time went on, and I gained proficiency, I was surprised at how right Debby's advice proved to be. Not to imply that I didn't get plenty of immediate rejections. That was par for the course. If I was allowed past the first three sentences, however, I knew I had made a serious inroad.

Once I had engaged the customer, I would tactfully try to extract as much information as I could, without the consumer feeling that I was probing. After all, when you're trying to promote something personalized like an insurance plan, you have got to know some basic facts about the potential customer's status and lifestyle.

I was shocked at how forthcoming people were. While some conservative customers were more reticent, I discovered that the majority of people out there had no qualms about telling a perfect stranger the details of their personal run-ins, the plans for their mom's upcoming birthday party, or the very explicit difficulties involved in raising their teenagers.

I found myself feeling rather unsettled by all this unbidden information. I was working in a women's-only office. As far as *tzeniyus* was concerned, the office appeared the picture of proper decorum. Still, I felt repulsed by the insidious attitudes seeping in through the phone lines.

When I shared my concerns with Debby, she waved them away.

"It isn't exactly what I'd call enriching, dealing with some of these people, but I've learned to live with it. I don't even hear these things anymore. It's just their way of talking; it has no practical impact on you. I've been working here for five years," she assured me. "And I don't think I've changed in the least."

Something about Debby's logic didn't sit right with me. It was true, I had no real contact with any of my customers, surely not with the people I was calling for the first time. Still, if I wanted to be successful, I couldn't remain aloof. Insurance was based on trust. And trust, in the perverted world we live in, had a casual tone to it. Much too casual for my liking.

Despite my subconscious disquiet, I was generally happy. I was busy juggling the challenges of keeping house and working five days a week. Binyamin was thriving in the *kollel*, and we often had *bachurim* as Shabbos guests. I felt a surge of fulfillment when I brought home my paycheck at the end of each month. I knew that the sacrifice of living far away from all our relatives, coupled with my *siyata diShmaya* at work, was enabling us to live the Torah lifestyle we both dreamed of. On hindsight, it was that sense of gratification that drowned out my misgivings about my job.

Each time I entered a new customer into the computer, I felt a sense of genuine pleasure. It was not just the simple victory of chalking another success to my account. My salary was configured on a commission basis. The more policies I sold, the more money I earned. And every penny, I knew, was going toward my husband's continued success in learning.

Baruch Hashem, our family grew. Working full time was an ongoing challenge, but I steeled myself to continue. I took shortcuts with my housekeeping and kept the cooking to a basic minimum. I had been promoted in the office and was doing so well; Binyamin was like a fish in water in his *kollel*.

In the meantime, subtle changes had taken place in the office. The "*frum*" in the "*frum* women only" clause had been dropped somewhere along the way, and new cubicles had been added to accommodate fresh employees. And employees, in our day, had no compunctions about what was considered requisite business apparel. Next to some of my new colleagues, I often felt like I was coming to work outfitted in bullet-proof armor. On second thought, perhaps I was. One thing was certain, *they* had definitely shed their shield to the rigors of the battlefield.

Most of us had been working together for several years. Though the men and women were careful not to address each other on first-name basis, there was an unmistakable air of camaraderie permeating the office. Teasing and banter, laughter and wisecracks were all casually tossed from the respective cubicles in a quick volley across the room. It may have been a subtle shift, but the general ambiance certainly didn't answer to the word formal.

Money is an addiction. So is success. As our company picked up, reaching out across the United States and Canada, and even as far as Europe and Eretz Yisrael, my boss began to place prosperity ahead of some basic standards. Our women's only office boasted two men now in the sales department. There were no separate offices. It was one family under one roof. A family splintered by multiple breaches.

Writing crystallizes feelings, especially when one is writing in retrospect. As I dash these words furiously across the paper, the signs seem so stark, the signals so clear.

Somehow, while it was happening, it took a long time until I really felt the accumulation of lint on the filter of my soul. Inertia has a way of propelling us forward down the assembly line of life; wake up, run to work, put up Shabbos, plop into bed. As long as we are generally moving in the right direction, it takes a calculated pause to check the filter, and question whether some outside elements aren't clogging our spiritual systems.

After the birth of my third baby, I began to feel the load of my dual responsibilities. Though I was fueled by my success at work, I was feeling depleted. *Perhaps I should consider some other field, something less demanding?* I mused. I had always enjoyed writing, and had an excellent working knowledge of both Hebrew and Yiddish.

We both knew, however, that sporadic writing couldn't compete with the steady income I was bringing home. Besides, I didn't have a clue as to how to make the necessary connections. I would have to relegate writing to my dreams.

We did decide to make some reforms, though. I spoke to my boss, and he agreed to curtail my hours. As long as I maintained the sales, I could come later and leave earlier, as I pleased.

The next thing I did was enroll in a women's *shiur*. I had been feeling a certain sense of apathy, as though I'd been numbed into running through my days like a robot on a treadmill. I hadn't engaged in spiritual and intellectual exercise in years. Perhaps a *shiur* would infuse me with the vitality I was missing.

The *shiur* was given by a special woman in our community, every Monday evening. She was a living example of her ideals, and exuded an air of *simchas hachaim*. I came home feeling refreshed in a way I hadn't felt in a long time.

It was as if someone had taken a giant pump and infused the picture of my life with dimension. I felt renewed meaning in the everyday acts I had become so accustomed to doing. Dressing the little ones, cooking for Shabbos, going to work, all these tasks seemed to puff up with a sense of mission, of spiritual fulfillment. I was feeling invigorated and accomplished.

And then, at once, sparked by this renewed awareness of what I was doing and where I was headed, I was suddenly struck by the disaccord between the two: where I was headed and what I was doing to get there.

Here I was, a hardworking mother, trying her best to support her family so her husband could learn undisturbed and so her children could imbibe the purity of a home saturated with Torah ideals. What was I sacrificing, though, toward that end? For a fleeting flash, I was able to see the office as an outsider, and I was horrified by what I encountered.

My sensitivities were being eroded by the slow poison of foul speech and immoral values coming through the phone lines. When I envisioned my husband, a sheltered *talmid chacham*, listening to some of the junk to which I was privy, I couldn't help but cringe. What made me think that I, the fortress of my household, was impervious to these slurs?

Life Insurance / 129

Besides, the office itself had lost the insulation that had characterized its structure at the outset. If I looked carefully, there was only the scantiest scattering of beams left where there had once been a proud sign, "*Frum* women only."

I made up my mind. Though I had consulted *daas Torah* twice over the years, it had been more of an offhand gesture to push the snooze button on my conscience. Both times I had been advised that I wasn't obligated to give up my job if I didn't have some other income set up.

This time, I was determined to shake myself awake. I knew that I hadn't presented the entire picture honestly, that I hadn't possessed the courage and candor to put our *parnassah* on the line, to set almost a decade of success in front of a Rav for his objective scrutiny. Now, I suddenly felt ready to do the right thing.

Binyamin and I sat down to seriously weigh our options. I could start job-hunting again, though I didn't quite know what field to target. I was wary of offices, and I wasn't interested in any line that required continued contact with the outside world. The idea of doing something with my writing cropped up again. Perhaps I could contact the editorial board of some newspaper?

Binyamin had begun tutoring *bachurim* in the evenings, several years before. Now, he considered giving up his afternoon *seder* to accept some more students. It still wouldn't be enough, though, to make ends meet. As it is, we just about managed to cover our expenses.

After tossing the alternatives back and forth for a while, we both realized we had reached a deadlock.

"Perhaps you can ask for some modifications at work?" Binyamin ventured. "I know the existing conditions are out of the question, but maybe things can be worked out somehow."

I shook my head. I felt as if the *yetzer hara* was closing in on us, just waiting for me to feel desperate enough to grab a loophole. I had already approached my boss on several occasions, and I had only gotten long-winded explanations in response. My boss was a nice person, but we weren't on the same wavelength. He was too bent on seeing his company take off, to tune in to subtle sensitivities.

"Don't you want to try seriously looking for something else, before you burn your bridges?" Binyamin asked. "Give it two, three months. Maybe something will turn up in the interim."

I understood his reasoning, but I stood firm. There were certain times a woman had to go by her intuition, and this, I felt, was one them. Something told me that I had to show my readiness before something else came up, that Hashem was waiting for me to relinquish my secure foothold before He lifted me over the chasm.

Binyamin respected my feelings. The very next day, I approached the boss and asked him if I could have a few minutes with him privately. He looked at me in surprise; then his eyes flickered with understanding as he glanced at my name posted on the bulletin near the copy machine. *She probably wants a bonus,* he seemed to register.

"Yes, Mrs. Gross, what can I do for you?" my boss asked when I was seated in his office.

"I would like to resign," I said quietly. " I'm willing to wind up whatever I'm in the middle of, but I don't intend to continue with the company."

My boss was taken aback. It took him a full minute to respond.

"Can I ask you what spurred your decision?"

"It was a decision based on personal considerations," I sidestepped his question. I wanted to leave no margins for negotiations.

"Hmm, I understand. Would a raise in salary affect those considerations?"

"Thank you, but no, not at this point," I replied. I had expected the question.

My boss looked thoughtful. "Well then, the company will be very sorry to see you leave," he managed to say, biding for time. Then as a last-ditch effort, he asked again.

"I understand there's something specific you're planning to go into?"

"Actually, I have no prospects lined up. I would like to find something in the writing field."

I stood up to leave.

"Can you do English-Hebrew translating?"

I steadied myself, looking at him in shock.

Life Insurance / 131

"We were actually going to bring someone in to do that kind of thing. Our company is opening an Israeli branch and we need someone to do foreign correspondence. We also want to have pamphlets and brochures written up and translated. Today, e-mail is a cheap and easy means of communication. We need someone creative to come up with the right wording for the constant flow of offers and updates we feed into the system."

"I'd need a private office," I said flatly. The words were out of my mouth before I had a chance to formulate them. I was surprised by my own response. I knew I sounded unsuave, perhaps even rude, but I was tired of wavering. I wanted all my cards out on the table.

"No problem," my boss said evenly.

I thought I was hearing things.

"Not just a separate cubicle," I explained very clearly. "I want an office with a closed door."

"Yes, yes, Mrs. Gross, I heard you. I believe we can accommodate you."

"And I want no direct contact with customers."

I don't know what gave me the courage to fling demands when a job offer was hanging precariously in the balance. Reflecting back, though, I think I was more afraid of losing my resolve than of losing my job. I had come to terms with leaving. I didn't want to rescind my pledge.

My boss seemed to sense my hesitations.

"Look, Mrs. Gross, the offer stands. Separate office, no customer service. The company has grown enough for us to hire an in-house writer/ correspondent. I've seen your work in the past, and you wouldn't have to learn the ins and outs of the company. Think about it. You can let me know when you decide."

I had stood at the foot of the mountain for so long, contemplating an alternate route. I had wavered and deliberated, considered, then tottered. And suddenly, just as I'd girded myself to climb, just as I'd let go of the weights keeping me chained to the valley, the mountain vanished before my eyes.

Binyamin and I had a lengthy discussion with our Rav. I had been so mentally geared to climbing, I was nonplussed by the abrupt turn of events. It was as if the script I had practiced so conscientiously had suddenly been altered by the unexpected appearance of a new character on stage. Who was this new character? Was it the *yetzer hara* trying to suck me back onto his turf?

The Rav smiled.

"As long as your conditions are met," he said slowly, "I don't see any problem with the offer. The *Ribono shel Olam* doesn't need our *korbanos*; He wants our *retzonos.*"

He let his words sink in.

"*Berachah v'hatzlachah.*

"*Man's livelihood is as difficult as the splitting of the sea.*"

And sometimes, when we mortals take that plunge, we are privileged to witness the parting of the waters.

A Steal of a Lesson

When I meet friends from the good old *mesivta* days, I brace myself for the inevitable gibes.

"*Nu*, Heshy, you're still wearing your bar mitzvah hat?"

"So, Heshy, how much money are you putting into savings every month?"

"Heshy, how many rings?"

I smile sheepishly. They don't have to say another word.

It was a group of us, back in those days, who would often

get together to learn *mussar* for 20 minutes before or after the regular night *seder*. Our schedule depended on Eliyahu, the *rosh hachaburah*.

Being that we didn't have a set timetable, we regularly parted after Minchah, promising to start a chain call before Maariv with the exact timing.

The script would repeat itself with unerring accuracy.

"So, Eliyahu, what time are we learning?"

"I don't know yet. I'll call Chaim Reuvain a little later with the timing. He'll start a chain call to the rest of you."

At that point, I would interject.

"Why can't we decide now? It's not a mitzvah to waste money on phone calls."

"I don't know now," Eliyahu would respond. "It depends on my father's learning *seder* with me."

"So let's make a code," I would suggest. "Three rings twice in a row if we learn before Maariv, five rings twice in a row if it's after Maariv."

"And how am I supposed to know that it's you calling?" That was Pinchus.

"Well, let's decide on a time. Eliyahu, what time do you think you'll know? Seven?"

"Listen, Heshy," Eliyahu would sigh in irritation. "Half the night will be over by the time we finish with these codes. Personally, I think I can afford the phone call. If you can't, then we'll put you at the end of the chain, so you won't have to let anybody else know."

The last line was uttered with a hint of sarcasm.

I never took the hint. Instead, I asked the rest of the *chaburah* if they minded if I was last. Nobody minded; they just got downright nervous from my idiosyncrasies.

I wouldn't take a bus anywhere if I could walk; I wouldn't buy a drink on the way even if I was fainting from thirst.

"There's a sink in the dorm," I would say, "We're almost there; it's a *shud der gelt (*a pity to waste money*).*"

"Come on, Heshy," Chaim Reuvain would chide, "don't be so *karg* (stingy); it's not healthy."

"I'm not trying to be *karg*," I'd counter, "it's *pashut a shud der gelt*."

That was just it. I never *tried* to be stingy. It came very naturally. My parents were that way; my grandparents were that way. And I was that way.

We didn't call it stingy. Thrifty. Economical. Prudent. No one was hoarding money under the floorboards, but if you didn't need to spend it, why spend it?

My father was a hardworking *balabus*, my mother a dedicated housewife. She was fond of repeating the Yiddish idiom that an efficient housewife constituted half a livelihood.

If anyone personified the expression, it was she. She took care of our clothing so that it lasted for generations, carefully sorting and laundering so that colors didn't fade and fabrics didn't age. Socks were darned, tears were mended, stains were scrubbed and soaked and sprayed until no sign of them remained.

My mother never wasted money on services either. She'd walk to the other end of town to save on deliveries and she did all the household cleaning by herself. She painted the house on her own and she shopped for her hosiery and dry goods in a basement store that didn't have any overhead.

Shopping, actually, was an art of its own. Or perhaps a science would more aptly describe it. My mother knew the prices in every store, just where the bananas were cheaper, and where the cleaning products went on sale. She bought the 16-ounce can of tomato sauce because it worked out a few cents cheaper, and the smaller boxes of crackers because the economy size turned stale, making them more expensive in the long run.

We did a good job of maintaining the ozone layer, too. Long before recycling was in vogue, my mother had it all figured out. Junk mail became shopping lists and scrap paper; plastic cups and foil pans, in the event that they were ever used, were rinsed over and over again for repeated use.

Electricity and water consumption carefully followed all the rules promoted by the environmentalists. During the daytime, Mother Nature did a very good job of illuminating the house and otherwise, fluorescent lighting was used only for as long as you were in the room.

This mind-set followed me into yeshivah. My roommates got an average of three hats before I ever thought of buying a new one, and my glasses were intact long after the frames were out of style. I took pride in the fact that I had never lost a pair of socks, never mind a towel or sweater.

My friends all knew. Heshy wouldn't go by taxi if he could take the bus, would never buy a *sefer* if he could borrow it from someone who wasn't presently learning the *sugya*. Though I was the butt of plenty of good-natured teasing, I never considered it a fault. On the contrary, I thought it to be a reflection of responsibility and maturity.

When I met my prospective *kallah*, we discussed anything and everything, from special needs children to the idea of mothers working. Although she came from out of town and I was a born and bred New Yorker, our backgrounds and upbringings were similar enough. We saw eye to eye on most issues, and shared the ideal of living a *kollel* life.

The one thing that we never thought important enough to discuss was our outlook on money. Everyone knew that *Chazal*'s counsel for a happy life was to live with the barest minimum. I was sure that any serious, responsible adult shared my view on these matters.

I was in for a surprise.

Actually we both were.

It started on the very first morning of *sheva berachos*. I came home from Shacharis to find a beautifully set breakfast table: rolls, spreads, and salad in the middle. The first thing that hit me were the rolls. What was wrong with bread? Rolls were three times the price.

I swallowed my impulse to say something. I knew that my new wife was eager to please me and that she had surely gone out of her way to set an especially appetizing table. I washed my hands and sat down to eat. Swallowing my first *kezayis*, I complimented my wife on the food.

When I finished the first roll, though, I just couldn't help it.

"Do we have any bread in the house?" I tried to be tactful. "These rolls are very good, but one is enough for now. You can put the other one in the freezer for tomorrow."

Esty blushed. "Um, actually, I don't think we have any bread. My sister dropped these off this morning; I asked her to get us a few rolls. Why, what's the matter, do you prefer bread?"

"No, I like rolls," I was quick to assure her. "but it's *pashut a shud der gelt*. I'm fine with bread; we never had rolls in yeshivah."

Esty seemed puzzled. I saw her make a mental note to get bread into the house. I hoped she wasn't offended; I hadn't meant to hurt her. I had just thought it was easier to make a casual mention of it right at the outset rather than turn it into an official issue later on. Although rolls were fine for *sheva berachos,* I didn't think it was a wise habit to feed.

Esty, I realized soon enough, was a wonderful *balabusta*, a warm, loving wife, creative, considerate, and generous.

Her housekeeping, though, was *not* half a livelihood.

By any stretch.

It was commonplace for me to come home to all the lights burning, the air-conditioner running, and the stereo on full blast. Without meaning to get angry, I would find myself irritably shutting the lights and switching off the air-conditioner. If the windows were open, there was a good breeze outside. It really wasn't necessary.

I understood the need for a light when one was working in the kitchen; I could even concede to the air-conditioning when it was really hot, though in our home it had been strictly reserved for Shabbos. This careless consumption, however, really annoyed me.

I found myself feeling curt and resentful when Esty breezed into the kitchen.

"Oh, you're home, Heshy?" she'd greet me cheerfully. Instinctively, she'd flick on the light.

Esty would ask me about my morning at *kollel*, and I'd find myself answering in distracted monosyllables. Why was she setting out blintzes when there was leftover tuna salad in the refrigerator? I tried to act grateful, but I found myself feeling tense.

Here I was walking all the way home from *kollel* to save on bus fare when she was splurging on indulgences. Didn't she know we were living on a very tight budget? What was this flippant attitude?

I found myself redoubling my own vigilance. Before we left the house for Shabbos, I'd make it my responsibility to switch off all the lights and appliances. I even unplugged the alarm clock on the night table near our bed. There were two other clocks in the house and we'd be away for three days; I'd reset it when we got back.

I was happy when I noticed Esty beginning to exercise more prudence. Apparently, she had picked up on my unspoken vibes. Though I hadn't made any outright mention of it, my body language must have spoken louder than words.

Still, it seemed to me that Esty was constantly asking for cash. Though I had strongly endorsed the idea of staying home for Shabbos pretty early on in the game, I found myself feeling anxious and skeptical. Why did making Shabbos have to cost so much? Wasn't there a way to do it more economically?

"If you're making the salmon for me," I told Esty, after our second Shabbos home, "then I'm okay with gefilte fish. It works out cheaper, doesn't it?"

Esty looked a little hurt.

"I mean I appreciate it very much; your sweet and sour salmon was delicious, but we're a living on a tight budget. We don't have to spend on unnecessary things."

"Oh." Esty looked genuinely surprised. "I thought *hotzaos Shabbos* didn't count."

For a minute, I was thrown off. Indeed, hadn't I been raised on the story of *Yosef Mokir Shabbos*? What was I, the miser next door?

Something about the argument, though, rang hollow. Whom were we fooling? Were we eating the salmon in honor of Shabbos or in honor of ourselves? I sensed the same skepticism that I always sensed when my spendthrift friends waxed righteous about *emunah* and *bitachon*.

To me, it was laziness masquerading as holiness, a perfect cop-out for squanderers.

Of course one had to have *bitachon* that *Hakadosh Baruch Hu* would provide, but that didn't exempt one from keeping a careful account of one's expenditures. I felt frustrated by Esty's lax demeanor.

When I asked her what she had paid for tomatoes one day, she didn't have a clue.

"I heard that the tomatoes are very expensive now," I commented. "Maybe we shouldn't be eating them."

Esty looked incredulous.

"No tomatoes? How do you make salad without tomatoes?"

"I don't know," I answered, trying to be gentle. "Maybe you manage without salad for a while."

Esty laughed. She seemed downright amused by my proposition. I was insulted by her disregard.

She continued eating, while I toyed with my spoon. I had no appetite for the salad.

"I think you're going a little overboard, Heshy," Esty looked at me concerned.

"I'm not saying I can't learn to be a little more careful, but I don't think a person is supposed to starve himself to save a few cents."

I felt myself getting hot under the collar.

"I don't think not eating salad is called starving yourself. Please. Don't get carried away. We can have peppers and cucumbers and carrots and ... there's more than enough variety, I didn't say not to eat tomatoes forever, only to wait until they're more reasonable."

Esty remained quiet.

That evening, I came home from shul with a notice I had taken off the wall.

Wanted: graphics artist for local organization. Flexible hours. Can be done from home. Experience requisite.

Esty looked at the notice.

"You mean this besides for my morning office hours, or instead?"

"Well, we'd have to call to hear exactly what it entails," I suddenly felt apologetic, "but if it isn't too many hours, maybe you could fit it in during the evenings."

Esty sighed.

"I guess I'll call."

I couldn't understand her reluctance. Esty was very skilled at graphics; it came easily to her. How many people had job opportunities knocking on their doors?

Esty took the job, but I sensed her indignation. She'd look at her

A Steal of a Lesson / 139

watch and sigh in frustration when I'd put the phone off the hook after supper so she could work undisturbed.

"You want the phone?" I'd ask, trying to placate her. "I was only trying to help you. You were just saying how crazy it is that you don't get to bed before 1 o'clock, what with phone calls and work."

"It is crazy," blurted Esty, "but I can't be cut off from the world. I work in the morning; in the afternoon I often have errands to run; the evening is the only time when I can socialize."

I felt bad. Perhaps it was, indeed, unfair to saddle Esty with an extra job. Then, suddenly, a well of resentment stirred inside me. Why was I being made to feel like an insensitive taskmaster? Weren't we in this together? Esty knew, just like I did, that we could use every extra penny that came our way. Living a *kollel* life had a price attached to it; a price we had both agreed to pay.

I felt as if I was doing my part, scrimping on anything I could get by without, picking up bargains in the supermarket, and helping with whatever I could to make Esty's workload easier.

Besides, Esty had a day off on Tuesdays and worked with a good friend in the office. It wasn't as if she was in total isolation. Why did she feel as if she was working solely for me?

Though we generally enjoyed a relationship of deep, mutual understanding, the money issue was a constant point of contention. I was frustrated and upset. I felt like a policeman standing guard.

Why didn't you go to Rosen's? Schmerler's is much higher on milk products.

Why are you throwing away this plastic container? What's wrong with it?

What did you tell Mr. Samson? Didn't he call you about doing a brochure?

I knew I sounded like a petty nag, and I hated it, but I felt that Esty wasn't doing her part.

After our first baby was born, the friction escalated even more. I hadn't realized that a baby entailed so many extra expenses, especially when Esty wasn't getting paid for her maternity leave. I found myself going through Esty's purchases, questioning the necessity of items she bought.

"Aren't there cheaper pampers to be gotten?" I'd ask. "I remember my mother buying irregular crib sheets. Don't they still sell them?"

Esty would patiently explain that the cheaper pampers often turned out more expensive because they had to be changed more frequently, and that the irregular sheets generally didn't fit properly. If I wanted, she could try another company.

If I wanted? I bristled. I didn't want anything. This was *our* burden. Esty's easygoing attitude chafed at me. I felt like I was carrying a refrigerator up the steps, heaving and hauling with every ounce of exertion, while my purported partner was tagging breezily behind, wondering why I was panting.

When I brought up my feelings one evening, Esty looked puzzled. She clicked the mouse to save the ad she was designing on the computer and swiveled around to face me.

"What you're saying is, that you feel as if you're carrying the whole weight on your shoulders."

I nodded. I hadn't said it in so many words, but if she had, then it was just as well.

"I don't know," said Esty slowly, "Maybe I'm wrong. But I don't think it's a question of you or me. I think you're carrying a burden that neither of us has to carry."

"Hu?" I was shocked. Esty was usually very reasonable.

She shut the computer and joined me at the table.

"I don't think either of us should be worrying," Esty repeated. "Worrying is a waste of energy. After all, *parnassah* is in Hashem's hands."

I felt the resistance mounting inside. *Here we go,* I thought, *putting it all on Hashem.* I knew the line.

"I don't mean that we have sit back and wait for money to fall from the sky, or that we should splurge unrealistically. A person has to do *hishtadlus* to earn money and try to spend within his budget. Which I definitely think I'm doing."

A jumble of thoughts flashed through my mind. There was no denying it; Esty *did* work hard to earn an income. What was it then that bothered me so much?

A Steal of a Lesson / 141

"I just don't come across as taking the burden," she continued, "because I don't. I'm only an employer doing my job. My worrying isn't going to help the *Ribono shel Olam* manage."

It took me a minute to respond. I had lost my own fragile thread of thought.

Hishtadlus. That was it.

"I feel like I'm the one forcing you to do the *hishtadlus*," I finally hit on the underlying point. "I'm forever having to nag you to compare prices, figure out cheaper menus, to pursue job offers that come your way."

"You don't *have* to," Esty smiled. "No one's stopping you from stopping."

"But you're right," she conceded, "if you weren't after me, I'd definitely take a more passive stand. I don't think I would run across town to save 9 cents on a pound of apples, or push another five hours of work on *erev Shabbos*, when we're having company."

Those weren't random allusions. They had both come up the week before.

"I am in this as much as you are, Heshy, believe me," she pleaded, "but I don't think *hishtadlus* means functioning like a pressure cooker. We have to do our share, and leave the details up to Hashem. Sarah Chana needs a calm mother, you need a happy wife, we all need sleep and clean clothing and nourishing food."

"Well, we need money for everything that you just mentioned. How do you think it'll work with your laid-back attitude?"

"Heshy," she appealed, "Give Hashem a chance to figure it out. It might be too hard for us, but I'm telling you, it's not too hard for Him."

I remained silent. I had a lot to think about.

Esty made sense, and I did admire her calm disposition and generosity of spirit. She wasn't talking about giving up her job or going on a luxurious vacation. She was talking about relinquishing our fastidious hold on every penny, pennies that added up and inevitably cost our family's happiness and peace of mind.

Theoretically, she was probably right, I just had a lifetime of baggage countering her logic. Much as I saw her side, it was so hard to leave go of habits I had been born and bred with.

Though it sounded ridiculous, even to my own ears, I almost felt anxious about not feeling anxious. I had been raised with the dogma of prudence and thriftiness, almost to the point of an obsession, and Esty's relaxed attitude hit a wall of cognitive dissonance.

Almost as if he had been in our dining room, the *Mashgiach's* Thursday night schmooze that week was centered around the timelessness of the *tzintzenes haMahn*, the direct correlation between *bitachon* and *hishtadlus* in our everyday lives.

I took it a personal sign that I was moving in the right direction.

Slowly, I learned to let things ride. It took more restraint than I had ever thought I had, but I would gag on my urge to ask Esty how much the mangos cost or when she was planning to finish her graphics project.

When a promising job offer came right after the birth of our second baby, I was the one to reject it.

"The money will come from somewhere else," I said, although every ounce of my inner being screamed that I accept the windfall. Esty smiled gratefully, echoing my sentiment that Hashem didn't lack for emissaries. There was no way she could know, though, what a spiritual workout it was for me not to lament the lost opportunity.

I patted myself on the back.

As skeptical as I had been, I had to admit that my new attitude didn't seem to affect our budget negatively. We had mangos and we had tomatoes, we even had tuna at 5 cents more a can, and we somehow made ends meet.

Esty had been right. We had only to allow the *Ribono shel Olam* to figure it out, and He did. Here and there, just when we were floundering, cash would appear from some unexpected source. A baby present from my in-laws, an old outstanding debt finally repaid, a refund for an appliance for which we had given up of ever receiving remuneration.

I was astounded by the clarity of *Hashgachah*. If one only let go of the reins, one felt *Hakadosh Baruch Hu* pulling the wagon.

And then came the big test.

A few months after our third son was born, Esty told me one day that her diamond ring was missing.

A Steal of a Lesson / 143

I was tempted to resort to blame. Esty was innately less careful than I was, and I had cautioned her on occasion that her rings would get lost one day.

"I know I put them in my drawer on *Motza'ei Shabbos*. I've started putting them away religiously before I do the dishes."

"You're sure they're not in any pocket?" I asked.

"No, no, I'm positive," Esty insisted. "I've already searched through every pocket. I can't imagine where they could be."

I couldn't either. We opened every drawer, searched through the closets, the toy box, even the garbage. No sign of the rings.

It was a few weeks before Purim. I was sure we'd find them when we cleaned for Pesach.

A week passed.

"I think my pearls are missing," Esty greeted me one day when I came home for supper.

Oh no, I thought. *First the rings, and now the pearls. What was happening?*

Suddenly, logic dawned.

"It must be the cleaning lady," I said gravely. "Who else has access to your drawers? Check if anything else is missing."

Esty came back, pale and alarmed.

"My gold necklace is not there either. That definitely was in my drawer. The only time I wear it is to weddings."

A hundred admonitions crowded my mind. Why hadn't Esty supervised the cleaning lady more carefully? Who kept jewelry in an open drawer with a cleaning lady in the house?

One look at Esty's miserable face, though, made my incriminations wither. We wouldn't get anywhere with condemnations. We had to get to the bottom of the mystery.

We canceled the cleaning lady, and hid the remainder of Esty's jewelry. Two days later, Esty's wallet containing $200 was gone. Vanished. Swallowed into thin air.

Someone was breaking into the house, and it was a very insidious thief. The wallet had been in the house in the morning and had disappeared sometime before lunch. The only place Esty had been in the interim was at the bakery.

We were stymied and scared.

Not for too long.

I came home from Shacharis the next day to find the door ajar. Esty was at a doctor's appointment, and I was on my way to *kollel*. Apparently, someone hadn't been counting on my appearance. As I entered the house, I saw him darting out of my bedroom. He stopped in his tracks.

It was Jack, my neighbor from the first floor. He was an old bachelor living with his mother, a pitiful drug addict to whom we had never paid much attention. Although he didn't exactly enhance our apartment complex, I had always written him off as harmless.

Well, here he was, harmlessly emptying my home of its valuables.

The blood drained from my face. I felt my knees giving.

"Jack," I confronted him sternly, "What are you doing here?"

"Oh, sorry, Heshy, sorry. Don't be mad at me; I didn't know you were coming home. I just needed the facilities."

You bet you didn't know I was coming home, I thought, the fury rising inside me.

"Where's all the stuff, Jack?" I demanded. "The rings, the necklaces, the money."

Jack sported this dumb look and tried to wriggle his way past me. I was too shocked to stop him. I felt as if I was experiencing a scene out of a contemporary high drama novel. A pretty far flung one, at that.

I immediately filed a police report and alerted the local equivalent of the Shomrim organization. By the time Esty came home, she found a very pale husband, a new lock being installed, and two police officers in the kitchen.

Jack, it seemed, had somehow procured a key to our door and had been digging into our assets to fund his addiction.

"He's not a malicious thief," said the officer, "but I doubt you'll see your valuables. They're probably long liquidated, sitting at the bottom of some drug dealer's safe."

I'm not here to tell the tale of Jack and our ensuing tribulations trying to get him out of the neighborhood. That's a story in itself.

For me, the harrowing ordeal was a pinnacle of sorts, a *nisayon* that somehow capped the mountain I had been sweating so intensely to climb.

Bitachon is not only the belief that Hashem provides regardless of our efforts; *bitachon* is also the acceptance of the fact that every loss is tallied Above down to the last penny.

I looked at Esty. She had been robbed of almost all her jewelry, but she hadn't been robbed of her serenity. Her complacence hadn't been a cop-out. She believed, truly believed, that Hashem was in charge of the ledgers, that He alone determined what a person would gain and what he would lose.

And I stood firmly alongside her in that belief.

It had taken several years of grueling, mind-twisting therapy, but I could finally say that I'd come around 180 degrees.

Gone were the condemnations, the regret, the calculations. I didn't even feel the heat of the inner skirmish I usually experienced, the clash between old ingrained ideas and new ideals.

We didn't have our valuables, and we would probably never have them.

But we had our *bitachon*.

And that, to me, was the ultimate steal.

Tools of the Trade

Nowadays, we're very into tools. A writer wouldn't think of pursuing a career without a computer; a seamstress wouldn't dream of going into the profession without a state-of-the-art sewing machine. We've made a lot of progress since the Middle Ages.

Somehow, when it comes to the more important aspects of living, we tend to shift into primitive gear. Parenting, improving, dealing with our mood swings; that's supposed to be inborn, isn't it?

I used to think so, before I became a parent. My own parents were so special, so warm and tolerant and giving, that raising us had almost seemed effortless. At least to us, it had. My parents had complemented each other so beautifully, had disciplined us so lovingly, and had commanded, rather than demanded, obedience and respect.

So when I became a parent, I was almost surprised by the multiple skills that the challenges of motherhood required. I had a model, though, to live up to and I was determined to continue the legacy. Together with my husband, I embraced the challenge, resolved to work at my mothering the way any professional works at a trade: industriously, consistently, skillfully.

I knew that running a home wasn't only about keeping the house in top order, about having squeaky-clean floors and a freezer stocked with cake. I knew that having it together meant more than even doing all of that and holding down my job as a tenth-grade *mechaneches*.

Running a successful home was primarily about navigating a family, about bringing the passengers on board safely and happily on their way to their destinations. And no matter what else I was involved with, my foremost goal was to be a successful captain on the home front.

The first experts I consulted were my parents. They possessed the wisdom born of experience, the know-how of what had worked and what had failed in their parenting. "How did you do it?" I pressed them. They were hard put to express their formula in words. It was something indefinable, woven of my mother's simplicity and my father's gentle kindness. My father smiled his soundless smile, eyes twinkling with good humor that conveyed his confidence in me. No one is perfect; parents are human. We can only try to do our best.

Infused with that positive outlook, I set out to find the approach that would work for me. I was constantly on the lookout for ways to brush up my communication skills. In my capacity as a *mechaneches* and an active *klal* member, I had the opportunity to discuss some key issues with several reputable *mechanchim*. I gained immeasurably from their wisdom. I also devoured numerous books on the subject, trying to cull the most potent techniques.

I gleaned some invaluable advice. Although each family is a small world of its own, rotating around the axis of its unique dynamics, there are certain universal tips that every parent can adapt to his personal challenges. Granted, one cannot parent from a book, and there are certain kids who seem bent on proving all the authors wrong. Still, cultivating tools is indisputably a positive step toward success.

One of the most important tools I mastered was a concept that seemed simple, almost elementary, but, as I realized, was so often not employed. I learned to function in a proactive mode rather than in a reactive one. In unadorned English, what that meant was practicing to foresee eventualities and brainstorming before the problems arose rather than as an involuntary response to provocative situations.

I would imagine Shmuly refusing to wake up in the morning, Chany coming home inexcusably late, Fraidy turning over her bowl of vegetable soup in the heat of a temper tantrum. I would project images of the boys tangled in a fight over the battery-operated tractor, of the girls whining in boredom on a day off, of the overly energetic child whamming into the kitchen with a ball.

Then I would mentally assess the most productive way of handling the challenge, and I would envision myself reacting. It was amazing how innovative I could be when I wasn't caught unawares by the immediate reality. Dealing with a theoretical situation rather than an actual one gave me the time, the resources, and the composure that real-life crises precluded.

I was gratified by the results I experienced. Though there is no magic formula that takes the element of hard work out of parenting, I immediately noticed a change in the atmosphere. Instead of feeling like a frustrated dictator, I felt the cool control that comes with forethought and mental readiness. My whole family enjoyed a calmer, happier, more cooperative household.

Unwittingly, I began to use proactive thinking in my own personal life. Being endowed with an active imagination, I found that envisioning inevitable scenes ahead of time empowered me with the skills to be able to deal with them in real life. As I would go about my household chores, I would become mentally involved in these hypothetical situations, almost to the point of actually experiencing them.

One day, as I was doing the dishes, I found myself thinking about my father. Unbidden, a smile played on my lips. My father was everything to me; I adored him and his affection for me was equally apparent. My father loved all of his children, but I think he derived unique pleasure out of my spunky nature. I was the youngest in my family, and I had always been Daddy's little girl.

He wasn't a demonstrative person, but he had always enjoyed my open display of affection for him. As a little girl I would unceremoniously dive into his lap and smother him with hugs. My father would laugh indulgently, not quite knowing how to reciprocate. "Rivkah'la," he'd smile, and there was all the love in the world in that one word.

Even as a married adult, I continued to enjoy my coveted place in Daddy's heart. My husband was his pride and joy; my kids were his life. We'd visit my parents and I would beam as I'd watch my father play with my little ones, observing their progress and enjoying their antics. My father followed every detail in my life and was always there to advise me and cheer me on.

All at once, standing there and washing those dishes, I was struck by the terrifying eventuality that, at some point, I would have to part with my father. The way of the world was that parents left this world before their children, and though my father was perfectly vibrant and healthy at the moment, it was a fact I would have to face.

I shuddered, just thinking about it. How would I ever be able to live without my father? How would I ever be able to go on? I was so engrossed in my thought process, I was barely aware of my tears cascading into the warm sudsy water. Suddenly, the slam of a door jarred me out of my trance. I almost laughed in relief. The power of imagination!

After that, however, every so often when I had a moment to myself, I'd consciously picture myself dealing with the loss of my father. I'd go through the motions of mourning and experience the excruciating pain. Perhaps, I reasoned, if I prepared myself mentally, the parting would be easier when Hashem saw fit to take him from me.

Little did I know.

Proactive thinking worked wonders with things like spilled juice or temper tantrums. Pain, however, real, wrenching, tearing, bleeding pain, couldn't possibly be bandaged ahead of time.

Not long after I had first contemplated the terrifying thought, my dear father was diagnosed with a terminal illness. I will forever remember the day my mother called me to share the devastating news. I was crushed. I remember, however, quickly stuffing the fact into a corner of my mind and throwing myself into my daily tasks with a fervor I had never known.

I took my kids to the library and baked cookies with them. I turned on a lively music tape as I bathed them and served supper. My husband was amazed by my strength. Honestly, however, I think it was a subconscious way of shielding myself against the terrible depression I feared would come.

It was *erev Succos*. I attacked my cooking and baking with gusto and threw myself into my Yom Tov shopping. My father was to undergo surgery immediately after Succos. I was in a kind of denial.

Exactly one year later, a harrowing year full of prayers and tears and flickering hopes, my father departed this world. It was *erev Succos* again. We sat *shivah* in a kind of unreal fog. The people didn't stop coming. People of all ages, from all walks of life, people we knew and people we didn't know, all bearing one thing in common. They had come to pay homage to a man who had helped them, a man who had touched their lives with his kindness in a meaningful, personal way.

When I think of that week of *shivah*, I remember the copious tears. Deep, retching tears that came from the most innermost place inside me, tears that choked my breath and blinded my vision and threatened to drown my soul. With each person who came, every anecdote that was related, the tears flowed again, hot and thick and salty, for the man I had loved so dearly and who would no longer be with us.

My father had been a simple *balabus*, but he had exuded greatness. He was a gentle, unassuming person, soft and soothing like a summer breeze. He had never imposed himself on anybody and accepted people just the way they were.

He had lived for *tzeddakah* and *chessed,* doing for others the way normal people pursue a hobby. Giving, to him, wasn't about having his name etched on plaques or the gold pages of the dinner journal. He would extend himself in the quietest way, without expecting anything in return, not even a simple thank-you. Actually, expecting is the wrong word. He never *needed* a thank-you. He was full to the brim with the satisfaction of having done another person a good turn.

In his own quiet way, my father had loved life. He had enjoyed nothing more than watching us kids have a good time, singing, dancing, kidding around. He had always been fascinated by nature, by the beauty of the autumn leaves or the sight of an exotic bird. He appreciated every facet of the *Ribono shel Olam's* incredible *beriah.*

My father had breathed the Jewish calendar. When it was Chodesh Elul, I knew from his somber humming, "*B'Rosh Hashanah yikaseivun, uv'Yom tzom Kippur yeichaseimun .... u'teshuvah utefillah u'tzeddakah maavirin es roa hagezeirah.*" He would go about his business, serious and reflective, like someone expecting a tax audit. When the *seder* night arrived, he looked like royalty, his face literally aglow as he recited *Hallel*. A Holocaust survivor, he considered every word a testimony to his own personal *geulah*. Watching my father go through any Shabbos or Yom Tov, there was no way to remain apathetic to *Yiddishkeit*.

And now he was gone. *Shivah* was over, and my family needed me to pull the strings together again. The Yamim Noraim and Succos were at the doorstep. There was shopping to be done and meals to be cooked. I felt totally detached, disconnected from reality. I felt hollow and burned out. Life would never be the same again. *I* would never be the same.

The month of the *sheloshim* passed. It was as if someone was propelling my body through time; first Sunday, then Wednesay, then Shabbos, and Sunday and Wednesday, and Shabbos and Sunday and Shabbos. It was an existence in a different zone, out of sync with myself, with my family, with the rest of the world. I didn't taste the days, or feel them, or see them pass. All I could feel was the gripping sadness. I had barely gotten up from *shivah* and the *sheloshim* was over. It was like living a month in emotional jet lag.

The grief wasn't rational or intellectual. It wasn't the tender sadness evoked by memories, or tears brought on by fragile longing. It was an almost physical sensation, like hunger or nausea or fatigue, that assaulted me in waves and clutched my heart so tightly, I felt like it was all I could do to breathe. Whatever I saw, whatever I heard, whatever I did was through that heart contracted with pain, constricted with anguish.

I tried to pull myself together, to pick up my life, my children, my pursuits, where I had recklessly dropped them in the shock of my loss. I tried to find the humor that had always winked at me from every situation, the fun I had always encountered in my daily duties. They seemed to have vanished from my life. All I could find was morbid despondency, black and heavy and choking, lurking in every corner, hiding behind every task.

I had always been a strong and upbeat person. I had embraced challenges with joy and had thrown myself into my tasks with fervor and zest. I was the kind of person others turned to when they needed some practical advice, empathy, or just a good word. On a more personal level, I had spent my whole married life cultivating my role as a devoted wife and mother.

Now, I was hard pressed to bring the most artificial smile to my lips. I just couldn't find joy in the things that used to uplift me and warm my heart. Most of the time I walked around in a distracted fog, and it took my most supreme efforts to do the laundry, put meals on the table, and smile to my husband and children.

My father had been everything to me. He had been a sterling role model and a source of inspiration, a constant bubbling flow of happiness and giving. He had loved me in the way that only a father can love his daughter; subjectively and unconditionally, taking full interest in every detail of my life. Now he was gone and I felt as if the turbine that had inspired my life had stopped.

The month of Kislev came dancing into the calendar, bringing the whiff of donuts and *latkes* and the soft glow of Chanukah flames into the humdrum of winter routine. My kids brought in the mail, breathless with excitement, assaulting me with the latest advertisements, nudging me to study the myriad color splashes announcing concerts, plays, midwinter sales. I felt numb, impervious to their thrill.

Chanukah had always been such a beautiful time. We had always gotten together with the family in the evenings and enjoyed the mornings off baking or frying donuts. I tried to go through the motions, but no one was fooled. My heart wasn't in it; I was frozen in pain. It seemed that the part of me that had loved, celebrated, enjoyed, was extinguished forever.

Time is the greatest healer. I had heard the cliche in the past, had seen it transform other people from dispassionate mourners into effectual, albeit hurting, people again. What a mirage. It was so much easier to toss cliches when the mourning wasn't yours, when the pain wasn't wedged in your very own heart, pinching with every breath.

Perhaps I, too, appeared to be healing. I certainly wasn't anyone's picture of a pitiable orphan. I was a grown adult, happily married, blessed with children. I had supportive friends, an enviable job, a wonderful mother. In the contemporary proliferation of heart-wrenching tragedies, my own loss seemed almost mundane. To everybody else, perhaps. Not to me.

I saw my father at every crossing, heard him in every conversation. I woke up aching for him, and I went to sleep aching for him. In between, I dressed and washed and cooked and spoke and listened. I went to PTA and paid the grocer and greeted my children and thanked the mailman, but the pain didn't let up. Sadness was my constant companion, clutching tightly at my chest, twitching at the corners of my mouth, stinging right beneath my eyelids with unshed tears.

It was a strange feeling. I had never before known unremitting despondency. I had dealt with disappointments and difficulties in my life, even loss, but never had I known this cleaving, crushing hopelessness.

I had always loved the outdoors, the song of the birds chirping, the beauty of trees in bloom. I had taken pleasure in music, writing, art. Our house had been a lively house, full of fun and laughter, full of sharing and giving. I had always taken an active part in my children's lives, keeping track of their school projects, taking interest in their friends. I had been an energetic wife and mother, doing, nurturing, in love with life.

It's incredible what an illusion of control emotional stability affords. Every person has ups and downs, but as long as one can rise above one's inner pain, he/she feels in charge of his/her state of mind. I had always belonged to that class. I had never known what it meant to have every dimension of one's existence flattened by one's mood. All at once, I felt small and vulnerable, pinned down by an oppressive force heavier than myself.

I didn't recognize myself. Neither did my closest family and friends. My husband was lost. He tried to lift my spirits, to tune-in to my feelings and be helpful with whatever he could do. My friends were wonderfully supportive. No one could relieve me, however, of the choking sensation I felt inside.

"Rivky," one of my close colleagues said one day, "This can't go on. You're doing a great job treading water, but who's to fool? You need help. Been there, done that. I know what it means. I'm giving you a name and number. Do it for yourself."

She fumbled around a moment for the paper, and I didn't even have it in me to protest. Chaya knew me too well for pretenses. She was right. I was drowning.

I was churning with ambivalent feelings. On one hand, I felt relieved, exonerated. It was soothing to have a good friend say it out loud like that; like letting someone into the dark dreary solitary confinement of the past few months. So I wasn't alone, and this wasn't normal. There was help to be gotten out there.

On the other hand, something inside me felt defensive, almost rebellious. Me? I didn't need help. I just needed some time; I was still grieving. Seeking professional help insinuated that I was a case, unstable, incapable of dealing with emotions on my own.

I couldn't help reflecting on the irony of it. All my life I had been on the giving end of the emotional spectrum. I was the one with the insight, the encouragement, the solutions. I was the kind of person others automatically gravitated toward for some sunshine and sensible advice.

And now, I was one of those people. I couldn't find even a glimmer of sunshine within myself. I was honest enough to admit that. It would take an act of supreme humility and courage, though, to turn my soul inside out to someone else.

Drawing on my innate confidence, I swallowed hard and mustered my coolest voice. "I would like to make an appointment," I said, subconsciously sitting up tall as I spoke. Sometimes one has to swallow one's pride in order to preserve one's dignity.

It was strange going for the appointment. If anyone saw me waiting there, the thought struck me, they'd assume that I was coming to confer with a professional about a third party. So be it.

My turn came. Closing the door behind me, I took a deep breath and squared my shoulders. I knew that talking about my loss would be painful, and I was determined to maintain my equanimity. When speaking of my father, though, my lips began to quiver uncontrollably. Before I knew it, I was crying freely, not bothering to regain my composure. This was what I had come for, and I would have to let my guard down if I wanted to be helped.

The therapist was very understanding. "I see you're extremely in touch with your feelings and you seem to have a strong support system. I don't think therapy is what you need. You have sustained a major loss and could probably use a low dosage of an antidepressant to help you deal with the grief."

I thanked her and took the prescription. As I took the paper, I felt the strength that comes with courage, the serenity of spirit that settles when one knows he/she has done the right thing. The hardest step was behind me. Now I would have to follow through.

All the way home, my mind was plagued with thoughts and questions that have probably troubled anybody with any sort of emotional issue requiring medical help. I was well aware that people were on antidepressants, but did I really need it? I was such a normal, healthy individual who had always had a positive outlook on life. It seemed like a cop-out to resort to a pill. Weren't there techniques that I could learn to help me handle my feelings?

In my heart of hearts, I knew the answer. I knew there was a difference between pain and paralysis. Sadness was part of the human condition. It was an inherent part of loss, and it hurt. Badly. When that sadness turned into its own entity, however, when it smothered a person's spirit to the point of dysfunction, it was like any other medical symptom that warranted intervention.

I had no qualms about taking Tylenol to soothe a bad headache, or antibiotics to treat a strep throat. When I had encountered challenges in child-rearing, I had had no hesitations about hunting for tools that would help me succeed. Now I needed tools to help me deal with my grief. The *Ribono shel Olam* had put those provisions into His universe. He wanted me to make use of them.

I took the pills the way I did everything else in my life, conscientiously, consistently, for the first time in many months, happily. Not to say that I was immediately transformed into the exuberant person I had always been. Slowly, though, I felt a part of me thaw, the part of me that had smiled, that had sung, the part that had experienced the buoyancy of joy and love.

I was still terribly sad, but I was a master over my sadness. I was able to vacuum up the despondency that had spread throughout my body and contain it in a special chest. I still went to that chest very often, opened it up and cried as I held my father close to my heart. I was able to close it, though, when I needed to. I was able to fulfill my responsibilities as a wife and mother, to nurture and love and live once again.

Under the close supervision of my doctor (okay, psychiatrist!) I continued with the medication for about a year, until shortly after my period of *aveilus* was up. I cannot say I am the same person I was before. I am improved, humbled, uplifted. My father taught me a lot in his life, and he taught me even more in his death.

Growing in this world is not about doing the things that gain us acclaim. Neither is it about reveling in the natural gifts that Heaven has endowed us with. Real growth is the thing that happens with sweat and humility, the buds that sprout when one buries his/her ego and feels his/her fragile dependence on the Ultimate Gardener.

As I go about my life today, I appreciate my regained spirit. I appreciate the calmness within, the dissolution of that tight knot inside my chest. I appreciate my ability to twirl a baby around with lighthearted joy, to laugh together with my teenagers, to enjoy shopping with a friend.

Most of all, though, I am deeply grateful for the wisdom. The wisdom to have been able to see past external considerations and look myself straight in the eye. Because at the end of it all, we are accountable for only one thing: the choices we make regarding that person in the mirror.

And I chose life.

Righting a Wrong

Playgroup teaching isn't often recognized as a talent. *Oh, anyone can be a playgroup teacher*, common sentiment has it; what does it take to occupy a bunch of 2-year-olds?

It's interesting how many people voicing this opinion can't seem to occupy a single toddler for more than a few minutes without turning restless. I don't usually take offense, though. If no one else knows what it takes, then I do. Running a playgroup draws on an endless reservoir of patience, resourcefulness, and love. It requires unusual amounts of stamina, creativity, and physical energy. Loads of physical energy.

Which is where my story started.

By the time I was married 10 years, I jokingly told my husband I could relinquish my last name. All anyone ever called me was *Morah Breindy*. If they hadn't personally been in my playgroup, then I had been the *Morah* of their sibling, cousin, or child at some point or another. I felt like the Mommy figure of the neighborhood.

"It's because I keep the groups small," I always maintained. I prided myself on knowing each and every child like my own.

When we moved to our own house, however, practicality overrode sentiment. The spacious, finished basement easily was large enough to accommodate 20 toddlers; even if I hired an assistant, I could significantly increase my income. Registration was closed before I could even advertise. I thanked Hashem for my reputation and found myself redirecting my prayers. Now I was in desperate need of a capable assistant.

After a few dead-end attempts, my prayers were answered in the form of Fraidy. Fraidy was a former neighbor of mine who had a special rapport with children. Her own two little ones were out in the morning and I knew she had been searching for some kind of job.

As I had expected, Fraidy seemed excited with my call. Yes, she was definitely interested; could she discuss it with her husband and get back to me?

I felt my stomach flutter with a mixture of apprehension and anticipation. On one hand, there was a twinge of loss. Together with the thrill of roomy, new quarters, a large group, and an assistant, I was saying goodbye to the cozy atmosphere, to the privilege of serving as the exclusive Mommy to 10 or 12 toddlers.

On the other hand, the prospect of being able to brainstorm with someone else, of having an intelligent partner to discuss things with, was definitely appealing. And the simple notion of having an available pair of hands to put on coats and unzip boots was a welcome thought.

Fraidy and I started the year with a group of 18 children. An intrinsically warm person, she had a wonderful way with the kids. I quickly realized, though, that discipline and order were not Fraidy's strong points. The children took advantage of her easygoing attitude and lack of experience. I couldn't seem to count on her to come on time or clean up at the day's end the way I had expected.

If I was slightly frustrated, I was grateful for an assistant who loved the children as deeply as I did. People weren't perfect, I reminded myself; we had to take them as a total package. In Fraidy's case, that meant paying for her devotion to the kids by taking responsibility for a lot of chores normally taken care of by assistants.

As the year wore on, I sensed Fraidy picking up my techniques. My heart swelled with the gratification of having trained somebody in a job. The parents were thrilled and I thoroughly enjoyed her company. I couldn't imagine a more ideal arrangement.

We ended the year with warm feelings. Fraidy and I had formed a close relationship. It went without saying that our setup would continue the next year. This time, considering Fraidy's experience, I allowed myself an enrollment of 19 children. I looked forward to an even better year than the year before.

The trouble began shortly before Chanukah. I began to feel wiped out in a way that I had never experienced before. In the beginning, I blamed it on recent family *simchos* and my 6-month-old infant who had been up a lot at night. After a few days, though, I realized there was more to it. I was barely able to get through exercise and *davening* before I asked Fraidy if she minded tending to the kids while I stumbled upstairs for a nap.

Though Fraidy assured me it was fine, I was alarmed. What was happening to me? I had been a playgroup teacher for nearly 12 years and had never experienced this type of fatigue. After two or three days, it suddenly struck me. Hepatitis. At once, everything made sense. The symptoms, the fatigue, and the yellowish tinge that was beginning to color my eyes. The blood test was the only confirmation I needed.

Writing notes to the mothers in my playgroup, I felt a sense of relief wash over me. So there was a reason for the way I felt. A reason that would, hopefully, run its course and blow over.

In the meantime, though, I couldn't leave Fraidy on her own. Faint with exhaustion, I made some calls. After about a dozen fruitless attempts, I finally cajoled my neighbor, Chaya, into trying. Though I hated to recruit a reluctant candidate, I had no choice. I informed Fraidy that Chaya would be assisting her and promptly dissolved into weightless oblivion beneath my quilts.

The next thing I consciously registered was the cordless telephone on my pillow.

"It's Fraidy, Ma. She said it's very important."

I felt the wisp of some incoherent dream float into the distance as I struggled to open my eyes. A wave of weakness knocked me back onto my pillow. I felt so vulnerable, so feeble, so hopelessly detached from my usual, robust self.

After a long moment of lying listless, I willed myself to lift the receiver.

"Hello?"

Fraidy was horrified.

"Oh boy, Breindy, you sound really bad."

I didn't have the strength to answer her.

"Sorry to bother you, I didn't realize you were that sick; I just wanted to know what you want me to do tomorrow."

Fraidy, I felt like saying; *I don't want a thing right now. Sing, dance, paint, play; do whatever you like. Right now I barely even know what my own children are up to.*

My words, however, remained annoyingly soundless. My voice seemed buried somewhere, together with my initiative.

"Breindy? What did you say?"

I didn't say anything.

"I'll send my husband with my file." I managed

"Just do — whatever you want."

If Fraidy was mystified by the ambiguity of my instructions, she was perceptive enough not to persist.

"*Refuah sheleimah*, Breindy. Rest up."

Only after I heard the dial tone droning into my ear did I realize I hadn't even asked her how it had worked out with Chaya or if she had agreed to continue the job. I felt as if a leaden fog had settled over me. I would worry about the playgroup some other time. Right now I couldn't even focus enough to worry.

The ensuing weeks felt like a night flight in turbulent weather. Fastened to my bed, I felt myself being bounced over the lurches and bumps of day-to-day challenges. My husband valiantly tried to man the controls; I struggled to retain some sense of balance. Meals were sent, bought, warmed. Clothing was changed and somehow laundered. My nieces came over to help my kids with homework and my cleaning lady showed up twice a week to keep the place in minimal order.

All throughout, I tried to keep my tabs on the playgroup. Whenever I ever felt a trifle better, I picked up the phone to call Fraidy. At one point, I detected a strange note in her voice.

"How are you going to manage painting with all of them?" I inquired, concerned. We had always painted a picture of the *Kosel* in time for *Asarah b'Teves*.

"Oh," Fraidy chuckled. "It's not exactly the first time I'm painting with them." Her chuckle rang a little hollow.

"You were so out of it last week, I didn't even bother reminding you about the *latkes* arts and crafts and the stuffed *dreidel*."

There was no mistaking the defensive pitch. I had unwittingly ruffled her pride. Mentally backtracking, I tried to figure out what had set Fraidy off. Had my inquiry come across as an insult to her competency?

You were so out of it, I didn't even bother reminding you about the latkes arts and crafts and the stuffed dreidel.

The irony of her statement hit me. *She* hadn't bothered reminding *me*. As if I had been somehow skirting my responsibilities, while she had been righteously shouldering more than was her due. It was more than insult. She sounded resentful, taken advantage of. Underappreciated.

Instinctively, I was tempted to nurse hurt with hurt. What did she think I was doing, having a grand old vacation in bed? Hadn't she thought of asking *me* how I was managing with meals and housework?

I quickly steered my thoughts clear of these emotional potholes. I knew they would only get me mired in a ditch of self-defense. Fraidy was simply overwhelmed with the playgroup; all she needed was my genuine appreciation.

"Oh, I can't believe I forgot," I quickly amended. "I didn't doubt you for a minute. I'm sure those *dreidels* came out adorable with your artistic touch."

Fraidy's tone softened, but I later looked back to that 3-minute conversation as the subtlest turning point in our relationship. We had always worked as a team; suddenly I sensed a hint of competition straining our conversations.

If I ever offered to help, Fraidy politely declined my offer.

"You just rest up. Between me and you, what are 19 booklets to staple when I have to be up all night preparing the hats anyway?"

I heard the undertone. Anything I would do was an imperceptible drop in her overfull bucket. She preferred being the martyr to affording me the illusion that I was doing something to make it easier.

"How's Chaya working out?" I innocently wondered. I hadn't heard much about Chaya the whole time.

"I guess you could say it's working out. She's not thrilled about the job, but she's doing it. She said she hopes it won't be much longer."

I certainly hoped so too. As I felt my strength coming back, I ventured an hour or two here and there. I told Fraidy that if she wanted, she could come at 10 o'clock, and I would get things going until then. I was happy when Fraidy accepted my offer. I sincerely wanted to alleviate the burden she had carried for close to two months.

Not that I was able to handle a full day yet. When Fraidy arrived at 10 o'clock, I nearly threw the reins into her arms as I staggered upstairs to bed. Chaya would join her until 12 o'clock when I felt ready to tackle the rest of the day.

The parents were none too happy with the setup, but there was little I could do. I knew the constant switch-off of *Morahs* was not the ideal arrangement for toddlers, though I suspected that the parents felt more gypped than their 2-year-olds. Most of the kids seemed to take the situation in stride.

"Well, their parents certainly don't think so," Fraidy retorted when I shared my opinion. "Ask my husband. That's all I heard every day for two months; how upset the kids were that you were out, and how they never would have registered had they known that Breindy wouldn't be there. I felt really great."

I winced at Fraidy's sarcasm. The bitterness was right beneath her taut smile. So *that* had been what had been eating at her all this time. Why couldn't people be more sensitive? Hadn't they realized that their constant griping about my absence had slapped Fraidy's best efforts in the face?

There was nothing much I could say. I hoped that things would slowly get back to normal so that we could both forget bygones.

It was a hope in vain.

As Pesach drew closer, piling extra stress on my already strained schedule, I felt myself buckling again. *Oh no*, I panicked; *not now*. I had the desperate sensation of driving a stalling vehicle right toward the middle of a busy intersection. *Please,* I prayed, *just let me make it to the other side; just let me get past Pesach.*

I did. Rolled with my last dribbling bit of inertia toward *bedikas chametz*. And then my engine gave out.

Relapse, the doctor pronounced; mono, my alternative practitioner diagnosed. It didn't really matter much to me what it was called. I knew that my motor was badly burned out. I could barely move off my bed. Pesach was the first hurdle; then I would have to see what to do with my playgroup for the remainder of the year.

Though I dreaded facing her, Fraidy made an effort to be nice. Sensing my helplessness, she assured me that everything would

Righting a Wrong / 163

work out. I tried to let her assurances assuage my feelings of failure. I knew I had miserably disappointed the parents, confused the kids, and overburdened Fraidy. I tried to take comfort in the fact that it had been unforeseeable.

I also tried to compensate to Fraidy whenever the opportunity arose. I raised her salary significantly, although I was nearly running at a loss. I had absorbed the cost of an additional assistant and had been forced to hire substantial cleaning help. The basement had become an unrecognizable mess in my absence. It was more than I could expect for Fraidy to keep the place in order.

When Fraidy asked me if she could use my basement to host her brother-in-law's *sheva berachos*, I graciously acquiesced. Although I knew it would be an imposition on my already difficult routine, I was glad for an opportunity to demonstrate my appreciation. I didn't say a word when her *kugel* spilled all over my oven or when I found residues of sticky sherbet all over. I had taken the extra mess into account when I had agreed. It was well worth the good feeling between us.

Only toward year's end did I begin to feel uncomfortable vibes once more. Perhaps it was the fact that I was getting back to myself, I mused. I wasn't sick enough to arouse pity anymore; on the contrary, the sight of me lounging around probably provoked Fraidy. Here she was scurrying breathlessly to prepare for graduation while I drank my morning tea over a leisurely telephone conversation.

Though I knew I was following strict doctor's orders, I cringed every time I heard Fraidy coming up the steps. I wished she didn't have such free access to my upstairs. If only she knew how gladly I would have traded positions with her.

One evening Fraidy called.

"We have to plan next year, Breindy. What do you have in mind?"

An uncomfortable silence charged the connection.

"Well, actually, I have a full enrollment already."

"And?"

"Well, I really hope we'll be able to work together again."

"Aha."

Why did she sound so funny?

"I'll tell you," Fraidy blurted, "I didn't think you would be up to doing the playgroup. It's only three months away, and you're still recuperating. I thought that maybe I would take over your registration and pay you to rent your basement and supplies. That way, it could work out for both of us."

Work out for both of us? I couldn't think of a more miserable idea. That was all I needed, another year of walking on eggshells around Fraidy, another year of misunderstandings and messes. Besides, my basement was part of my house. It doubled as my playroom and it wasn't for rent.

"I don't see it happening, Fraidy," I said, struggling to keep my voice from sounding stilted. "I think we either stick to our old arrangement, or, if I see I'm not up to it, just cancel."

"Fine."

Fraidy sounded anything but fine.

It was dead silent for a moment.

"I'll let you know what I decide, so you can make a decision, okay?" I couldn't stand the lilt at the end of my sentence. It sounded so overly sweet. Anything, however, was better than the deadlock of a moment before.

I spent the next few days in limbo. Yes, no; yes, no. The wavering accompanied me through breakfast and lunch, distracted me throughout bedtime and storytime. Would I be ready to undertake another year, or was it wiser to take a break? My husband and good sense finally won over. The way I felt, there was no way I could make a fair or realistic commitment to 20 toddlers and their parents.

Last year had been one thing; to knowingly repeat the disaster would be quite another

"Look," my husband finally swayed me, "You've established a name in the neighborhood. You're not saying goodbye to this forever. Even if something opens next year, I'm not worried. *B'ezras Hashem*, when you'll feel ready to reopen, you'll have kids."

I hurried to dial Fraidy before my resolve faltered again.

"I've come to a decision," I informed her. "I won't be opening next year. If you want to take my registration, the basement of the *shul* next door is probably available for rent. I'm not sure, but you can find out."

Righting a Wrong / 165

Fraidy sounded excited. I was happy to have helped her out.

Two days later, after I had called the parents to update them, Fraidy got back to me.

"Um, about next year …" Fraidy ventured awkwardly.

"I have to sign a contract with the *shul*. Preferably, they want to sign a lease for two years."

I picked up her insinuation.

"Breindy, at this point I have no way of knowing if I will or won't reopen my playgroup in two years' time. It really all depends on what I'll be up to."

"Aha."

Fraidy lapsed into thoughtful silence. I took the opportunity to interject.

"If you're afraid of investing too much," I offered, " I'll be happy to rent you my tables and toys. That way, you can always decide later on."

Fraidy happily took me up on my proposal. Finally, I felt the forced diplomacy of the past few months dissolve. Now that there was no more rivalry shading our relationship, we could be best friends again. I was thrilled.

Over the course of the summer, I spoke to Fraidy often. I lent her my file of arts and crafts ideas and songs and reviewed the curriculum with her. We reminisced about our first year together and were even able to joke about the difficulties of the past few months.

Whenever I met mothers whom I knew had children enrolled in Fraidy's playgroup, I would rave about her qualities. It was as if I had a personal stake in her success. Whenever I passed her place at dismissal time, I derived a special sense of satisfaction from seeing her kids waving the familiar arts and crafts projects. Fraidy would smile and we would stop to chat for few moments before she hurried home.

"I still have to make a *cheshbon* with you about the stuff," she would invariably call after me as we parted.

I would wave my hand obligingly.

"Don't worry about it, Fraidy; whenever you want, we'll discuss it."

For my part, I wasn't in a rush. I was happy to have a year off to be able to recoup my depleted resources. I ate well, attended an exercise gym, and had time to tend to neglected chores. It was the first time in about 13 years that I wasn't working. I felt like a new person.

As Purim approached, I was bombarded with calls regarding my plans for the coming year.

"I really don't know yet," I responded. "Call me back after Pesach."

When I met Fraidy at a school function, I casually mentioned that we would have to discuss our plans for the next year. Fraidy paled and then turned a deep crimson.

"Plans?" she stammered, as she picked at the peeling bulletin board. "What kind of plans?"

"I'm not sure yet," I returned, "but I think I feel ready to reopen. Parents are asking me about registration. Do you want to figure out an arrangement with me? It doesn't have to be like our original setup. You have more experience; we can do something more worthwhile for both of us, like doing two groups or else alternating hours."

Fraidy looked like the life had gone out of her face. She took a tissue out of her pocket and got busy pleating it into a fan.

"No, I don't think I'm interested," she said evasively.

"Tell me, Fraidy," I probed, "what bothers you about it?

"Well, I'll tell you the truth; it really isn't worth it for me. I worked like a horse last year. Between me and you, I think I should have gotten the full pay of any self-employed *Morah*."

By that time, I realized I had made a mistake to approach Fraidy on one foot. I hadn't dreamed the issue was so charged. The buzzing school halls were not the place to settle our score. Fraidy forced a smile to a mutual acquaintance as we silently agreed to freeze the conversation for the way home.

I barely slept that night. Fraidy's words rang in my ears, stung deep inside until I felt tears trickling onto my pillow.

Why did Fraidy keep clinging to last year's fiasco? We both knew that last year hadn't been in my control. I had expressed my heartfelt apologies so many times for the way things had worked out. I guessed it wasn't the apologies. Fraidy had felt underpaid. Didn't she realize that I hadn't made a cent on the playgroup?

Besides, she wasn't taking into account the ideas I had provided her with, the basement and supplies, the fact that she had never had to stay to clean up. Didn't she notice the difference now that she was on her own?

My face was wet with tears. I felt hurt and betrayed. Had Fraidy ever thanked me for my file, for my ideas, for every detail of her playgroup that was a takeoff on her experience with me?

When I had mentioned it on our walk home, Fraidy had turned defensive.

"Oh, yes, my husband keeps saying we have to pay you for everything."

She had completely missed the point. Not everything could be measured in cash. Her drudgery last year couldn't be compensated with money, and my gesture of gratitude could not be bought off with money either. My files were not up for sale.

Only I knew how many hours of painstaking work had gone into each sample, how many years of trial and error had gone into perfecting the songs and techniques. Each *parashah* song, every arts and crafts was the outcome of years of experience. I wouldn't sell them for any money in the world. I had willingly given them to her as a favor and all I wanted in return was for that favor to be acknowledged.

I had been too hurt, though, to respond then.

Fraidy had taken my silence as a cue to explain her surprise.

"I didn't dream you were thinking of reopening the playgroup. Besides signing a two-year lease, you can't imagine how much I invested in the basement."

Again, I felt instigated. What did she mean, *she didn't dream*? I had explicitly told her that I had no plans for the future. If she had assumed I had finished my career, it wasn't my fault. Besides, how could she bemoan one year of investment when I had 12 years of elbow grease behind me?

When Fraidy called me the next day, there was an affected eagerness in her voice.

"You know what, Breindy? You open registration; accept as many kids as you want. Ten, twelve, as many as you were planning. And then, after you close your registration, I'll advertise. That way, we won't be stepping on each other's toes."

I wasn't fooled. I knew the dynamics of registration better than to think it was an open-shut affair. Besides, I didn't like the shift in Fraidy's tone. She suddenly sounded aloof, almost smug; she was *willing* to let me have the first round.

Her attitude irritated me. I had clearly told her my stance before she had signed her lease. She was stuck now and I was expected to take my hat off in deference to her selflessness.

"That's not the way it works, Fraidy." I said quietly. "Registration takes a long time. And you're not stepping on my toes. I don't mind if you open registration together with me."

Fraidy was silent. A few more ideas were raised and discarded. Finally we settled on what seemed like a fair division. Fraidy would accept the younger set, and I would open a group for older children. That satisfied both of us. Fraidy would have the large group she wanted, and I would take the few older ones, whose parents, for whatever consideration, preferred a private playgroup to a school nursery.

It was what I considered a cold truce. We parted formally, Fraidy's amenability of a few moments earlier slightly diffused. I tried to put my resentment aside and plan for the coming year.

Fraidy avoided me over the summer. She sent her assistant to pick up some missing papers, and left a message with my daughter regarding a tune to a certain song. When I bumped into her in the fruit store, she stiffened and forced a smile.

"You know, I still have some *schmuntzes* (odds and ends) of yours to return." She said as she threw peaches into a bag. "We better make a *cheshbon*."

Schmuntzes? I felt stunned. Did she, by any chance, mean my tables and chairs, my Lego and riding toys, my dolls and dishes, tapes, books, and puzzles? I had amassed a considerable collection over the years and had kept everything in almost new condition. By whose definition was that called *schmuntzes*?

"Yes, we really better," I replied, ignoring her slight. "I'll need my stuff back soon."

"I mean, you could imagine what everything looks like after a year of wear and tear; some of the Lego got lost and two of the trucks are broken. I guess that's part of it."

Righting a Wrong / 169

Fraidy laughed. I found it hard to join her. She had taken all my stuff, had ruined a good part of it, and had sufficed all along with some vague reference to a *cheshbon*. Forget about a *cheshbon*; couldn't she sound apologetic?

I felt myself burning with indignation. Flashes of memories flitted through my mind as I bagged my fruit order and went on to the butcher.

I was in a turmoil. On the one hand, I so badly wanted to forgive and forget. I knew Fraidy surely had her own side of the story and that she wasn't an ungrateful person. *You're not a baby,* I chastised myself. *Can't you rise above the resentment? Just put it behind you, and that's all.*

No sooner had I resolved to wholeheartedly cleanse my heart of ill will, then I found myself rehashing old scenes. Fraidy coming perpetually late, Fraidy making *sheva berachos* in my basement, Fraidy leaving a mess every day after playgroup. Hadn't I given for giving's sake? I berated myself. Giving didn't come with returns; giving meant swallowing one's need for acknowledgment and credit.

I made a firm commitment to forgo payment for the equipment Fraidy had rented from me. Perhaps if I bent over backward to show her I really had her welfare at heart, I would feel that peace I craved.

My emotions were like a maze. For several days, I went around convinced that I had almost gotten to the end. Circumvented the quirks of pride and rivalry blocking the path to true love. Then I met Fraidy at The Copy Counter, and I felt myself tighten. This definitely was not love. I would have to retrace back to the beginning and see where I had gone wrong. Would I ever feel the liberation of reaching the other end?

And then, suddenly, as I stood in front of the machine, watching the bulb move up and down in time to a rhythm, it dawned on me. I had been taking the wrong path.

Who said silence was always golden? Wasn't silence sometimes a steel bolt? Didn't silence sometimes imply that one gave no credence to the other person, that one had full confidence in the validity of one's own position? I had so sincerely wanted to give; I had wondered why it wasn't fostering the love it was supposed to breed. What I had failed to take into account was that love had no chance to grow in a wordless climate.

Fraidy and I each had a side to the story, a side that we fully understood. If we wanted to make that perspective understood to each other, we had to talk. Trying to swallow resentment and force smiles was like spraying air freshener in a room with a rotting potato. The unpleasantness was bound to overpower the mist.

That night, I called Fraidy.

"Fraidy, I think we have to make a *cheshbon*," I stammered the time worn line.

"Yes, yes," she said hurriedly. I could feel her blush, could feel the tension crawling into the wires. I plunged into an explanation before I lost the courage to continue.

"Not a dollars-and-cents, *cheshbon*" I clarified. "That'll come later."

Fraidy was quiet. She sounded taken by surprise.

"We're each starting a new year right next door to each other; we can be ideal working partners. Why should something as trivial as a *cheshbon* get in the way?"

Talk is easy to come by, the dictum goes; it's action that takes commitment.

On that Monday evening, I discovered how very difficult talk can sometimes be. How very difficult, and how very enlightening, and how very rewarding …

It was so much easier to sulk in passive silence, to exult in the self-righteous pride of being a martyr. It was so alluring to convince myself that I was doing the loftiest thing there was by remaining silent and trying to transcend injured feelings.

I had never transcended them.

I had been walking around in denial, cleverly masquerading as forgiveness. *Me?* I was the ultimate peace-lover, the forgoer. Bring up old hurts? I had forgiven already.

But there was one catch.

What I didn't realize was that forgiveness left a sweet taste in its wake. It planted love in one's heart and a sense of real peace in one's soul. Forgiveness didn't keep retching old hurts, didn't pull one's smile too taut for comfort.

Denial was integrally different. Denial was emotional indigestion. It started by swallowing a mass of unchewed feelings, and it ended with severe heartburn.

If I wanted to forgive, truly forgive, I would have to go through the unpleasant process of bringing up all those old sour feelings again. I would have to be ready to break them down, one at a time, until they were ready to be swallowed, and then listen to Fraidy do the same. It wouldn't make me feel like the saint I wished I was, but it would free me to become the person I knew I was meant to be.

I listened quietly as Fraidy shared her feelings: the flak she had faced day in and day out from the parents, her husband's displeasure with the situation, her feeling that she had been underpaid. She described the intensity of having invested everything in her playgroup, the feeling that she had been deceived.

I let go of my defenses and listened, really listened, the way I had always listened to Fraidy, the way I'd have listened had she been unburdening to me about an encounter with someone else.

She was my friend and these were her feelings. Feelings weren't right or wrong.

Then I aired my own perception of things: how grateful I was to her, how I felt she had rebuffed my overtures to help, how sorry I was that her workload had been doubled by the insensitivity of people.

"I wish I could have paid you more," I told her sincerely, "but I was paying you more than the standard salary for a substitute, and I was running at a loss as it was. I so badly wanted to compensate for your devotion by giving you things that money couldn't buy. Things like my warmest recommendations to parents, my songs and ideas and activity sheets.

"Now that you have your own playgroup, you know the time and effort that goes into cleanup and preparation. I tried so hard to ease that burden, although admittedly sometimes it wasn't easy for me."

I paused, and I saw Fraidy listening, really listening, the way she had always listened to me. And in the openness of that moment, I knew one thing.

Feelings weren't right or wrong.

Sharing them, however, talking and listening and accepting them, had the power to right a wrong.

וְאֶת־יִרְאֵי ה׳ יְכַבֵּד;

... but who honors those who fear Hashem;

Walking the Tightrope

Brisk-walking up one of Yerushalayim's famous hills together with a friend, I stopped to catch my breath.

"I guess that's the price we pay for living here," my partner touched her racing heart, "the hills."

"Hm," I nodded, not skipping a beat. *That's the price we pay for living here; the hills.*

She had no inkling how on target she was.

I grew up, your proverbial Mimmy, right out of Yaffa Ganz's storybook. Not that I was an only child. I had four brothers, older brothers, three of whom were learning in Eretz Yisrael, one in a local yeshivah. Everything else, however, fit to a tee.

From the pretty pink room to the closet full of clothing, I was the envy of any little girl. I had enough dolls keep a kindergarten class happy, games and books, art sets and craft kits. The only thing I was missing was a sibling with whom to share my time and toys.

Unlike my classic counterpart, though, I didn't spend my days dreaming about Simmy across the street. Living in a congested *frum* neighborhood in England, I usually had half the block over at my house playing, or else there were friends from school. As soon as I was old enough, my mother enrolled me in art and music lessons.

Though I was never cut out to be a painter, my piano teacher immediately noticed my talent. I picked up the basics with ease and was quick to graduate the first few elementary books. My parents bought a baby grand piano and delighted in my nightly practice.

Reading this back, my description sounds like the picture of a frivolous, pampered child. Surprisingly, I never fit the bill. In fact, even as a very young child, I remember going out of my way to befriend the shy girls in my class. I would let them play with my dolls and try their hands at my piano. I derived genuine pleasure out of sharing.

Growing up as the only girl in the house gave me a special opportunity to cultivate my relationship with my parents.

"Should I tell you a secret, Tzippy?" my mother would wink. "You're my favorite daughter!"

"And you're my favorite mother," I would invariably laugh and give my mother a hug.

For years, this joke was part of my nightly bedtime ritual, after I'd shared my daily rundown. Then I'd collapse, giggling, into my pillow, and my mother would playfully flap the quilt over me until my nightgown ballooned in the simulated breeze. That done, she'd tuck the quilt snugly beneath me and blow me one final kiss before she shut the light.

Though I was the only one home, my mother never worked in any official capacity. Her days revolved around my needs, and I never remember her being too busy to listen to me or to help me with my homework. My father, too, was involved in every aspect of my upbringing. From treating me to my favorite Danish, to researching a question in the *midrash*, he was always there for me.

My three older brothers were married in fairly quick succession and moved to Eretz Yisrael. They had been learning there for years and having married Israeli girls, it was natural that they settled near their wives' parents. My next brother married a girl from New York and moved to Boro Park.

The adjustment was difficult for my parents. Although the boys had been in yeshivah for years, it had always seemed like a temporary situation. Now that they had married girls from overseas, there were slim chances of them ever settling nearby.

My brothers would send pictures and occasionally come for Yom Tov, but it just wasn't the same as having them live close by. The grandchildren spoke mostly Hebrew and it was difficult for my parents to have any meaningful relationship with them.

"When you get married, Tzippy," my mother would say, only half-joking, "we're going to buy you a house right next door to us. Don't you think I deserve some real live *nachas* already?"

In the meantime, my parents relished every minute of having a teenage daughter around. I would bring home friends to study and we were always the address for sleepover parties and class picnics. As I became more adept at playing the piano, I often brought home choir groups to practice in our large den. My mother loved listening in and serving refreshments.

"Doesn't Tzippy play like a professional?" she would marvel, embarrassing me time and again. I let her indulge, though. I knew I meant everything to her and it was just her maternal way of sharing her pride.

When I became of age, the propositions starting coming fast and thick. My father was a well-off businessman who supported many Torah institutions, my brothers had sterling reputations, and I myself was, *Baruch Hashem*, a successful seminary graduate.

The first condition my parents always set down, even before they heard the name, was that the boy agree to settle in London. After a few failed attempts, we realized that it wouldn't be as simple as we had thought. Most of the serious boys that had been suggested were learning in either Lakewood or Eretz Yisrael. England didn't hold much of a future for them.

When one of my brothers suggested an outstanding boy from the yeshivah where he was a *maggid shiur*, my parents were more inclined to listen.

"What about living here?" my mother inquired. "Will he be willing to move to England?"

"Look," my brother said, "I don't think he'll agree to settle in England right after the wedding. He's an Israeli boy and he's learning here; but I imagine that after a few years he'd be willing to consider the move."

After some phone calls back and forth, *Hashgachah* simply took the reigns out of our hands. One thing led to another, and before long we were engaged. The plate was broken, the *Mazal Tovs* resounded, the *tenaim* were signed and read. I paid little attention to the terms printed above the dotted line. Wasn't the *tenaim* merely a formality, an excuse for an official celebration?

The main thing was that I was a radiant *kallah*, the *chassan* made a wonderful impression, and all our friends and family took part in a warm and joyous affair.

The first four months after our wedding were a blissful period for my parents. Though we had our own apartment not far away, we practically lived in their house. They insisted that we be their daily guests for dinner; after all, we would have enough time on our own when we left.

I tried to make my husband feel as comfortable as possible. Though my parents showered him with attention, he was, after all, a complete stranger to London. He couldn't read or speak the language, and he didn't recognize a single soul. To add to that, the *derech halimud* in the *kollel* was very different from what he was used to.

My husband reassured me that as long as it was only temporary, he was fine.

"Four months pass quickly," he chuckled, "Soon *you'll* be the one adjusting to my country and family."

I was glad my parents hadn't overheard. They wouldn't have taken the joke in very good humor.

Four months *do* pass quickly, whatever way you look at them. Before long, we were seriously packing to leave. My parents had a hard time watching. Though we had agreed upon that specific amount of time before the wedding, time always moves faster than anticipated in these instances.

"We've barely had a chance to spend time together," my mother moaned one night after supper, "The first month passed just recuperating from *sheva berachos* and these past few weeks have been so hectic getting ready to leave. Maybe you'll stay another few weeks?"

"Ma, come on," I said, feeling my muscles tense, "There's no chance. You know Gershon wants to get back for the new *z'man*."

My husband entered the dining room.

"*Nu*, Gershon," my father turned to him, smiling, "What do you say. Is it really that bad here?"

I cringed as I watched my husband blush. What was he expected to answer, that he felt like he was in exile in their home? Thankfully, my father let it go as I awkwardly tried to change the subject. The tension, though, was palpable.

As much as my parents had known that we'd be leaving, it was hard for them to face the actual departure. Their lives had been so full during the past few months. First there had been the shopping and preparations preceding the wedding; then there had been the constant cooking and hosting, the excitement of having a young couple around. My father had learned with my husband, and my mother and I had spent so much time together. Their lives would be so empty now.

I felt selfish and guilt ridden thinking of my parents' pain. On the one hand, I knew I was married now, and that my husband's wishes were my first priority. On the other hand, I just wished everyone would want the same thing. Why did my husband's happiness have to conflict with my parents' foremost dream?

It was a question I would ask myself many times, over the next few years, a question that had a longing, tearing quality to it and no viable answer in response.

As anyone who has ever settled in a new country knows, it isn't easy. There is a new language to learn, new food products to get used to, new customs to adapt to. During those first few weeks, I found myself unsettled and disoriented, homesick for everyone and everything I had left behind.

Harder than anything else, though, was the pressure I felt to conceal my hardships from my parents.

"How's everything, Tzippy?" my mother would inquire.

"Great!" would be my unwavering reply. The food was great, the weather was great, our apartment was great. Yes, my in-laws were helping me find a job, and Gershon came home for lunch and I had English-speaking neighbors. It was all just wonderful.

Sometimes I wished I could tell my mother that it was boiling hot and that I hated squashing into my in-laws' apartment and that I found *sponga* so difficult to get used to. I knew, though, that if I wanted to keep my parents' pleas at bay, I would have to make things sound as rosy as possible.

Parents are still parents, and my mother wasn't totally convinced. She took any opportunity to send frozen fish, meat, even farmer cheese. She'd send decorative knickknacks for my apartment, soaps for the bathroom, anything she could think of that would constitute a touch of home. This was all in addition to my father's monthly check that generously covered our living expenses.

We were barely in Eretz Yisrael for a month when my mother broached the topic of Pesach.

"Ma, we're not even up to Chanukah," I chuckled. "Who's thinking about Pesach?"

"Well," my mother countered, "Aren't *you*? I thought you were dreaming of coming home. I mean, I don't know, maybe you don't mind being at your in-laws for Yom Tov."

I was quick to patch the booboo.

"Oh please, Ma, of course, we can't wait. All I meant was that it was really too early to plan the technicalities."

"Not at all," my mother said emphatically, "I don't want any more misunderstandings. Just make sure Gershon doesn't plan to come the last minute or something."

I felt provoked. What did she mean, any *more* misunderstandings? What had been the first misunderstanding? As far as I knew, the terms had been agreed upon beforehand. I forced myself to remain calm and reassuring.

"I'll talk to Gershon; I'm sure he'll be flexible."

The truth to tell, I wasn't all that sure. Something about the accusing shadow tingeing my mother's words, however, compelled me to paint my husband in the most positive light.

Walking the Tightrope / 181

After that, there was always some mention or other of Pesach. Esther Tzucker said the tickets were cheaper if you came for Purim already, Breindy Mahn's son told her that the yeshivah was emptying out earlier since Rosh Chodesh fell on Shabbos.

For some reason, my husband seemed to be the only one who thought that *bein hazmanim* started on the fifth day of Nissan, and that Chaim Mahn was going home early for a wedding. I tried to stay noncommittal, reassuring my mother that we would come as early as we could, all the while signing to my frantically gesticulating husband that I wasn't saying anything definite.

I felt like an embattled ambassador, embroiled in the middle of everyone's feelings. I felt driven to explain my parents' stance to my husband; then I would turn my rationale inside out and present my husband's logic to my parents. It was the most tedious job, carefully unraveling conversations and restringing sentences so that they smoothed everyone's sensitivities the right way.

In my desperation to appease everybody, I didn't even know what I wanted myself anymore. Oh sure, once upon a time I had wanted to go home for Pesach; if it were up to me, I'd have flown for Chanukah.

But it wasn't up to me.

I wasn't my own person anymore, and I didn't want to be.

Time is a fickle catalyst. Sometimes it eases feelings; sometimes it intensifies them. Pesach came and went. Spring turned into summer and summer turned into fall. Sarah'la was born in the middle of Cheshvan. Though it had meant botching his winter *z'man*, Gershon had agreed to fly to England for Succos and stay on for the birth. We both knew how much it meant to my parents to be part of our *simchah*.

Though I felt like I was always flying off to England, and my Israeli neighbors certainly did, my parents never had enough of us.

"Your visits are always so short," my mother lamented. "We barely get to enjoy you and you're packing your bags again."

"At least you don't have to share us with in-laws when we come," I tried to quip. Humor, I learned, usually took everyone off the defensive.

The joke was lost on my mother.

"What do you mean, *I don't have to share you with in-laws?* I share you all year long!"

Though I loved visiting home, nothing could compensate for the anguish in my parents' eyes as we departed at the airport, the tears in my mother's voice every time we came back.

"Tzippy, the house just feels so empty, I can't get myself to do a thing. Is it normal that we have five married children and I don't have a single one near me? My friends are so busy with their kids, cooking for this one, baby-sitting for that one, hosting couples for Shabbos. Don't you think we deserve a little bit of *nachas*?"

I would listen in misery, not knowing what to say.

"Can't you explain it to Gershon? Your in-laws have nine children, all of them living near them. They wouldn't even know the difference if you lived here."

I ignored the slight to my in-laws.

"It's not a matter of explaining, Ma. We've discussed it so many times and Gershon understands you. It's just that he feels he wouldn't be able to grow in England."

It was like pouring gasoline into a fire.

"Oh don't give me that line; you think there's no Torah in England? It's all a matter of attitude. If he wanted, he could find plenty of *ruchniyus* on this side of the ocean."

I was beginning to feel my strength giving. I was a new mother; how was I supposed to handle all of this?

When Sarah'la got her first tooth, I called home, excited. I heard my mother sniffling at the other end.

"I guess it's just too much to ask to have one grandchild close by. You'll see what it means now that you're a mother. You give and give and love with all your heart. I hope Sarah'la doesn't ever do this to you."

I felt helplessness and hurt stinging my eyelids.

"I feel so bad for you Ma, I really do." I almost gagged over the lump in my throat.

"I know you do. That's why you're back in Eretz Yisrael."

I felt the bitter edge of her sarcasm pierce the oversized lump in my throat. Tears cascaded down my cheeks, running into the little holes on the receiver. My mother's voice sounded distant and garbled.

Wet phones sounded that way.

So did hurt feelings.

I hung up feeling drained and confused. What *was* I supposed to do?

Kibbud av va'em had always been a primary mitzvah on my list. Over the years, I had done everything in my power to bring my parents joy. I had bought them presents and written them poems, made surprises and brought back souvenirs. They had always known that they occupied the most treasured place in my heart.

And suddenly, my hands were tied. They didn't need my presents or my poems, my surprises or my souvenirs. They needed *me*. And I couldn't give them that.

With no affront to anyone, Gershon just couldn't see himself acclimating to life in England. He'd been born and bred on the holy soil of Eretz Yisrael, in an atmosphere of simplicity and *ameilus b'Torah*. Without his oxygen, his *chaburos* and his *mashgichim*, he couldn't imagine maintaining the same level of *avodah*.

I knew I could never convey these feelings to my parents. My father was the first one to uphold Torah; that's why he had chosen Gershon in the first place. It wasn't a question of logic. It was a question of love. And love, as *Chazal* have noted, can twist the straightest line.

I noticed an obvious change in my parents' attitude. There was a definite aloofness, a distance completely uncharacteristic of them. The fish rolls had stopped coming. So had the clothing. Though I was surprised, I chalked it up to forgetfulness, to preoccupation with my grandparents who had been unwell recently.

"Ma, Sarah'la's undershirts are getting snug on her already," I told my mother one day. I knew she'd be only too glad to send me the next size.

"Don't they sell undershirts in Israel?" my mother feigned surprise.

I got the barb. If we don't mean enough to you, then have it your way. Live in Eretz Yisrael; buy fish there, buy undershirts there. Just leave us out of it; it hurts too much.

My father's checks stopped coming. My husband was angry. I was sad. I knew my parents weren't trying to be mean. They were desperate. *Perhaps if they'll need their sustenance*, they reasoned, *then they'll come.*

At that point, I broke. It wasn't the withholding of the funds that finished me. It was my parents' utter devastation with our decision. It was my husband's negative view of my parents. It was the pressure of my parents' pain dangerously sawing at the taut bond between my husband and myself. I needed to have my conflict resolved by a *gadol*.

I made an appointment with my husband's *mashgiach*.

The *mashgiach* listened to my plight and conveyed his empathy. Though he had all of his own children living on the same shores, he could only try to imagine the anguish of parents who had all their children living far away.

"Believe me," he smiled, "I have two sons living in B'nei Brak, and it's far enough for me."

"*Kibbud av va'em* is one of the *Aseres HaDibros*. One cannot underestimate its importance. When a woman gets married, however, this mitzvah takes on a deeper dimension. Ultimately, a Jewish parent's foremost wish is that his child build a lasting Jewish home. And the cornerstone of a *bayis ne'eman b'Yisrael* is that the wife defer to her husband's wishes."

He paused to make sure I was following. I nodded.

"Women are innately loyal; their very essence is submission. Yet if their loyalty is tugged in two opposite directions, they aren't free to move forward, to perpetuate the chain. Fortunately, the Torah foresaw this conflict and very clearly *paskened*: a married woman's first loyalty belongs to her husband.

"Of course that doesn't mean that you should be insensitive or ungrateful to your parents. Try to honor them and appease them in every possible way. Call them, visit them, send them pictures. Do your best to show them how much they mean to you.

"And as far as *parnassah*, I'm sure they'll come around. In the meantime, though, try to cultivate your own source of income, so that you won't feel so helpless and resentful."

Walking the Tightrope / 185

He added another few words of *chizuk* along with his heartfelt *berachos*. I felt strengthened and uplifted. I wasn't cutting ties or showing ingratitude. I was welding my link in the chain, bending my destiny in the direction *Hakadosh Baruch Hu* had blazed for me. And ultimately, I was embodying my parents' sincerest dreams.

Fortified by the *mashgiach's* advice, I looked for a job. Incredibly, *Hashgachah* sent one right to my door. A seminary in my neighborhood was looking for a pianist to play for their concert. My neighbor, who was a secretary there, remembered that I played. I was hired for the job.

I threw myself into practice with a fervor I hadn't felt in a while. Playing was therapeutic for me. The theme of the concert was *Eishes chayil*, and the songs all spoke to my heart. My fingers flew across the keyboard as I thrust my heart and soul into the words. My voice soared along with the notes, filling me with an inner peace I hadn't known in a while.

My parents were still giving me the cold shoulder. I tried to share, to tell them about little Sarah'la, about the upcoming concert. I even begged my mother to come for the event. She had always loved hearing me play.

"Me?" my mother retorted wryly. "I thought children were supposed to visit parents; I didn't know it went the other way around."

I almost gave up.

And then, two and a half weeks before the concert, my father called.

"Tzippy, I'm booking you a ticket."

"Now?" I spluttered. "We're in the middle of January."

"I know. I want to surprise Mommy. A few families here are grouping together to spend the winter holiday in a hotel in Arosa. We were offered a cheap rate, but Mommy had no desire to go. 'If Tzippy and the baby could come along,' she sighed, 'it would be a dream come true.'

"Tzippy, I know Gershon wouldn't want to come now in the middle of the *z'man*, but I'm not taking a no from you."

I felt every muscle in my body tense. *Please, Ta,* I begged inwardly, *don't do this to me. Gershon and me, we're one unit now. I can't just pick up and leave in the middle of everything.*

And even if Gershon agreed, I suddenly thought miserably, *the concert is in two weeks. How could I get away now?*

Something inside me, however, told me that this was the opportunity I'd been waiting for, the chance to show my parents that I was ready to sacrifice for their happiness. My mother knew about the concert. She knew how much pressure I was under with practice. If I came now, she'd be certain I was still her little girl who loved her.

It was *Motza'ei Shabbos*, 11:30 at night. I had just spent a beautiful Shabbos with my parents in Arosa, and now we were having a *melaveh malkah*.

"Why don't we have a *kumzitz*?" one of my mother's friends suddenly suggested. "The men are still dancing in the other dining room. How about closing the lights?"

"Tzippy," my mother nudged me, "There's even a piano. You know how I love to listen to you play."

A few women overheard my mother's suggestion and joined her. I acquiesced.

Sitting at the piano, I played with all my heart and soul. The women started hesitantly, but the singing soon picked up momentum. There was a warm sense of togetherness and longing in the room.

As the last notes died, I lifted the microphone, and said there was a song I wanted to dedicate to my mother. It was the finale song I had composed for the concert.

> There's a special chest on High,
> Gilded clasp, jeweled walls,
> Waiting, waiting, up on High
> Filling as each teardrop falls,
>
> There's a special chest on High,
> For those tears that mothers shed
> As they nurture, as they cry,
> Until every child is bred.

Salty tears, dancing flames,
Burning, yearning, churning pleas,
Heartfelt prayers, whispered names,
Begging for the proper keys,

Raking furrows, planting seeds,
Tears and more tears as it grows,
Pruning petals, pulling weeds,
Work only a mother knows,

And then, alas, the flower's grown,
Plucked out of her loving clasp,
And transplanted on its own,
Far away, out of her grasp,

There's a special chest on High,
For those tears that mothers shed
As they nurture, as they cry,
Until every child is bred.

There's a special chest on High,
Where tears turn into shining gems,
Where pearls grow out of every sigh,
And love returns to where it stems.

I looked up. My mother was bawling. There wasn't a dry eye in the audience. My mother got up and embraced me. We held each other tightly for a long time. This time, it wasn't my talent that touched her. She knew I had sung from my heart, from the depths of my soul. She knew now with all the certainty in the world that no matter how deep the ocean that separated us, it was an ocean of love, not hurt.

Epilogue: Tzippy is still living in Yerushalayim with her family, still struggling to be that loyal wife and loving daughter at the same time. It isn't easy, she says, and it takes a lot of prayer, forethought, and constant juggling.

"Knowing what my task is makes it a lot easier," she says.

"And just a word of caution to those innocent bystanders who can unwittingly pour salt on an open wound: never approach a married daughter in her mother's presence and ask her questions that can be a point of strife between them.

"I've had countless needless clashes with my parents, when people would thoughtlessly remark, 'Nu, Tzippy, when are you coming back to live here? Didn't you originally plan on settling here after a few years?'"

It's a precarious enough maneuver, trying to keep one's balance on the tightrope between spouses and parents. One little sway from a spectator can send the tightrope walker tottering to the depths.

I Lift My Eyes to the Mountains

I'm not much of a writer and I'm certainly not much of a mountain climber. My story is about as ordinary as you can get. Still, perhaps it is that very ordinariness that is giving me the impetus to put pen to paper. If, from my vantage point, I can toss a rope to one person struggling at the foot of the mountain, I will feel I have truly gained by sharing. And then again, if I can salute the true mountain climber in my story, then I will feel a trifle better about the many times I've slid downward.

I grabbed the cordless from the dining-room table, looking furtively in my mother's direction. Walking down the hall to my bedroom, I jabbed the familiar buttons. Why wasn't Miri answering all afternoon? Frustrated, I glanced at my watch and reluctantly returned the phone to the base.

"You seem desperate to reach someone. Whom are you trying?" my mother asked, as she watched me check the time. I felt myself blushing guiltily.

"I'm just looking for someone to come shopping with me," I answered, busying myself with a pile of books on the table. I knew that my nonchalance was transparent, even to my mother.

"What kind of shopping?" Something about my mother's unsuspecting tone made me falter over my response.

"You know, clothing, shoes for Shabbos *sheva berachos*, some housewares; I've hardly done anything yet."

"You mean *chasunah* shopping? No problem," my mother replied, a defensive note creeping into her voice, "I'm ready to go with you whenever you want. *I'm* the one who keeps nudging you to get the shopping behind you."

I felt the familiar bubbles of tension rising inside me, tingling all the way to the tips of my fingers. I hated being caught in this internal crossfire, trapped between my desire to please my mother and my need for independence.

"Ma, thanks a million, I really appreciate it, but I actually wanted to go out with Miri." The words came out hurried and strained. I knew I was hurting my mother, but I couldn't help it.

"You know, it's different," I fumbled for words, almost pleading for her understanding. "Girls at my stage know what's in style, what the *kallahs* are wearing these days. It's important to go with someone who knows."

My mother shrugged. I could see the pain in her eyes.

"Look, in my day a *kallah* went shopping with her mother, but if you think Miri knows better ..." she let the rest of the sentence wilt in the air.

"It's not that I think she knows better," I said, tripping over my words in an effort to patch things up. "It's just that her sister recently got married, and so did two of her first cousins. She knows what goes."

To tell the truth, my reasoning sounded foolish, even to my own ears. My mother had married off 12 children, seven daughters among them. She certainly had more experience than Miri, whose resume totaled a single sibling's wedding.

Still, surveying my mother's profile, from her short layered *sheitel* down to her sensible oxfords, experience wasn't what I sought right then. I wanted to enjoy the fun of choosing, the thrill of buying. I knew that my mother's experience threatened to iron the whole adventure of shopping flat with one stodgy criterion: practicality.

"If you're so reluctant to go with your mother, then I won't force myself on you. I'll give you a rough estimate of the amount you can spend, and you can use your own judgment. Or Miri's." Despite herself, an edge of sarcasm shadowed her tone.

"Just make sure the clothing you choose goes along with acceptable standards of *tzeniyus*."

I was flooded with relief. For the sake of momentary satisfaction, I was even willing to swallow the slightly sour aftertaste of shame. I was smart enough to realize that all the tact in the world couldn't soften the cutting implication of my request to have a friend accompany me. Still, for then, I was thrilled to have my mother's okay, albeit a reluctant one.

I tried to avoid her gaze as she came out of her bedroom carrying her purse. Grabbing my pocketbook and bus ticket, I uttered a breezy thanks and hurried out to meet Miri.

As I walked to the stop, I tried to analyze the situation objectively. I was and, always had been, the baby of the family. As the youngest of 13 children, I enjoyed both the advantages and disadvantages of my position.

My mother was a youthful, energetic woman who invested all her time and energy into her children, married and unmarried unlike. She'd divide herself between the children, shopping for this one, baby-sitting for that one, cooking for the third. Our house was always simmering with activity, alive with my mother's many multifaceted projects

Still, the generation gap between my mother and myself was definitely more pronounced than it was with some of my friends.

Why, my mother was the same age as some of my friends' grandmothers. Though I took tremendous pride in her, our opinions differed sharply when it came to superficial matters like shopping and dressing,

I had always had an eye for fashion and aesthetics, while my mother, though neatly groomed, focused very single-mindedly on durability and practical value. All her suits were navy and black, of the most classic cut, and I could predictably determine what she would bring home from any given shopping spree.

Spree, come to think of it, was the wrong word to describe my mother's calculated shopping habits. She never splurged on impulsive purchases; neither did she find any pleasure in browsing or window-shopping. She'd hold the hanger up, crumple the fabric in her fist to see if it creased easily, and then quickly figure how many months of the year the outfit could be worn.

We had always had a hard time shopping together. Now, however, it wasn't a matter of one isolated purchase. I'd be shopping for a whole new wardrobe, and I had my heart set on shopping with a friend who was on my wavelength.

Miri was my closest friend, who also happened to be in on the latest word in fashion. It wasn't only fashion; Miri knew everything about everything. She was the second of five siblings and did all her mother's shopping every season. She knew the stores inside out and had our itinerary mapped out before we even greeted each other.

"I don't know how to thank you, Miri," I gushed. "This is going to take your whole afternoon."

"Please," she objected, waving away my thanks. "You know this is just down my alley. I love shopping, especially for a *kallah*."

"I hope I'll be able to reciprocate when it's your turn," I responded, closing my jacket against the brisk air.

"Forget about it," Miri laughed, "by then you'll be a working young wife, too busy for friends."

"What are you talking about?" I protested, horrified by Miri's casual prediction. "As busy as I'll be, I'll never be too busy for you."

"You think so," insisted Miri," I know how it is. With the best of intentions, friendships cannot be the same afterward. You know how close I was with my cousin Shanny? Now that she has a baby, she hardly even picks up the phone to say hello. Whenever I call, she's either busy with her husband, the baby, or preparing for school."

We continued on our way, chatting and philosophizing as we stopped in front of the storefronts to analyze the fall displays. Miri pointed out a stunning wool suit that her sister had just gotten, and we went inside to try it on. It was a thrilling experience, shopping together with cash at our disposal, free to speculate and choose as we saw fit.

We got two *sheva berachos* outfits, a lightweight jacket, and one better weekday suit. "Let's stop into the housewares store now. I know he's running a special on pots."

Taken by Miri's confidence, I followed her into the store. We chose a set of enamel cookware, white with a border of delicate pastel flowers around the rim.

"These are stunning!" I enthused, "so much prettier than my mother's stainless steel pots. Just looking at them makes me excited about cooking."

I came home at about 5:30 to the smell of vegetable soup and stewing chicken. "Hi, Ma," I called out as I dragged the bulging bags through the door.

My mother was anxious to see my purchases. She wiped her hands on a towel, and came into the living room where I had deposited my bags. I pulled out the wine-colored suit, eager to win her approval.

My mother, though, had noticed something else. She bent down and peeled the large shopping bag off the cumbersome box on the floor, revealing a colored picture of a set of white pots.

"Enamel pots? What in the world made you get a set of enamel pots?"

I tensed up. "Why, what's wrong with enamel pots?" I asked. "Look how pretty they are."

"Pretty? That's a new one. What good is a pretty pot if it's not useful? Enamel chips terribly and is not a very good conductor of heat. Besides, these handles are going to be impossible to lift when they're hot. I hope you made sure these pots were returnable."

I Lift My Eyes to the Mountains

I accepted the criticism in silence, mentally praying that sale items were indeed returnable. Why hadn't I thought to ask? After all, when it came to the kitchen, my mother was undeniably the expert. I draped the wine-colored suit over the couch, hoping to get off to a better start with the clothes.

"This is pretty," my mother conceded. "But it's always going to look creased," she frowned, scrutinizing the inner label. "And the shell is hand washable only."

"That's not a problem," I countered feebly. "I'm not starting out with 13 children."

I pulled the next thing out of the bag, but the wind was out of my sails. The suits had lost all their charm; as far as I was concerned, I was ready to return the whole lot.

Later that night, after discussing it all with Miri, I felt some of my confidence restored. The pots had been a mistake, but the outfits, she maintained, were all good brand names that ought to last well. Look, she chuckled, dressy suits aren't meant for careless wash and wear. All good clothing has to be handled carefully.

My wedding was an emotional one. My mother danced the *mezhinka* broom dance, sweeping the last of her fledglings out of her nest, while all my siblings stood in a circle, clapping enthusiastically. I detected tears in my sisters' and sisters-in-law's eyes.

My mother was the stereotype of a *Yiddishe Mamme*: warm, simple and selfless. She had nurtured 13 children with every fiber of her being, and now she had just led the last of them under the *chuppah*. No one knew better than we children what this moment meant to her. Grabbing my mother's hand to dance, I felt a deep tug of affection for her.

Swept on that swell of emotion, I felt sure that my wedding would herald a brand new era, an era in which I would relate to my mother with renewed trust and understanding. I didn't realize that waves of sentiment had very little holding power, surely when it came to changing deeply rooted attitudes. I was caught by surprise, then, when I found myself consulting with Miri about what to wear for a lunchtime *sheva berachos*.

That wasn't the last issue I took up with Miri. She was my springboard when it came to anything from menu planning to figuring out a workable housekeeping schedule. Never mind that she had never run a home in her life. Miri had great ideas, and for experience, she always had her married sister to fall back on.

My mother invited us for meals, and gladly gave me advice when I asked for it. Most of the time, I chose not to.

As far as meals went, my husband, Menachem, was thrilled to eat at home. He complimented my cooking and constantly told me that there was special *yishuv hadaas* in eating by ourselves in the privacy of our own home. Over our meals, we would share the events of the day, discuss *hashkafah,* and contemplate plans for the future.

Soon enough, the job issue came up. I had graduated the two-year Israeli seminary program the year before, and we had gotten married in the beginning of the winter. I still had no prospect of a job. Teaching positions in Yerushalayim were hard to come by, if not impossible.

"I might be able to exercise some connections," said Menachem one lunchtime. "I have an uncle in Chinuch Atzmai who may be able to pull some strings."

"Teaching?" I asked incredulously. "I didn't even bother hoping in that direction."

"Look, of course you need credentials," my husband countered, "but I believe that my uncle could get you a decent job in some local Beis Yaakov."

I smiled at the irony of his proposition. Fancy, securing a job with pull. After all those self-righteous speeches I had given the year before about the unfairness of young teachers weaving their way into the system via some hotshot of an uncle on the board of the school. It had almost become a matter of principle with me. Still, how could I pass up the prospect of getting a good job? I decided to ask my mother what she thought of the whole thing.

"I don't think it's for you, Shevi," my mother dismissed the idea, without even paying it any serious thought.

I Lift My Eyes to the Mountains / 195

"Why not?" I asked testily.

Never mind that I had harbored my own serious doubts just a moment before. Somehow, the way my mother had phrased her response put me on the defensive.

"It's not the issue of the pull that bothers me. If I thought teaching suited you, then I would advise you to go for it. Connections are also Hashem's emissaries."

"But?" I prodded, impatient to hear the end of her reasoning.

"I just don't think you're cut out for it," my mother said simply.

I was hurt and taken aback. I had always been a straight A student and was surely just as capable as anyone else. *I guess my mother still doesn't trust me,* I thought bitterly.

"I'm not worried about your intellectual abilities," my mother continued, sensing my wounded silence. "I know you're perfectly capable of preparing lessons. It's just that I wish I could see you doing something you'd really enjoy. Disciplining takes loads of patience, and isn't always easy."

I was sorry I had ever asked. Perhaps I wasn't your most patient specimen, but I certainly thought I measured up to the average teacher in the system. What did my mother think, that all teachers were tolerant angels?

Suddenly, all I wanted was to get the job. When Menachem broached the topic again, I skipped any mention of my mother's opinion. To him, I was the most wonderful candidate around, and our relationship was much too fresh for me to spoil that image. Menachem called his uncle, and I waited with bated breath.

Within two weeks, his uncle let us know that he had arranged for me to take over for a teacher who had taken an unexpected leave of absence. I was to teach *Navi* and *Parashah* in the seventh grade of a school not far from our home. I couldn't have asked for a more prestigious position.

Prestige, I learned soon enough, was pretty ineffectual when it came to classroom management. My students were wild and unruly, determined to make a flop out of my teaching career. My sternest measures didn't seem to daunt them. I tried contests and promises, with no relief. It was the middle of the year and the class had locked itself into a rebellious mode. There was no getting them back on track, especially not by an inexperienced greenhorn like me.

In the beginning, I tried to put on a valiant front and assured Menachem that it was only a matter of time. Inside, I felt tense and pressured. I would come home, my confidence wrecked, and try to smile the sweet smile of success. After three weeks of this harrowing charade, my facade gave. I found myself sobbing to Miri on the telephone.

"You have to be honest with your husband," Miri advised, "there's no sense putting yourself through this misery. I'm sure he'll understand; not everybody is cut out to teach."

If I recognized the line of reasoning from somewhere, I didn't admit it. I felt miserable enough without adding extra guilt to my burden.

"Don't worry," Miri tried to lift my spirits. "We'll think of some other line that suits you. Maybe telemarketing; it's a very big business today."

Menachem was understanding, as Miri had predicted. He empathized with me and stated unequivocally that nothing in the world was worth his wife's happiness. I smiled through my tears.

My mother was nice enough not to remind me of her unheeded advice. She supported my decision to leave the job, and tried to help me brainstorm for some other occupation.

"Maybe you should think in a more commercial direction," my mother ventured. "Perhaps you could sell something in the house."

I was mortified. My mother and her old-fashioned notions. "Miri mentioned telemarketing," I suggested, ignoring her proposition. "She said that's what goes today."

"Telemarketing?" my mother echoed skeptically. "Hm, I don't know."

Here we go again, I thought. What was wrong with telemarketing? My mother had this built-in resistance to anything up to date, that was all. I would have to discuss the matter with Miri. I didn't want to broach the idea with my husband until I was more certain about it.

I Lift My Eyes to the Mountains / 197

Surprisingly, Miri seemed to have forgotten all about telemarketing when I called her in the evening.

"Oh that?" she asked unenthusiastically. "I just threw it out as a suggestion. I don't know how practical it actually is. But listen," she said, the excitement in her voice carrying the promise of some new, undiscovered horizon. "I thought of something else."

I smiled in anticipation. I knew I could trust Miri to come up with the right thing.

"My sister told me that there's this new store that just opened in B'ne Brak. They sell everything for little boys, *yarmulkes, tzitzis, sifrei Torah*, little books, puzzles, and *siddurim*. I think it could be a real hit in your neighborhood. These are all specialty items for which people generally have to go to Geulah."

"A store?" I asked lamely. It was the last thing I'd expected Miri to come up with.

"You're artistic, Shevi; you could personalize all the items, and you could prepare gift arrangements for little boys getting *peyos*. The more I think about it, the more I like the idea."

"What about money, though?" I grabbed at the obvious technical hitch.

"I thought about that. I have a sum of money put away in an account. It's not a huge amount, but it's something. My father agreed that I lend you the money so you can make the initial investment. Don't forget, I don't have my own expenses yet, for the time being. You'll pay me back slowly, as the store takes off."

"If it takes off," I interjected, still skeptical.

Miri's enthusiasm, however, wasn't lost on me. I was overcome by her generous offer to lend me the capital to start, and immediately asked my husband for his consent.

"What does your mother say to the idea?" he asked.

Actually, my mother sounded quite surprised by my change of heart. Why, just the day before, I had responded so indifferently to her suggestion that I start a business. She quickly switched her tone, though, to one of genuine approval, when she heard the idea.

"I think it has a lot of potential," she said optimistically. "And what's more important, I think you'll enjoy it."

She offered her wholehearted assistance and even thought of some contacts who might be able to help me. I hung up the phone, feeling confident and happy, grateful to Miri for her brainstorm.

Within a month, I had signs and flyers posted all over my neighborhood. The striking logo announced the grand opening of *Hamalach Sheli*, My Little Angel, the name my husband and I had chosen for the new store.

The little sale in my dining room soon mushroomed into a full-fledged store. We rented a small *machsan* next door, and spent hours setting up shop. My mother worked industriously, helping me organize and unpack the merchandise. Miri came by and admired the way things looked. I reveled in her compliments.

Our move was blessed with *siyata diShmaya,* and we began to see returns. Word of mouth got around that we had good prices and excellent service, and I found my hands full. It was gratifying work, selling *yarmulkes* and *tzitzis, Alef Binahs* and little *bechers* to pure little *yingelach,* getting their first taste of Torah. I loved the actual work too, setting up gift displays and shopping for merchandise. The business was truly successful and I was genuinely happy.

One evening, long after I had repaid Miri's loan, I found myself reminiscing with her.

"Remember my teaching fiasco?" I reminded her.

"It's hard to believe that was only one year ago," Miri commented. "Things have really turned around since then."

"And it's all thanks to you," I said sincerely, "I don't think I can ever really repay you."

Miri looked uncomfortable. "Shevi," she said, "I hope it's okay that I'm telling you the truth, but I can't take this pretense anymore."

I looked at her strangely. What was she trying to tell me?

"This whole idea had nothing to do with me." Miri blurted, "It was all your mother's doing, from beginning to end."

"My mother's?!"

If she had told me she had gotten engaged last night, I wouldn't have been more stunned.

"Wwwhat?" I asked, my mind reeling. "What do you mean?"

I Lift My Eyes to the Mountains / 199

"Your mother called me one evening last year and told me she wanted to discuss something confidential. She had always thought you would do well in a line that combined your business efficiency with your flair for pretty things. She had thought of a novel idea, but she was afraid you wouldn't accept the suggestion if it came from her."

I was overawed by the thought. *Hamalach Sheli*. My mother had set this whole thing up without my ever knowing.

"What about the money?" I asked suddenly. The pieces were falling into place.

"Oh, it was all your parents' contribution," Miri said simply. "Your mother thought of every detail to make this work."

I walked home in a daze.

My dear mother. How could I ever give voice to the feelings that crowded my heart, that threatened to smother me with the deepest sense of love and the deepest sense of shame?

Long after she had let go of my hand, long after I had let go of hers, my mother had always been there, holding me without me ever knowing it, providing me with everything I had without me even acknowledging it.

I thought of my mother in her simple navy Shabbos suit, her support stockings, and sensible oxfords, and my heart surged with pride. Yes, my mother was a woman of true class; she believed in durability, in things that had long-lasting value. Things I had missed somewhere along the way.

I would try and pick them up now.

And perhaps, if you happen to be on my path, you will squint upward and pick them up too.

A Child in Pain

My inner landscape is not the sort of terrain anyone would consider mountainous. I'm of an even-keeled, measured temperament, consistent, no nonsense, predictable. I'm not a writer, and I certainly don't fit the stereotype of someone who would spill his personal struggles on the pages of a newspaper. Still, I feel an inner compulsion to share an experience that has significantly changed my life.

Different things cause different people to climb. The frightening thing with me was that I never even realized I had a mountain to scale. Self-assured and in control, I didn't doubt my firm footing for a moment. Fortunately, Someone above rattled the pebbles beneath my feet, until I was forced to confront the one person I had never confronted before: myself, and take hold of my life. And if I can find it within me to share my story, then I'll know that I've truly climbed.

Even as a young child, my extraordinary leadership skills were apparent. I was always the spokesman, the student in charge, the one arranging our class's affairs. When I spoke, it was with a confidence and authority that commanded a certain respect. I remember my *rebbeim* laughing. "You'll be a *menahel*, yet, one day," they prophesized.

It didn't take that long for the prophecy to come to be. After learning in *kollel* for several years, I was offered the position of principal in a new Talmud Torah that had opened in a growing city, half an hour's drive from my neighborhood. Though I had no previous experience, my employer had confidence in my abilities, and I accepted the job. It was the perfect opportunity to actualize my potential while earning a respectable income at the same time.

I worked there faithfully for nine years. During my ninth year there, I was offered the opportunity to be a *menahel* in a prominent *cheder* whose principal was due to retire. The salary was considerably greater than the one I was presently receiving, and the *cheder* was in my own hometown, a fact which would preclude my daily commute to and from work.

Unlike my previous job, where I had personally hired the *rebbeim* and had established the institution from its inception, I was now entering a flourishing Talmud Torah where things had been running a certain way for years. It was a completely new type of challenge for me. Though there were unofficial rules by which the school ran, the environment was generally looser, or in my terms, unprofessional.

Financially, too, it was apparent that things had run loose for too long. The classrooms were crowded and the payment of teachers' salaries was terribly backlogged. The hallways were in desperate need of a painting, not to mention bulletin boards, which were completely absent from the scene. I frowned in disapproval at the sight, determined to bring matters under control.

A few weeks before the beginning of the new term, I called a staff meeting. After a short introduction, I outlined my goals and expectations, and proceeded to list, very explicitly, the rules by which things would run under my jurisdiction. The *rebbeim* weren't surprised. I already had a reputation as a tough captain who ran a tight ship. I told them that I would make every effort to ensure that their salaries were paid on time, but by the same token, I expected that they come through with their obligations.

Right from that first meeting, one particular *rebbi* rubbed me the wrong way. Everyone fondly referred to him as Reb Mendel and he was a stocky man of about 40 who sported a perpetual broad smile. To me he looked like the typical town jester in the books. His top button was open and his beard seemed to fly in the wind. Something about his demeanor provoked me.

I don't know if it was his *tallis katan* sloppily slung over his shirt, or his unkempt *peyos,* but the combination of his casual appearance and jolly attitude went against my staid approach to life. It was almost as if he was mocking me with his easygoing manner.

Reb Mendel, I observed disapprovingly, as I continued to watch him in *cheder,* seemed to have no cares. I couldn't understand how a man of his years could still be so childishly cheerful. Didn't he carry any burden in life?

Maybe that's why the children relate to him so well, I thought cynically, as I watched his second grade students tumble out of their classroom for recess, hanging on to his every word. He never bothered to get them into a straight line as he continued to dramatize the story he had been in the middle of. Even in the playground, he seemed to live it up with them. "Reb Mendel, Reb Mendel," the kids would chorus from their various perches, and he would swing them around playfully, enjoying their antics.

"Reb Mendel," I approached him one day, " I've noticed that you are often late handing in your sheets. I would like to see your *parashah* sheets on my desk by 11 o'clock Thursday morning. At 11:30, all the sheets will be sent down to the main office where they'll be copied and collated."

"Certainly," responded Reb Mendel heartily, "we'll certainly try."

I nodded stiffly, purposely not reciprocating his friendly style. *He better not try,* I thought; *he better* do *it.*

For the first few weeks, things ran smoothly enough. I was pleased with the reforms I was making in the yeshivah, and the *rebbeim* seemed satisfied as well. One Friday, I bumped into the secretary, who was frantically making his way down the stairs with a few sheets of paper in his hand.

"Where are you headed?" I asked curtly. If there's one thing I dislike, it's people scurrying in the hallways when they are meant to be at their desks.

"Uh — I just have these copies to make," stammered the young secretary.

"What kind of copies?" I shifted my gaze to the big clock across the hallway with emphasis.

The secretary looked flustered. "Uh — just these *parashah* sheets for Reb Mendel."

I was infuriated. Reb Mendel had circumvented my instructions, and had been stealthily handing his sheets to the secretary on Friday mornings. Instead of taking all the sheets down on Thursday to be copied in an orderly fashion, the secretary had to make a special trip down at the last minute in order to accommodate Reb Mendel's lax behavior.

"If one of the teachers finds it too difficult to comply," I said icily, "let him take it up with me. Your job is to follow orders, not to enable others to mess up the system."

During the recess break, I confronted Reb Mendel and had him know that I wouldn't tolerate these deviations from administration policy.

"Oh, you mean the *parashah* sheets?" he asked complacently, as if he had never heard the rule. "*B'seder, b'ezras Hashem*, I'll have them ready by Thursday."

It didn't end with the *parashah* sheets, though. When I surveyed the *cheder* a few months into the year, I felt more than a tinge of pride at what I had managed to accomplish over a short period of time. I had instituted regular staff meetings, weekly planbook checks, and careful assessments of every single *talmid*. The halls were adorned with new bulletin boards, and the teachers were receiving their salaries on time.

The place was running like a well-oiled machine. But for one kink.

Reb Mendel.

If the whole *cheder* marched like an army, Reb Mendel's class always seemed to have one foot out of the line. While all the *rebbeim* had their students in their chairs, *davening*, at exactly five minutes to 8, from Reb Mendel's classroom, you could still hear a happy ruckus all the way down to the office. If I ever stuck my head in to see what was going on, I would be met by a jumble of children chattering as they hung their up lunchbags, blissfully oblivious to my presence.

Reb Mendel, noticing me, would wave, completely unfazed, from wherever he was sitting, and call out a friendly good morning. It was as if I had never spoken to him about the importance of order and punctuality.

The last straw came one morning, well into the year. The *cheder* was bursting at its seams, and I had been working tirelessly on fund-raising efforts that would allow us to build a new wing. I was thrilled when a delegation from a philanthropic American family I had contacted expressed their interest in coming to see our institution. I set up an appointment with them for the following Wednesday morning. Then I got to work preparing for their visit.

Not that there was much work to be done. When an institution is in top form all year, I reflected, there's no need to engage in last minute patchwork in order to impress company. Just to be certain, though, I posted a notice in the teachers' room letting the *rebbeim* know that we were expecting important visitors on Wednesday morning and asking that they all be especially well prepared.

During the recess break, when I met with the teachers, I pointed out that the guests were modern Jews from America and would be dressed accordingly. I requested that they explain this to the students in advance in order to forestall any awkward situations.

On Wednesday morning, I greeted the delegation in my office, where some pastries and drinks were set out tastefully on the table. I introduced them to our institution, told them a little about its history, and described some of the activities that took place in our classrooms.

They listened attentively and then asked if they could catch a glimpse of the classes in session.

"Sure," I responded courteously, "it would be my pleasure to show you around."

The tour got off to a pretty good start. The students rose respectfully and then continued to participate in the lessons, as the visitors hovered near the doorway, observing with interest. As soon as we entered the hallway of the second floor, though, my stomach tightened. From the end of the corridor came the unmistakable sound of chairs screeching and children giggling with glee.

I tried to remain cool. Steering the guests away from the noise, I pointed to a particularly striking display that the sixth graders had built, depicting the different types of *succos* that were described in *Mishmayos Succah*. The visitors, though, seemed more interested in the tumult.

"Sounds exciting in that classroom," the senior member of the delegation chuckled. "Let's see what's going on there."

I felt myself blushing, imagining the scene that was about to greet us. Inside, I was seething. *There goes Reb Mendel again*, I thought. *That man is absolutely impossible to depend on. Well this time, he'll pay bitterly. He'll learn that actions exact consequences. A person can't just keep breaking the rules, and expect to iron things out with a smile.*

The scene in Reb Mendel's second-grade classroom surpassed my worst scenario. There was Reb Mendel crawling on all fours alongside a clan of romping, braying students, while the rest of the children jumped up and down in their seats and in the aisles, hooting with excitement.

I stood in the doorway, the visitors peering over my shoulder, while my whole insides contracted with rage. What in the world was going on in this room? If eyes had the power to burn, I would have roasted Reb Mendel right there under the fury of my gaze. I couldn't even find a word of explanation to offer to the delegation. My mind was too busy churning with thoughts of the harsh tongue-lashing I would mete out to Reb Mendel.

Reb Mendel and his little charges, though, seemed to have no compunctions. The kids, distracted by the sudden appearance of a group of adults in their classroom, began to call out.

"Hey, who are these people?" and worse yet, "*Menahel*, how come they aren't wearing *yarmulkes*?"

I stood there sweating, not knowing how to extricate myself from the uncomfortable bind.

If Reb Mendel was perturbed, he definitely didn't show it. He stood up, and without even dusting off his pants, greeted the visitors warmly.

"*Shalom Aleichem!*" he extended his whitened hand. "It's my pleasure to have you join our classroom. Please feel free to come in."

I forced a polite smile, and refused his offer with a wave of my hand. Then I tried to shepherd the group out of the classroom as elegantly as I could. They plodded reluctantly after me, their eyes still riveted to the action in Reb Mendel's room.

"A lively class," one of the visitors commented.

I mumbled some kind of noncommittal response.

"Have the students in your school really never seen Jews without *kippot*?" another one asked.

That question sealed Reb Mendel's fate. All my well-laid plans for this visit had gone up in smoke thanks to Reb Mendel's breezy attitude. He wouldn't get away with it. *Not this time,* I thought; *he'll learn, for once and for all.*

The rest of the visit was somewhat strained. My nerves had been shot by the incident in the second-grade classroom, and though I continued to show the visitors around, I was withdrawn and distracted. My heart wasn't in it anymore. I felt that Reb Mendel had ruined our chance to impress these unaffiliated American guests.

As soon as the delegation had left, I summoned Reb Mendel into my office. He walked into the room, his *tzitzis* swinging, apologizing broadly that he had entirely forgotten about the expected visit.

"I don't think any harm was done, though," he added. "So the visitors saw some kids acting like kids."

And a grown rebbi acting like a kid, I thought, the fury mounting inside me again. Didn't anything fluster this man? I ignored his apologies and stared at him frostily. *Just be quiet,* I thought; *I'm sick and tired of your easy complacence.*

In a restrained voice I told him that as far as I was concerned, his career in our Talmud Torah was over. We would pay him anything we owed and he would receive his salary for the rest of the month.

I think it was the first time since I had met Reb Mendel that I actually saw the color drain from his face.

"You don't mean that seriously," he tried to protest, but I wasn't moved.

"I'm serious about whatever I say," I answered evenly. "Too bad you never realized that before."

I went back to my paperwork, insinuating that our exchange was over. Reb Mendel stood in his place, twisting the ends of his beard.

"I have eight children to provide for," he pleaded. "Can't you overlook a little mistake?"

This was no little mistake, I felt like roaring. This has been months of violating rules, big and little, of defying my authority, of fostering a lax atmosphere in the entire *cheder*. A person is accountable for his actions. Someone like you doesn't belong educating the next generation.

I left all that unsaid.

"Your little mistake today caused our institution an irreversible monetary loss. Had the visiting delegation found our *cheder* fit, we stood a good chance of receiving a grant to build a new wing. Now that chance is lost, and so is yours. Not every chance returns." I looked at him with a penetrating gaze.

For once, Reb Mendel remained silent, his mouth drawn into a pensive line. For a moment, admittedly, I felt a little surge of satisfaction at seeing the humor in his eyes extinguished. After all these months, my words had finally made some dent in his impermeable spirit.

Two days after the incident, I came home from Maariv to find my wife in a state of near hysteria. My 2-year old daughter had high fever, and nothing seemed to bring her temperature down. At the advice of a Hatzolah member, we tried sponging her with cool washcloths, and dipping her socks in vinegar. The fever went down for a short while, but then began to climb again.

Close to midnight, my wife suddenly called out in alarm, "Esty's bed is shaking; I think she's having convulsions."

I felt myself break out in a cold sweat. Pushing myself against waves of panic, I grabbed the receiver and called an ambulance. Then I ran to Esty's bed where my wife stood, helplessly wringing her hands.

At the hospital, we were immediately admitted. The doctors tried to bring down the fever, and simultaneously ran a battery of tests to try and determine the reason for the fever. In the meantime, the temperature stabilized under the influence of the medication. Esty looked like a sleeping angel, so tiny and vulnerable under the hospital sheets.

My wife and I stood by her bedside, barely exchanging a word. We were each lost in our own thoughts. My wife murmured quietly from the *Tehillim* she had brought along, while I went to try and find the doctor. We fervently hoped that the crisis would pass quickly.

As soon as the effect of the medication had worn off, though, Esty's fever began to rise again. This time, the medication was impotent against whatever it was that was causing the raging fever. The doctors fluttered around her, talking in grave tones. At that moment, ice-cold fear gripped my heart. Our baby's life was in danger.

Aside from the immediate peril, the doctors feared that the prolonged high fever and convulsions were likely to cause brain damage. The room swarmed with medical personnel; doctors hurrying in and out, nurses drawing more blood, and more nurses swathing Esty in wet towels. Accustomed to taking action in a crisis, I suddenly felt lost by my powerlessness to do anything.

Suddenly, a light flickered in my mind. Why hadn't I thought of this earlier? I hurried out of the room with my cell phone and proceeded to dial the number of a renowned *Gadol* in Yerushalayim. Though I wasn't personally affiliated with any particular following, I had gone to him on numerous occasions for a *berachah*.

Nervously, I listened as the phone rang. I was too emotionally overwrought to notice the hour. At the second ring, a *gabbai* answered. I quickly explained the urgency of my situation and requested that he ask the Rebbe to intercede on our behalf. The *gabbai* listened sympathetically, and wished my daughter a speedy recovery. He told me he would speak to the Rebbe, and that I should call back in 15 minutes.

I spent those 15 minutes pacing the hall. The doctors were still hovering over Esty, and from their grim expressions, I surmised that her condition hadn't improved. I told my wife I had called the *Gadol*, and that I was waiting for a response. Her expression eased for a moment.

I dialed again. When I heard the *gabbai's* voice on the line, I felt a gush of reassurance. This wasn't solely on our shoulders anymore; we had a *Gadol* intervening for us. We had someone who would help us storm the *Shaarei Shamayim*.

I was expecting to hear the standard wishes for a *refuah sheleimah b'karov*, perhaps even a promise that Esty would pull through, unharmed. Instead, I heard words that sounded cold and threatening.

"The Rebbe said," the *gabbai* fumbled for a piece of paper, and I held my breath. Then the *gabbai* read, citing the Rebbe verbatim, "If one hurts a *Yid*, it is no simple matter. Your daughter cannot merit a *refuah sheleimah* as long as the *Aibeshter's* child is in pain. You must first ask *mechilah* of the person you have hurt."

I was stunned. I thanked the *gabbai* feebly and hung up. Suddenly, I felt alone and vulnerable. I was standing in front of a sealed gate that even the *Gadol* couldn't help me open. I had locked the door with my own hands. Now I would have to search for the key in my very own heart.

It took a few minutes of careful recollection before I made the obvious connection. Reb Mendel. Although from the inside of the hospital ward the incident seemed miles away, I knew the *Gadol* was clearly referring to that episode.

Replaying the story in my mind, I felt strangely detached, as if I was watching a soundless filmstrip. I saw the drama unwinding, just the way it had happened, and yet suddenly, I could muster none of the passion I had felt at the time. All I felt was a chilling urgency to call Reb Mendel and receive his pardon.

Again, I disregarded the unearthly hour and dialed Reb Mendel's home. The phone rang several times. I shuddered with each vibration. Each ring seemed to jar my soul, to drill right into my heart.

I could visualize Reb Mendel jumping out of bed, swinging his *tallis katan* over his shoulders, and rushing to the telephone. I could see him waving his hand broadly, and dismissing my apologies. I suddenly felt mortified that I had ever resented his resilient nature.

Reb Mendel finally answered. He croaked a terrified hello, and sounded shocked when he heard me on the other line. I, the proper, prim, *menahel* who had just fired him, was calling at 3 o'clock in the morning. I wasted no time on formalities. My 2-year-old daughter was in critical condition, I hurried to explain, and I was desperately entreating him to forgive me for the way I had treated him.

"*Machul, machul, machul,*" came his voice, clear and resounding. "You have my *mechilah gemurah*. I must admit, I've spent these two days in a state of real anxiety, but now everything is fine. May your daughter have a complete recovery."

I knew Reb Mendel, but still, I was dumbfounded by his response. For the first time, I felt dwarfed by this giant of a man who had place in his heart even for the person who had just caused him so much anguish.

Esty's condition slowly began to show signs of improvement. The fever started to go down, and for the first time since we had been admitted, the doctors claimed that she was out of the crisis. They still had no clue as to what had caused the strange phenomenon.

I didn't need any clues. I had found the key.

Esty's mysterious condition and miraculous recovery left me deeply moved. When I entered my office two days later, I found two messages waiting for me. The first was a letter from the American philanthropists who had visited several days ago. They had decided to come through with the amount needed to build a new wing. Their decision, they wrote, had been primarily influenced by "the impression that your school is a place where children can grow, a place that is bent on liberal ideals that encourage freedom of expression and creativity."

I nearly fell off the chair.

The second message was from Reb Mendel. Though he assured me once again that he had completely cleared his heart of resentment, he wanted to let me know that he had accepted a position in a different *cheder* and wouldn't be returning.

The third message, unspoken, unwritten, yet almost tangibly woven by the first two, was a message straight from Above.

It was a message that gave me the impetus to climb a steep mountain that I am still climbing today. It is the mountain from which I view people from a different vantage point than I have ever seen them before. From my new stance, high above the ground, I can see my employees, my neighbors, my children, and *mechutanim*, in a new light.

Gripping the slippery cliff, I have shed my rigid perception that there is one way to ascend. I have tossed to the ground my notion that either punctuality and precision, or warmth and creativity, are the sole measures of perfection.

Today, I can see people who are each different, but are each right. I see people who have flaws and shortcomings, but at the same time, possess invaluable abilities and virtues. I see people who have different bridges to cross, and different waters to tread. And most of all, I see people who, as varied as they are, are each one of the "*Aibeshter's* children," trying to climb to the top.

נִבְזֶה בְּעֵינָיו נִמְאָס,

... in whose eyes a contemptible person is repulsive,

Riding the Roller Coaster

There are certain topics that make classical material for debates. Does a person shape his environment, or does an environment shape a person? Personally, I never went in for staged sparring. Life, however, turned me into a live specimen.

Let me start from the beginning, though.

I had a pretty uneventful childhood, happy upbringing, positive school experience, normal adolescence. If life was a ride, then I was your typical nondescript passenger traveling coach class.

Marriage, *Baruch Hashem,* proved to be a rather non-dramatic turn off this pleasant freeway. The standard yeshivah couple, we moved to Lakewood, where apparently, we fit right in. I found a job; my young husband learned full time.

For me, a fairly quiet person on the outside, those first few years pinned a prototypical identification tag to my lapel. Name: Shaindy Brody, occupation: *kollel* wife/secretary, status: newly married. My name could have easily been interchanged with any one of the dozens of bustling women whom I courteously nodded to on my way to work. There was nothing, superficially at least, that set me apart from them, or that connected us in a real and meaningful way.

"Status" was thankfully replaced by mother of one and then two, *Baruch Hashem*. By the time our family numbered four young children, we faced a crossroads of sorts. My husband was offered a position as a *rebbi* in an out-of-town community, a beckoning proposition considering our financial difficulties.

Our children were young enough to be thrilled with the adventure of the change, and admittedly, I was more than a little excited myself. Though I felt a slight tremor of apprehension every time I thought of uprooting and settling in a new, unfamiliar neighborhood, I looked forward to joining a small, close-knit, Torah community.

My sense of anticipation proved to be well founded. As soon as we arrived, I was able to sense something different, something warm and welcoming about our new surroundings. From the signs on the door to the cake and drinks on the kitchen table and supper in the refrigerator, we felt as if we had come home.

Wherever I went, people warmly took note of the fact that we were the most recent addition to the community, that I must be the wife of the new seventh-grade *rebbi*, that my kids had to be their children's lovely new classmates. I was showered with invitations, with offers for meals, baby-sitting, and the use of a car until we got settled in. Though I felt shy, being the spotlight of so much attention, it was a wonderfully reassuring landing to a new destination.

The true test of social acceptance is the subtle progression from recipient to contributor. Giving is a sign of generosity, but taking is an indication of true parity. My heart began to swell as I saw the tiny buds of these new relationships sprouting. Neighbors knocked on my door to borrow from me, my kids' classmates would come to our house to play.

I joined the car pool and happily took my daughter's friend for Shabbos when her parents visited New York. Soon enough, I got a job in the school office, working part-time as a secretary. I felt the petals inside me unfurling, the delicate hues of my personality coming out in full color.

I had always been a warm and affectionate person. My closest family knew me as a talkative and sensitive soul with a fabulous sense of humor. In public, however, I had always donned a reserved facade, fading like a solar-operated calculator out of the direct light.

Now, enveloped in the closeness of a small, informal community, I shed my inhibited veneer and embraced all my friends as family. I spoke with newfound confidence and didn't hesitate to share my droll comments in a crowd. I joined the local ladies auxiliary and helped organize various extracurricular projects in school. Always a creative person, I used my talents to set up community *simchos,* and later to direct the summer daycamp. I felt infused with a new sense of life, of giving and belonging.

During my second year, I gave birth to my fifth child, a baby boy. A real part of the community by then, I was able to recuperate, secure in the knowledge that my family was being provided for. When my mother expressed her concern over being so far away, I reassured her. "There's nothing like a mother, Ma, but my friends here are determined to disprove that."

My kids were divided among friends and neighbors, and my husband and I were smothered with thoughtful care packages and delicious meals. After a week or two of this pampering, I looked forward to getting the family back together again.

I didn't know that I would have to remain suspended on the taking end for quite some time. When I found myself feeling chronically depleted, I attributed my weakness to normal postpartum exhaustion. My baby was up a lot during the night, and caring for a family was tiring. I soon came to realize, however, that the all-consuming fatigue was more than just par for the course.

By the time I sent my four older ones off in the morning, I was spent. I felt as if some automated system was closing the shutters on my eyes, on my brain, on my plans for the day. It was the most helpless feeling in the world. Despite my most desperate protests, I felt my body going limp, deadweight into bed. I would leave the beds unmade, the breakfast dishes untouched, a trail of tights and pajamas on the floor, and dissolve under my covers.

After a few weeks of just barely treading water, I was finally diagnosed with Epstein-Barr virus. It was a relief to know what was wrong after weeks of feeling like a half-dead zombie.

Knowledge, however, never cooked anyone supper or washed laundry. Fortunately, my neighbors did.

In the most unassuming, considerate manner, they set up a rotation system where different neighbors would volunteer to take my kids out, do the supermarket shopping, and help with the laundry.

More than all of this, though, was the fantastic emotional support my friends provided. They would drop by for short visits, send cute cards full of warm humor, and ply me with reassurance that my situation was only temporary. If not for these hands and hearts so readily extended to make things bearable, I cannot fathom how we would have pulled through the crisis.

Fortunately, the symptoms began to lift as they had appeared. Slowly, I felt my strength coming back, my ambition and stamina returning. I was overcome with gratitude, with the enormity of these simple gifts I had taken for granted. As I put a basic meal on the table or read my kids a bedtime story, I felt the joy of finding a treasure that I had given up for lost.

Though I was grateful for my restored health, months of not functioning had left me on an emotional low. I knew I had to channel my energies toward reestablishing the routine in my home, yet something inside me yearned to reach out, to tap into my talents, to undertake something that would make me feel actively productive. Once again, my friends came to the rescue.

"Shaindy," the principal in my daughter's school approached me one day, "I don't know if you've heard, but Morah Weissman, our first-grade teacher is moving to Eretz Yisrael. We're looking for a teacher, and I think you would make the perfect candidate."

"Me?" I croaked. Though I had taught when I was single, my skills were rusty, and besides, I had never taught first grade. In my mind, a first-grade teacher was someone skilled, experienced, someone with professional techniques and years of expertise.

The principal waved away my objections. Experience, she claimed, was something everyone had to acquire at some point, and she was willing to hire me despite my lack thereof. As far as skills, I had the rest of the spring and summer to brush up and she was confident that Morah Weissman would help me with whatever I needed.

"Trust me, Shaindy," she said, "I've discussed this with more than one person, and everyone feels you'll make a natural first-grade teacher. Personally, I have no doubts, and my intuition usually doesn't let me down."

Propped up by the principal's confidence, I approached Morah Weissman. Taking extra household help, I threw myself into the preparation for my new job with enthusiasm and vigor.

My new preoccupation was like a balm to my soul. I walked around the house humming and tended to my household chores with a lightheartedness and purpose I hadn't felt in a long time. My husband and children were thrilled with the change in me. They had just about gotten a mother back, and now she was becoming a teacher too.

Becoming a first-grade teacher, indeed, was a turning point in my life. I loved my little students to bits, the shy, serious ones nodding earnestly in their seats, and the boisterous effervescent ones who were always losing pencils and never remembered to raise their hands.

Like the community at large, my class was small and close knit, 18 girls who were mostly familiar with one another. I was like a Mommy to them. We learned the letters, sang and drilled, and in between I got to hear whose grandmother was coming to visit and whose baby brother had gotten new shoes. They eagerly drank in the stories I told and just as eagerly gulped my warm, loving compliments.

I found every aspect of the job rewarding. Artistic by nature, I had fun drawing pretty stencils and funny cartoons to make the learning more exciting. I encouraged my students' creativity, teaching them to decorate their notebooks and training them to resolve problems on their own. Though one can taste success without anyone telling one how it's supposed to taste, it was heartwarming to receive waves of positive feedback wherever I went.

Whether it was in the supermarket, at a bar mitzvah, or at the yeshivah's dinner, I always met some enthusiastic parent or grandparent, aunt or neighbor, who came rushing over to tell me what a wonderful job I was doing.

"You can't imagine what a different child she is," they would gush. Or "It's incredible how much fun learning can be." "I wish all my kids could go back to first grade."

Success breeds success. If I had never seen it in actuality, then I certainly experienced it that first year. I had the little first graders eating out of my hands, and what was more, they were all reading confidently and fluently as the year drew to a close. In addition, I worked on cultivating other skills outside the classroom, teaching them to successfully jump rope and catch a ball. It was gratifying to see even the shiest among them infused with social confidence.

By my third year of teaching, I felt like I'd been teaching first grade forever. I had mastered the techniques of teaching reading and was constantly looking for ways to improve my methods. The parents all clamored to have their daughters in my class, and first-grade teachers the world over were constantly calling to borrow my stencils.

Mentally rewinding four years, I thought back to the time when I had been chained by the shackles of a virus, weak and incapacitated, skeptical that I would ever function as a normal productive human being again. Shuddering at the memories, I couldn't help but offer a heartfelt prayer of gratitude. In the blink of an eye, Hashem had extracted me from the dismal valley and had lifted me to these dizzying heights.

Perhaps my prayer had been a shadow short of submission, of dependence, a shade too intoxicated with the heady feeling of success. Basking in my sense of fulfillment, I wouldn't have believed how quickly I could go plummeting down to the depths again.

As my third year of teaching came to an end, I wound up my affairs with a happy sense of accomplishment. Vacation was just around the corner, and I was looking forward to spending time with my children without the pressure of work. When I walked in from teaching one spring day to find my husband concluding a phone call, I suspected nothing out of the ordinary.

I kicked off my shoes, and got busy defrosting some chicken for supper. Breezing around the kitchen in a rush to get something underway before the kids came home, I hardly noticed that my husband looked tense and reflective. Stroking his beard nervously, he remained hunched over the chair upon which he had been leaning, lost in his thoughts. Finally he dropped the bombshell.

"They just called from New York to offer me an important position."

I spun around, stunned.

"Whaat??"

From the furrows on his forehead, I could tell my husband was serious. Dumping the chicken into a pan in the sink, I sat down to register what he was about to tell me. It was the first of many discussions, weighing a decision that would change our lives.

By the time summer vacation rolled around, our decision had been made. Though I knew it would be an enormous sacrifice on my part and a tremendous adjustment for the children, there were too many pros tipping the other side. We would be starting the next semester in New York.

Things moved at a furious pace. Friends helped us around the clock as we rushed to get the house packed up in record time. If we wanted to settle even somewhat before the new *z'man*, we had to make the move as soon as possible. The days and nights blurred in a whirlwind of activity and disbelief, as we were engulfed in warm wishes, heartfelt poems, tearful farewells.

Like a film on fast forward, the days jumbled over each other, as we dismantled our secure existence and packed the pieces of the past six years into boxes and suitcases. Two nights before moving day, the entire community surprised us with an emotional farewell party. There were speeches and *grammen*, songs and pictures, poems and letters. It was a warm, informal affair, with plenty of delicious refreshments and an atmosphere of closeness and love.

At the evening's end, I scooped up the beautiful album and the many warm parting letters from parents of students, neighbors, and friends. I knew there was no indispensable man, yet at that moment I couldn't help feeling that a void would be left in our place.

New York was a culture shock. Pulling up in front of a brick building on a double-parked street amid honking horns and throngs of anonymous humanity was a stark contrast to our arrival out of town six years earlier. There were no signs on the door, no welcoming committee upstairs, no cake on the table. In contrast to the lovely house with the shrubbery and greenery, there was a dingy apartment with old linoleum and even older plumbing.

I tried to keep my spirits from flagging. This had been a conscious decision and I had known it wouldn't be easy. I tried enlisting my sense of humor, and believe me, during those first few weeks, there was plenty to joke about. As hard as I tried, though, not to send negative vibes, the kids were perceptive enough to absorb the differences on their own. They didn't need anyone to point out the hardships.

The real test came with the new school year. My husband had begun an important administrational job and was under a lot of stress. The kids, who had been so confident and well adjusted in their classes out of town, became shy and fearful. My second grader boarded the bus each day amid a trail of tears, promises, and prizes. Actually, boarded the bus each day is a terrible exaggeration. Most of the time, she kicked up a scene so severe, it was impossible to get her to the bus. We were both miserable.

I knew that if I wanted to make social contacts and create a niche for myself, I had to get out of the house and find a job. Though everyone had warned us that job-hunting in New York was doomed to failure, I had an advantage. Armed with my principal's raving recommendations, I went for interviews in several schools. My principal, a respected person in the educational system, contacted these employers and extolled my virtues as her most creative and successful teacher. Within two weeks, I was flooded with positive responses from various schools in the neighborhood.

The one catch was that none of the schools had a first-grade job slot available. Though I especially wanted to accept the job offer in my daughter's school, believing that my presence near her would help her adjust, I was more than a little hesitant about taking on a seventh-grade classroom.

I was used to first graders, innocent little children with round eyes who were so easy to enchant. I was familiar with the curriculum and had experience teaching reading. Seventh grade was a daunting proposition: lively kids who had already donned the sophistication of adolescence and hadn't quite shed the boisterous mantle of immaturity.

Whomever I shared my reservations with, vehemently dismissed my fears. "You have such a magic spell in the classroom; you'll see, you'll succeed beyond anyone's imagination."

"You didn't think you could do first grade either, and look what a star teacher you became. You have everything it takes; just go for it."

If I still harbored qualms about teaching seventh grade, my ego was certainly inflated. Reminding myself that my first-grade career had also initially been grounded on self-doubt, I accepted the job.

Headlong into the lions' den.

Thirty-four seventh-grade New Yorkers, I quickly learned, are not double of 17, out–of-town first graders in any equation. They are a completely different breed, an entirely altered composition. Love and humor may be the way to a child's heart, but it is also the way to a teacher's heartache. If it isn't tempered by stern discipline, it is a quick recipe for chaos and disorder in the classroom. And once you've shown the soft hand, I discovered, it's too late to don the steel glove.

The first day was not bad. I got to know the students' names and introduced them to the basics of each subject. After that, though, it was downhill. What started off with giggles and whispers turned into a rowdy convention of sarcastic interchange, silly comments, and open disinterest in anything being taught.

I felt the powerlessness of a captain losing the ship. While there were four or five girls who took pity on me and tried to participate, the general atmosphere was one of loose abandon. The girls mimicked my accent and echoed my questions, laughing hysterically at their own theatrics.

Though I tried to act cool, I felt the desperation forming a tight knot in my stomach. Trying to get through my lesson was like trying to ride a flat-tired bicycle across the beach. It was tiring, dispiriting, and humiliating. I could barely last the torture until recess; how was I going to plod through a year of it?

The worst part of the ordeal was the burning shame that accompanied me in and out of the classroom. The teachers on the staff shared a warm camaraderie, yet I was much too self-conscious to even get close to their circle. I didn't fool myself; I knew everyone saw me as the new teacher from out of town who couldn't control the class.

I couldn't look the secretary in the eye either. My classroom was located not far from the office, and she was privy to the unearthly ruckus that rose from my room. If anyone came near my corner, I'd pretend to be busy searching my cubby, or sorting through papers, anything to avoid the embarrassing confrontation.

It was like solitary confinement in a buzzing hall, like being lynched every day all over again. I tried initiating contests, projects, rewarding diligence and decent behavior with nosh. As I tried, I knew I was making a fool of myself, unabashedly pulling at loose straws to grab some sort of foothold. These kids were seventh graders, shrewd enough to see through such transparent maneuvers and snide enough to let me know.

In school, I managed to put up a front. I always came dressed to a T and kept a polite smile on my face. At home, I shed my veneer together with my *sheitel* and smart suits. My self-esteem was in shambles, my motivation to do anything was numbed. I felt like one big failure, a capable adult humiliated beyond belief by a bunch of 12- and 13-year-olds. If kids only knew the pain caused by the power they wield.

I was irritable most of the time, nauseous and dizzy from my daily ordeals. I had approached the principal several times to tell her I had made a mistake and that I wanted to leave. Not believing how bad the situation was, she had brushed me aside and assured me that things would be fine.

After a few weeks, however, the principal called me aside to tell me she was receiving complaints from the parents. Though it came as no surprise, it was degrading all the same. As if the parents had to tell me something was amiss. If I had known what to do, I'd have done it ages ago.

I came home in a state. I told my husband I wasn't stepping foot into the school again, come what may. He gently suggested that I take a short leave, which we would use to visit the community we had left. I was only too relieved to oblige.

Indeed, going back was like a cool compress on my wounded ego. We were greeted with open arms and all our neighbors and friends vied over the privilege of hosting us for meals. My former students came over to visit, singing songs they still remembered and looking at me with undisguised admiration and affection in their eyes.

So I was a person after all, an admired individual, a successful teacher. New York was all a bad dream, a drab, dreary nightmare that had turned me into a flop. Sitting in the company of close neighbors and colleagues, I almost didn't believe it myself. My friends, accustomed to my dramatic flair, were regaled by my accounts of my teaching fiasco. Try as I did, I couldn't get them to believe the severity of my plight.

I went back to New York, a revived person. I had extended my vacation and spoken to many experienced *mechanchos* who shared their empathy and wise counsel. Though I knew I would never be the shining star I had been, I was willing to give it another try.

Somehow, I got through the rest of the year. Stumbled may have been a better word. I never covered half of the curriculum, neither did I achieve the sense of gratification that teaching had always provided me with. But I wasn't a loser; I stuck it out, like a kid gagging on every last spoon of his oatmeal.

The day I walked out of that building for the last time, I felt like a prisoner who had just ended his sentence. I was free, liberated; I wasn't bound by any contract to a miserable job that made me sick to my stomach each day. The birds were chirping, the sun was shining; I could be a person again.

When I put away that briefcase, I did it with pomp and ceremony, certain that I was preserving a symbolic relic of my bygone days as a teacher. I would be a secretary, a party planner, an accountant, anything but a teacher. Let anyone try and make me set foot into that school building again.

Summer passed, and slowly I felt my self-esteem returning. On the second day of school, I had to drop an important form off in the office of my daughter's school. My muscles stiffened involuntarily. I couldn't think of walking past those doors, into the office that had witnessed my shame. Mustering all my strength, I drove to the school. I couldn't spend my life hiding under a blanket.

The power of association is incredible. Just the smell of the office, the copy machine, the air freshener hanging near the secretary's desk, made my stomach lurch. The dean greeted me. I forced a smile to my face. I handed him the form and turned around to leave. I had made it.

"Mrs. Brody," the dean called after me, "we've just started a monthly nit-checking system in our school, and we don't really have any volunteers yet. Would you be interested in the job?"

My first impulse was to run. I felt stifled, trapped, afraid of being conned into staying in the miserable place that held the ghosts of my failure in its walls. Then the preposterousness of his suggestion hit me. Nit-checker! Of all the glory in the world. From dethroned teacher to celebrated nit-checker.

Still my natural resilience, and my even more natural need to bring in some sort of income, made me press him for details.

"What does coordinating the project entail?"

I had occasionally stumbled upon a nit, but I certainly had never entertained the thought of turning it into a profession. Visions of a white-haired school nurse poking around with a tongue depressor came to mind.

"Well, it would mean coming in twice a week and tackling two classes a morning. It would also mean drawing up parent lists and trying to recruit mothers on a once-a-month basis to assist you."

"Hm."

For some reason, his offer struck my funny bone. Wait until my friends heard about this. For lack of anything better, though, I relented. My pride had already been lost in this place. What else did I have to gamble?

At first I felt like a certified idiot, sitting in a chair, sifting through strands of hair opened loose all over my lap. So this was what I was doing with my credentials, with my talents and experience. I quickly tossed that attitude aside, though. My ordeal the year before had done something to me. It had planted a seed of humility in my soul, a deep and honest recognition of who I was and what made me into a valued person.

I had suffered enough having my identity defined by the prestige of my job. The mental equation had cost me my health, my happiness, nearly my emotional sanity. I now knew that it mattered not what one *did*, but what one *was*. I was determined to make my job fun for myself and for the kids.

I greeted them cheerfully, took interest in their activities, joked around with them. I conscripted mothers to volunteer for the program and got them to join the spirit. Always good with people on a one-to-one basis, I received positive vibes from the kids and the mothers alike.

"Mrs. Brody," one mother greeted me laughingly one day, "You're the most popular figure in the school. My third grader had to write a composition about what she wanted to be when she grew up and she said she wanted to be a nit-lady!"

It took an extra measure of courage to face the eighth graders, my former seventh-grade students, but I crossed that bridge too. It was easier, dealing with them one at a time, in a setting that was supposed to be relaxed. Ironically, they suddenly appeared timid and shy. What nit-checking could effect!

At home, I prepared a poster-sized adorable caricature of a terrified louse being banished by a scowling nit-checker. I hung the colorful sign over my little corner. After all, I was also entitled to put out a shingle, even if the letters M.D. didn't quite fit.

I saw the principal smile with amusement when she noticed the sign. "You did that?" she asked incredulously. "I didn't know you were artistic! We're desperate for someone to do the monthly bulletin boards."

And thus, I became officially promoted from nit-checker to interior decorator. Make that educational interior decorator. In no time, I became a popular member in the office and the teachers' room and began to bond with the staff in the personal way I had so missed the year before. I've gotten to know many mothers and I have an excellent rapport with the students.

Our private minutes together lend themselves to a very unique kind of relationship. The kids' defenses are down; I'm not a person of authority. They feel comfortable airing their frustrations and I'm glad to lend a listening ear.

No, I'm not a teacher, but I certainly am a student of life.

I've paid a steep price for my tutorial, the price of humiliation and shame and misery. But I've learned. The ultimate success and failure of any venture is in Hashem's hands. Sometimes He deems us worthy of reaping the rewards of our efforts, and sometimes He makes us taste the humbling pill of defeat.

Dignity, however, is what one does with that failure. It is the ability to shake the mud off one's clothing, and start the painstaking climb all the way up from the bottom again.

And one doesn't have to ever reach the top.

As long as one is climbing, he is a person of stature.

Breaking the Pattern

"Mooooomy!"

Bleary eyed, I glance at the alarm clock on the night table beside my bed. Two a.m. Basya must be having a nightmare. My head sinks into my pillow for just another split second of sleep, just another whiff of oblivion, before I spring out of bed to comfort her.

No need. Soft padding of little feet. The velvety brush of a furry blanket and the groan of the mattress springs, as a cuddly little figure snuggles up close.

"Mommy."

There is relief in her voice, as her hand gropes under the cover to feel my reassuring presence. I hug her to me and stroke her hair. "Mommy loves you, Basya; was that a scary dream?"

I make room for her in my bed. Though it is 2 o'clock in the morning, and I'm exhausted, my heart expands. I feel an old scar healing just a tiny bit more.

When I was Basya's age, I suffered from nightmares too. But they were living nightmares. And I didn't dream of crying out "Mommy" the way Basya so instinctively does. Oh no, I didn't dare.

My Mommy *was* my nightmare.

Tall and unpredictable and volatile, my mother was the monster in my life. Squeezing my eyes shut against my fear, I'd shrivel under the covers as she went into one of her hysterical rants. It was all I could do to hope she wouldn't get close to my room. I had only myself to turn to in the caverns of my big, dark room. And myself was a frightened, vulnerable little girl who had not a clue what the words love or security meant.

My mother suffered, and still suffers from, bipolar disorder.

I don't know when the exact diagnosis was made, but she has had fluctuating phases of mania and depression ever since I've known her. Her manic stages would come in fits of unreasonable rage, as if a steamroller had entered her personage, steering her on a crazed route of violence and wreckage. During those days, she would vent her fury and frustration on the most hapless victim in her path: me.

On other days, just as unpredictably as the tempest storm that had preceded them, I would come home to a dark dreary house. The lights would be out, the shutters drawn, and my mother would be hovering like a gloomy cloud, slumped in a chair or lying in bed, motionless. She wouldn't so much as acknowledge my entrance, as I sadly put away my briefcase and sat down to do my homework.

I don't know which was worse, the melancholic apathy or the seething fury, but one thing was sure; never did I get the tiniest taste of what it meant to be loved, to be missed, to be welcomed by the affectionate, giving person other people called a mother.

Now, through my retrospective adult lens, I can try and separate illness from the person who inflicted so much pain on me as I was growing up. I can recognize, if only intellectually, that somewhere in the recesses of her heart, unaffected by the malady that distorted her sentiments, she really did want the best for me.

Back then, though, as a frightened little child growing up without siblings, I couldn't possibly make sense of my mother. For me, there were no formal introductions to the world of mental illness. I never had the chance to meet the symptoms of bipolar disorder in a textbook, to study them through the safe distance of a laboratory lens. I was born into the vise of its terrifying grip.

My mother came into marriage weighed down by a generation or more of emotional baggage. Her father had suffered from depression for many years and her brother had ended his life. The family had lived on welfare and her parents had gotten divorced when she was a teenager. Her difficult childhood left its marks and by the time she grew older, she was plagued by a host of fears and phobias. When she met my father, she was already a prisoner to her violent mood swings.

My father was the one ray of sunshine in my life. A gentle and loving soul, he lived at my mother's side and tried to navigate the unpredictable waters of our existence. It is to him that I owe any semblance of normalcy that I had growing up. Actually, it is to him I owe my very existence.

After they married, my father looked forward to building a family. My mother, however, aware of her shortcomings, was terrified of the prospect. She knew that in her depressed, confused state, she didn't possess the tools to nurture tender children. My father pleaded and cajoled, begged and encouraged. My mother agreed to seek help so she would be better prepared for motherhood.

Today, there is more awareness of mental illness and its causes. With medication and willpower, a patient with bipolar disorder can keep his mood swings under control. Back then, though, things were different. Though my mother went for therapy, her condition was never properly diagnosed or treated. She had long sessions with a therapist, presumably plumbing the depths of her subconscious, yet was never prescribed the medication she so badly needed. Years passed, and still there were no children on the horizon.

Along with therapy, my mother decided to pursue a degree. In her mind, a college-educated woman had better chances of being a competent mother. Ironically, the key she sought was nowhere in the tomes of physics or language arts. It was lost somewhere within her very own soul.

After 15 years of marriage, when the sand in the timer had nearly run out, my father finally prevailed. At 40 years old, my mother gave birth to their first and only child, a little baby daughter. Thus, my dubious destiny began.

I have the murkiest memories of my very early childhood. There is one thing, though, that I know for certain. I was never cuddled, hugged, or even held by my mother. My bottles were propped or held by my father in the scant hours he spent at home. Though he loved me dearly and openly demonstrated his affection, he had built a protective world for himself. He had thrown himself into his career as an engineer, and was usually absent from the house. My mother, the natural primary caretaker, remained detached and aloof, and perceived my crying as a deliberate hindrance to her freedom.

So it was that the first word that came out of my little mouth directed all my adoration to the one person I knew really treasured my existence: Daddy. I instinctively saved my antics for him when he came home; around my mother I quickly learned to suppress my curiosity and mischief and behave as close to an angel as any little toddler ever behaved.

Not that it seemed to help much. None of the rules that governed the cause and effect in most children's lives seemed to hold any relevance for me. I could be the sweetest little girl, dressing myself and eating my cereal down to the last spoon, and still evoke a violent tirade. My mother would call me stupid and lazy, blaming me for anything and everything that went wrong. Then I could pout and mope all I liked and inexplicably, the harangue would come to an end.

That, in recollection, the utter unpredictability of my mother's whims, was the most frightening aspect of my childhood. Children crave consistency. Even children of normal parents become confused and insecure when their normal routine is disrupted. For me, there was no normalcy and no routine. It was like walking through a spooky house, blindfolded, never sure of what lay around the next bend. From the youngest age, I'd wake up in the morning and tiptoe out of bed, carefully checking the coast for signs of the day's emotional forecast.

I remember being about 4 or 5, when my parents took in an exchange student to board with us. Her name was Ann, and I was absolutely delighted when my mother told me she was my older sister. I had so badly craved a sibling, any sibling, and though I had thought that they only came in the form of newborn babies, if Heaven had sent me an older sister, my joy knew no bounds.

I walked the streets, my hand proudly linked in Ann's, introducing all my friends to my older sister. I showed her my private little knickknacks and even let her use my pillow. I had finally found an island of comfort, an older sister whom I could learn to trust.

After two weeks, I came home from school to find that Ann had vanished. Just like that, with no warning, the older sister whom I had grown attached to was whisked off the board of my life. My mother looked at me frostily and offered no explanation. Ann was gone. She had been there yesterday, an integral part of my life, and today she was no more. Just like the rest of my existence, precarious and uncertain, prone to the winds of my mother's impulses.

Though my father tried his best to infuse me with his love, he was trapped himself. Trying to salvage his own sanity while carefully skirting my mother's quirks, he would try to smooth over my aching hurt with bland clichés: "It's not that bad," "She doesn't really mean it," "Don't take it to heart."

It wasn't only love and security that were absent in my life. My mother was so wrapped up in her neurotic fears, she had no presence of mind left to teach me the very basics of organization and personal hygiene, the things most mothers impart without even being aware of it.

It was from comments tossed unwittingly by friends that I slowly learned to shower consistently, to brush my teeth and cut my nails, to wash my hair and have it cut from time to time. I was a keen observer and picked up the subtle cues in my social environment. It didn't take long for me to learn that my house was a source of embarrassment and shame.

Though my father earned a comfortable living for a family of three, my mother held on to her imagined belief that we were decrepitly poor, a hangover from her impoverished childhood. She scrimped on every drop of water, neglecting to flush the toilet and letting mold grow in the shower stalls. The state of the house revolted me, and I cringed at the thought of inviting friends inside. Other than my closest friend, an asset I fortunately had, I never harbored a thought of letting classmates visit my home.

Even outside my house, though I tried my best to look neat and put together, I was ashamed of my appearance. My mother, locked in her notion that we couldn't afford the basic necessities, refused to buy me clothing. She accepted hand-me-downs from some pitying neighbors, outmoded and outgrown articles of clothing that I was loathe to wear.

When she finally did relent and agreed to take me shopping, she always bought two sizes larger than I needed, convinced that she was getting the most for her money. A self-conscious teenager, I walked around in these sloppy outfits, my ears burning with shame. My pleas for nice, normal clothes like all my friends wore fell on deaf ears. My mother was impervious to the ocean of hurt lapping within my soul.

When I turned 16, she treated me in honor of my birthday. It was one of those isolated demonstrations of her bizarre sense of love that stands out in my memory. She took me to an exclusive department store and went on an extravagant binge, buying me thousands of dollars worth of jewelry: gold necklaces, diamond pendants and bracelets, a silver and onyx brooch, a sapphire ring. It was benevolence bordering on lunacy, completely out of character and completely out of proportion.

Neither my father nor I, however, had any hope of making her see the almost comical absurdity of the situation. I was walking around in virtual rags, imploring her for the most basic clothing, while she was plying me with jewelry fit for a princess. If only I could have cashed in some of those diamonds for normal sweaters and T-shirts, shoes, boots, and coats. My mother's perverted logic, however, didn't allow for such exchanges.

While I was growing up, it wasn't unusual for me to come home to an empty house. Of course, no warning or explanation ever preceded these sporadic absences. My mother would simply disappear for the day, checking into some hotel, and leaving me to wonder about her whereabouts. I always felt somehow responsible for her disappearances, as if I'd somehow overburdened her into escaping.

It wasn't guilt born of imagination. My mother gave me good reason to think I was selfish and inconsiderate, stupid, uncaring, and incompetent. She generally scowled at me, lashing out at my friends, or else gave me the silent treatment for days. When I was in my late teens, my mother disappeared one day at the beginning of the summer. I took her disappearance in stride, sure that she would surface again, raging or sulking, within a day or two. This time, however, I was in for a surprise. My mother had flown off to Israel, leaving my father and me alone for the summer.

At first, I felt angry and deserted. As much as she was virtually nonfunctional, I still liked to harbor the childish illusion that I had a mother. The fact that she could walk out on me for two months without any qualms shattered that notion into a million shards all over again.

Before long, however, my sense of abandonment gave way to a feeling of euphoria. My mother was gone, abroad, safely out of range for two whole months. I took a deep breath and filled my lungs with the intoxicating scent of freedom. I could do what I wanted, invite my friends over, eat what I pleased, wear what I felt like. It was almost too good to be true.

My closest friend came over and we got to work, furiously cleaning the house. I couldn't believe how good the bathrooms could smell, how neat the kitchen could look, how inviting the living room could seem when the heavy drapes were parted and the sun was allowed in. We reveled in the new look, in the sweet fun of conspiracy, in the joint effort of working together.

Like a shadow never really lifting long enough to let the warmth settle, my mother called from Israel to tell me she had left me something very important. Despite my mind's admonitions, my heart fluttered with fragile anticipation, with the faint illusion that I was about to touch the fleeting flower of love. I gingerly removed the lid of the pot where my mother had instructed me to look for her parting gift.

I don't know what I expected to find; actually, I think I deliberately didn't speculate. For once, I had wanted to indulge in the delicious suspense of receiving a gift, something my mother had cared enough to leave behind as a surprise. What I discovered beneath that lid was like a kettle of hot water on an ice sculpture, melting my dreams in a minute.

It was a book, 80 pages long, written in my mother's penmanship: her lifelong legacy to her only daughter. It was a long, disjointed exposition on life, colored by her paranoiac view of people and of the world in general. She described this world as a dark and dangerous place, a bumpy road where peril lurked just around every corner and behind every bend.

She went on to exhort me that none of my friends really loved me or even liked me, that they only manipulated me with their own benefit in mind, and that I'd better beware. She listed my friends and classmates and brought proofs that they were all traitors who were secretly conspiring to see my downfall.

By the time I had gotten through a few pages, I was sick to my stomach. Gone was the silken ruffle of love that had palpated my soul just moments before. In its place was a sour pit, an oversized lump of rejection lodged in the middle of my throat. Sitting crosslegged on the kitchen floor, I fought tears of disappointment and disgust, tears for the love that never was, for the pain that would always be.

At that point, I was already attending college, and was trying to make a life for myself. It took every bit of effort on my part. When I'd leave our home in Florida for the semester, my mother would never accompany me to the airport, or even to the car. She'd stand stony faced at the door, like some prison warden letting her charge out on parole, and wordlessly stick out her hand to retrieve my personal set of house keys until I returned. Though it became a ritual, I wasn't spared the humiliation and pain each time anew.

One summer, when I was 20, I was in a terrible car accident in Syracuse, New York. I suffered multiple fractures and was hospitalized in the Intensive Care Unit. My parents were immediately notified of my condition. Though I was all alone, with no phone or any human connection other than the nurses in the ward, my mother insisted that they didn't need to come be at my side, so long as their intervention wasn't medically necessary.

Several of my friends later told me how badly they had wanted to come be with me during those difficult days. A visit meant airfare; however, their parents felt that it was my parents', and not their, duty to be at my bedside. Thus I was left abandoned in the hospital, my body badly injured, my heart broken beyond repair.

After two weeks, when I was about to be discharged, my parents finally arrived. Though my condition had drastically improved, I was not a very lovely sight. My mother took a look at me and emphatically declared that I wasn't fit to travel. No matter how hard the doctor tried to persuade her that I was ready to go home, she stuck to her stand.

She insisted that we check into a hotel for a month before we flew home. Feeling weak and vulnerable, I broke down in sobs. I didn't have much of a home, but the little bit of it that was mine, my own blanket and pillow and the familiar window over my bed, beckoned longingly after the traumatic ordeal I'd been through.

My mother shrugged, and went ahead with the check-in, leaving my father to fly home with me. I arrived home, weak and dispirited, crushed once again by my mother's indifference. She stayed a few days at the hotel, just to prove her point, and then came home.

When a month had passed, and my bones had healed enough to begin physiotherapy, my mother suddenly switched gears. She maintained that I had rested enough and demanded that I leave immediately for college. I looked at her in disbelief. My arm was immobile, and I was barely able to get around with a bad limp. Was this the same woman who had refused me entry to my home only four weeks ago on the premise that I was too weak to fly?

If there is one thing I learned from that bitter experience, it is that bones, no matter how severely fractured, are more easily healed than a crushed spirit.

Breaking the Pattern / 235

I graduated college with honors and went on to law school. I did well at my studies and had a devoted circle of friends. Still, as diligent and successful as I ever was, my view of myself and of the world was shaded by my mother's warped perceptions. My soul had been feeding on slow poison for years; I was a victim of emotional toxemia. Much as I tried to muffle the impact, I couldn't get rid of the accusing echoes of my mother's condemnations.

In fact my very decision to pursue law, an odd choice for someone soft and emotionally predisposed like me, was inspired by the closest thing to a compliment I had ever heard from my mother. "You argue so well," she would say cynically, "you would make a great lawyer." Though it was meant as a put-down, to a child starved for some sense of self, it became incorporated as an attribute.

Ironically, it was her own unreasonable demands and baseless accusations that forced me to resort to arguing. I knew there was no talking to her emotions, so I tried to appeal to her rational sense. What I didn't realize was that in my mother's world, there *was* no rational sense. She refuted all my arguments with her own upside-down logic, and if I ever did get her to see the validity of my point, she would punish me harshly for having won the round.

Fortunately, I had one priceless blessing in my life, the single anchor that remained stable despite the ongoing turbulence: my closest friend. We had bonded naturally as soon as we had met at age 9, and had remained faithful to each other throughout the years. She was privy to my deepest darkest secrets, and accepted me as I was. It was she who kept me from losing faith in myself, from succumbing to the negativity and pain festering inside my soul.

During the second year of law school, my friend began showing an interest in *Yiddishkeit*. Though it didn't put a barrier between us, it took me another full year until I followed in her footsteps.

Yiddishkeit opened a new door for me. Though I had always known I was Jewish, I had never realized the significance of the role it played in my life. As I slowly became acquainted with the world of Torah, I began to appreciate that religious observance wasn't a fastidious obsession with rules and rituals dating years back. It was a vibrant way of life, an exquisite formula designed to guide each and every individual through his personal struggle to grow.

Taking the first step in my break from the past, I enrolled in Neve seminary, and spent a year in Yerushalayim. Like a wilting plant transplanted from the arid desert conditions to fertile soil, I drank thirstily, absorbing the new attitudes permeating the lectures, imbibing the restorative warmth of the Yerushalayim air.

It was the beginning of a long and arduous healing process, a process of setting emotional and spiritual fractures that had grown warped and gnarled by years of neglect and abuse.

After a year in this therapeutic cast, my spirit had sufficiently healed to begin my lifelong therapy. I wasn't kidding myself; experience had shown me that corrective therapy was grueling work that took a superhuman amount of determination and grit. Still, I was resolved that with Hashem's help, I would be able to overcome the hurdles and plant a productive future where my rocky past lay buried.

As if Heaven was waving me on, I met my husband shortly thereafter, my faithful partner and forbearing therapist. Together, we embarked on our mission.

I cannot say it's been smooth sailing. Grit and determination are potent tools, but the weeds of constant and repeated negative messages have dug roots deeper and tougher than the hardiest spades. For me, it's a path of constant vigilance; no matter how far I've trodden, I can never afford to slacken off and revert to old, ingrained attitudes.

It's a struggle each and every day to believe in myself and in the people around me. With the unwavering support of my husband and the help of a wise therapist, I have learned to trust that I am indeed a capable and loving person, a devoted wife and competent mother.

It took years of sorting through the garbage of my upbringing before I was able to see the world as a safe place, and the people around me as kind and trustworthy. No matter how ludicrous I had always known my mother's fears were, no matter how wounded I had been by her verbal lashing, the child inside me had still viewed her as the significant adult whose truths were indisputable.

As a mother of a lovely family, I find comfort and peace in nurturing my beautiful children. There is strength in breaking a chain, especially when those shackles have held your family hostage for several generations.

If there is one belief I live with, it is that a person's past does not inevitably determine his destiny. Indeed, it is unimaginably difficult to wrench oneself away from one's roots, to record a new melody in place of a persistent erosive rhythm, but it is possible. Each morning is a new opportunity, each situation a new chance, and we all have it within us to choose life, thus beginning a brand new chain.

My children do not know what enormous reservoirs of strength I have had to draw from in order to function as a normal, loving mother. They take it for granted that they can play and make noise, bicker and cry, cut and paste, laugh and invite friends. They don't pay a thought to the fact that breakfast, lunch, and supper appear on the table every single day, that their mother is there to hug them when they come home from school, that they are disciplined with love and sensitivity when they need to be guided.

Yet their blissful unawareness doesn't make me feel unappreciated or resentful. It is actually the sweetest reward of my painstaking struggle to rise above the odds.

The fact that my children are positive and healthy, that they do not bear any vestige of my old scars, that they are returning my love and laughter, my encouragement and affection, all that, to me, is the delicious purity of the unpolluted air at the top of the mountain.

Unexpected Roadblock

"*Why is she repeating the* Rashi?" I remember thinking in annoyance, as my tenth-grade teacher explained a difficult *Rashi* yet again. *Can't we move on?*

I was one of those bright kids who got the gist of things the first time around, got annoyed the second time around, and was doing a crossword puzzle under my desk by the third repetition.

When our teachers returned our graded papers in order of performance, (cruel, but actually common, practice 18 years ago), I naturally listened for my name at the top of the list. The question was whether I would receive my paper first or second; it never went past that.

The funny thing was, I never perceived myself as being extraordinarily clever. The teacher explained the material and I understood it; I read the paragraph and I got the point. I knew no other reality.

Of course I was aware that some of my classmates grappled with math or spelling. And there were always those non-students who didn't participate in class discussions and never seemed to know which *pasuk* we were reading. Like most struggles that don't touch home base, though, I never paid much thought to those girls.

When I got engaged, our whole community rocked with excitement. Lazer Rothman was the *illui* of the yeshivah, the upcoming *Rashgabahag*. Wherever I went, I heard raving regards.

"My father-in-law claims your *chassan* is head and shoulders above the rest of the *shiur*. And my father-in-law doesn't just dispense compliments."

"Lazer Rothman? Is he the one who was in my brother Chaim Zev's class? He's a real genius! Well, actually, I forgot whom I'm talking to. I guess it's a *tzugepaste shidduch* (appropriate match)."

I remember fumbling to sound modest while I blushed with pride. I finally hit upon the right line.

"*Baruch Hashem*, we're very grateful."

"Well, you better get some advice on raising geniuses," well-wishers teased. I'd chuckle uncomfortably. It was awkward enough receiving personal compliments about a boy I'd hardly gotten to know; never mind children I didn't have yet.

When Hindy was born, my husband was a trifle disappointed she wasn't a boy. Of course, he was mature enough not to give voice to his feelings. We both knew such thoughts were frivolous. People poured their hearts out in prayer for a baby; any baby. Only a young couple boasting a baby on their first anniversary could fret, even fleetingly, about preferences of gender.

Still, Lazer had dreamed about his *bechor*, his shining star, the one who would learn to read at 3 and would be rattling off *mishnayos* by 5. "*Meila*," he resigned himself, "so she'll know how to *daven* at 3, and she'll be rattling off *chumash* at 5.

Little did we know.

Hindy was an adorable little baby. We watched in delight as she crawled around the house and learned to squeeze her chubby finger to her little nose on cue. She started to walk and talk pretty much on schedule to the applause of her proud parents and grandparents.

When Hindy entered first grade, I felt my heart flutter with excitement. Hindy was no longer our only child; she had a few siblings beneath her. Still, there is something about each first milestone with an oldest child that invites a tingle of emotion.

Hindy brought home her *nekudos* sheets and we hung expectantly on to her every syllable. Though she picked up the basics of reading with fairly little trouble, she definitely wasn't the genius of the class. Still, we were satisfied with her progress.

Second grade was unsettling for both Hindy and me. Six or seven weeks into the school year had me sitting over *parashah* questions with a frustrated 8-year old, trying to maintain my patience.

"Who was buried in the *Me'aras HaMachpelah*?"

"Uuum …" I'd encounter a befuddled expression.

"Come on, Hindy, think. Adam and …?"

"Um, Chavah?"

"Good. And who else?"

"Ummmm. Noach?"

"Nooo, One of the *Avos*."

"The *Avos*? Ummm. Avraham?"

"Good. And who else? Who was Avraham's wife?"

I sighed in exasperation, looking at the kitchen clock. This was only the third question; there were five more to go. If we continued at this rate, it would take us another half an hour to complete the questions. And there was more homework as well. *I better talk to her teacher,* I made a mental note. *Why do they give second graders such sophisticated assignments?*

When I met the teacher at a wedding the next week, I mentioned my concern. Wasn't it a bit much to expect second graders to complete five or six detailed *parashah* questions on their own?

"Look," Mrs. Miller replied. "It always takes a bit of time for the kids to get used to it, but if you noticed, we did the first few together in class. As the weeks go on, the kids will get the idea and be able to do it all on their own."

The weeks went by, but I saw no improvement. I was spending hours with Hindy doing homework.

"It's ridiculous," I complained to my mother, "they saddle these kids with much too much work. If homework in second grade takes over the whole household, what do they demand in high school?"

"Having a second grader nowadays is a full-time job," I would tell my friends only half in jest. "They flood them with sheets and assignments; the kids can't even keep track of their own briefcase."

Hindy's briefcase constantly looked like the typical executive's desk, cluttered with miscellaneous worksheets and old notices.

"Isn't this supposed to be in your *Chagim U'zmanim* notebook?" I'd ask her, pulling out a pleated paper from the bottom of the mess.

"Oh that?" Hindy would take the paper from me, her face puckered in strained confusion. "Yeah, I think so."

"I see it isn't filled in. Was it for homework?"

"Um, no. Yeah. I think so."

Now *I* was confused.

"Did you do this together in class or were you supposed to fill it in at home?"

Hindy blinked at me, as clueless as I was.

What was going on? Perhaps she was the typical absentminded professor, I thought optimistically. Something about the mystified look in Hindy's eyes, though, told me otherwise.

Somehow, we managed to flounder through second grade. Third grade was a slight relief. Mrs. Greenbaum, Hindy's teacher, was a laid-back, easygoing *bubby*, who reassured me that Hindy seemed to be one of those late bloomers who just took longer to catch on. When I mentioned her atrocious spelling, Mrs. Greenbaum dismissed my concerns.

"Spelling is inborn; you either have a knack for it or you don't. I don't think it's any indication of intelligence."

In the meantime, Sarah Baila, our second daughter, had entered pre-1a. Unlike Hindy, who had picked up the *aleph-beis* with ease, Sarah Baila seemed to be playing a guessing game.

"What's this?" I would patiently prompt her, and Sarah Baila would squint at the letter. "*Beis*?"

I would moan in frustration. This was not the way I had envisioned reviewing *aleph-beis* with my children. What was happening to my geniuses? Schools nowadays were so anxious to cover, cover, cover. What was the point of rushing ahead if the kids hadn't fully mastered the material?

When Hindy hit fourth grade, her progress had slowed down to a tedious crawl. The tension in the house became palpable, as I tried to tackle hours of homework and studying amid the thousand other demands of a hectic household.

Hindy hated going to school. Every day was a fight.

"Hindy!" I would call in alarm, "It's 8 o'clock; your bus is coming in 10 minutes. Why aren't you dressed?"

"My stomach hurts," she would whine, doubling over her pillow. "I can't go to school today."

Oh no, I'd feel myself tighten, *she can't do this. I have to be out of the house in 20 minutes.*

"Come on, Hindy," I'd cajole. "Hurry up and get dressed. I'll make you a tea."

"I can't; I can't. My stomach really hurts."

I forced myself to take a deep breath as the tension mounted inside me.

"I'll write you a note. If your stomach still hurts by lunchtime, you can call me."

Hindy made no indication of moving. She lay on her bed whining reluctantly.

I felt like I was going to explode. The baby was screaming to be held, Sarah Baila still needed her tights, and Motty wanted me to stand at the window so I could wave goodbye to him as he walked to the bus stop.

"Please, Hindy," I strained to control myself, as I stuffed pampers and a bottle into the diaper bag. "I have to be out of the house in a few minutes. If you get dressed real quickly, I'll give you a treat for recess time."

By the time I got to my high-school job at 8:30, Hindy's stomachache had caught up with me. My insides were a mess from the stress of the morning, my mind was frazzled and unfocused.

Why was Hindy always suffering from morning ailments? Why did she go into slow motion just when I was in such a hurry to get everyone out and leave for my job? Something was very wrong in school, even if I was loath to admit it.

I set out for the first PTA meeting, my taut smile belying the knot I felt in my stomach. I was a successful *Ivris* teacher in a well-known high school; my husband was learning in an elite *kollel* for gifted *yungerleit;* everyone around me just assumed I had come to reap my yearly *nachas* report. I walked into the classroom with a forced confidence in my step.

"Hindy's a very sweet girl," the teacher started out with a smile.

Yees? I thought, holding my breath. A teacher myself, I knew too well what "very sweet girls" translated into.

"She is mature and responsible and I can see she puts a lot of effort into her work." She shuffled through a few sheets, nodding to herself. "I can't put my finger on it, but she definitely seems to have a problem."

That's it. She had said it, given that daunting word to my niggling intuition. Hindy had a problem.

"I've noticed that her briefcase is in a constant state of disarray," I shared, suddenly anxious to contribute my own observation. "I was wondering if that was normal for a fourth grader."

"Well," her teacher chuckled, "messy briefcases are actually pretty typical of this age. What worries me is her disorganization across the board.

"If I ever hand out several stencils at once, like before Yom Tov, or at the beginning of a new topic, she seems completely lost. She also has a hard time following instructions and is completely overwhelmed with the math."

"Hmm," was all I could summon. I felt as if someone had extinguished a bulb that had been flickering for some time. Although I had known that Hindy was struggling, there was a marked difference between blinking premonitions and the grim finality invoked by a teacher's assessment.

"If I were you, I'd take her for an evaluation," Mrs. Stein advised. "She does seem to be a bright child. If you could pinpoint her difficulties, we could more readily help her."

If I were you. How many times in my capacity as a teacher had I uttered those words? From my stance as a professional, they had always seemed to exude empathy born of the mutual concerns of motherhood.

As a mother, the innocuous two-letter preface, *if,* was all I heard. *If* set us apart by a million miles, put us into two very distinctive classes. No matter how she phrased it, she was *I,* the tactful teacher, and I was *you,* the helpless mother.

I wondered: Had I, in that teacher's place, ever felt the sour taste of disappointment and shame that was lodged in my throat right then?

Putting my feelings aside, I consulted with my friend Shulamis whom I knew had a learning disabled child. I had the sense of knocking on the door to a room I had always seen, but had never entered before. That was Shulamis's room, the room I had always admired her for gliding in and out of so naturally, but had silently disassociated myself from.

Shulamis gave me the name of the top person in the field, and shared some personal coping skills. I had heard these things before, but I had never felt the acute kinship I felt at that point.

The results of the evaluation were both enlightening and discouraging. Though we were told that Hindy was an auditory, and not a visual, learner, and that she had language processing problems coupled by perceptual difficulties, the evaluation was very ambiguous in terms of what could actually be done to improve her skills.

It had taken such courage and candor to face up to Hindy's problems and seek professional help; I had expected that my efforts would yield a remedy for, or at least the proposed treatment of, her learning difficulties. I was disillusioned to find that even the experts were still stymied by many of the mental quirks tossed into the basket termed "learning disabilities."

There was no magic, I learned, no tangible prescription like glasses or hearing aids that would pull Hindy out of her misery and "fix" her learning disabilities. As we plodded through the remainder of fourth grade, I was faced with the bitter realization that Hindy's schooling would require ongoing trial and error, vigilance and repetition, and mainly sweat, a lot of sweat.

Though I was nearing my own 10th year of teaching, I suddenly found myself ever so cognizant of the struggling student. In my capacity as a high school teacher, I was constantly privy to comments strewn unthinkingly by frustrated teachers.

"I don't know what to do with Frumy," a colleague of mine announced one day, plopping her briefcase onto a chair. "As many times as I tell her that I want her to stick to the lines on the answering sheet, she always writes these long, rambling answers. What does she think; that I'm supposed to read a rewritten rendition of her notes and find the right answer somewhere along the way? That's it; I'm grading the first two lines of her answer and that's all."

I blushed. Was it a trick of my mind that I heard Hindy where she had said Frumy? My cheeks burned for Frumy's privacy and pride carelessly infringed upon in the name education. Not that I professed to be beyond making a mistake. I knew that no teacher deliberately inflicted pain. My own injured soul, however, winced instinctively at the flippancy of her tone.

Most teachers, I found, had been successful students themselves and had no concept of what it meant to be academically challenged. Hindy's own Hebrew teacher was a former student of mine, fresh out of seminary. She had been a straight A student all her life and had sailed through school.

Consequently, she had little understanding of what it took from a girl like Hindy to complete a simple set of *Chumash* questions. She had no inkling of the social stigma that accompanied having a tutor, the shame of receiving a special test, the emotional energy that went into guarding these secrets. *

Hindy was a bright 11-year-old girl who desperately wanted to fit in. She was a child who was frustrated beyond words trying to decipher a relentless jumble of facts and figures that never seemed to daunt her friends. She was a responsible oldest, brimming with common sense, whose cousins wouldn't dream had any difficulty in school.

Hindy's teacher, however, a young nineteen-year-old success story, saw a kid who doodled on her desk, looked at her in confusion when it was her turn to read *Rashi*, and handed in half-blank tests.

It hurt. It hurt to have my pride stripped in the face of my own student, hurt to see Hindy misunderstood and unappreciated by her teacher. Hindy worked so much harder than most of those honor students. She put in hours doing homework, walked to her tutor, rain or shine, and spent the bulk of her vacation studying. Was effort really awarded in our system, I wondered, or was it a tribute synonymous with academic failure?

In the meantime, my second daughter, Sarah Baila, was floundering in second grade. When her pre-1a teacher had allayed our concerns regarding her confusion with the *aleph-beis*, we had readily grabbed at her reassurances. After all, we were two exceptionally intelligent parents. Though we had no biological explanation for Hindy's disabilities, we had reasoned that anything could happen once. We didn't even entertain the thought that both of our daughters could possibly be learning disabled.

Unlike Hindy, Sarah Baila was a difficult child. She had a hard time obeying and easily flew off her handle. When she didn't catch on in first grade, we attributed her difficulties to her excitable nature.

"She likes action," her teacher had chuckled. "She'd much rather listen to the janitor drilling in the hall than repeat the *nekudos*."

In our desperation to smooth out the bumps, we accepted her logic. We repeated first grade in the hope that Sarah Baila would mature and things would fall into place.

Sarah Baila just about made it into second grade. That's when the trouble began. On the fourth day of school, Sarah Baila came home in a violent mood.

"What happened?" I tried to coax.

"My teacher said that if I'm so interested in what's going on outside, then I can stay there until I'm ready to come back in."

Sarah Baila was humiliated and hurt. From there, it was a downslide into a spiral of disruptive behavior, sarcastic barbs, and miserably failing schoolwork. We both sensed that Sarah Baila's problems weren't as benign as we would have liked to believe. As much as that recognition hurt, remaining indifferent to it was hurting Sarah Baila even more. Armed with the references we had painstakingly researched for Hindy, we had her evaluated.

When Sarah Baila was diagnosed with ADHD complicated by language-related disabilities I felt like my world was crumbling. What was happening to the family of my dreams, the children of my fantasies? How could two of my four school-aged children be suffering from disabilities when both my husband and I had no family history of anything remotely related?

These were questions I would learn to deal with in time. In the meantime, I had to handle the practical and emotional aspects of doing what was best for my children.

A specialist recommended that we pull Sarah Baila out of the school she was attending and enroll her in a framework targeted at learning disabled children. We were reluctant to take the step. There were so many stigmas attached to these specialized schools, so much misunderstanding in the community at large.

Still, our love for Sarah Baila and our concern for her welfare prevailed. As opposed to Hindy's difficulties which were solely academic and were perceptible only in the classroom, Sarah Baila's behavior required skilled management. It hurt my heart to see her being mishandled by teachers who weren't equipped to deal with her. While I didn't blame her teachers, I knew it was unfair to leave Sarah Baila in a setting that brought out the worst in her.

Unexpected Roadblock / 247

Evaluations can be neatly categorized and graphed. Children can never be compartmentalized that way. Although Sarah Baila's problems were in large part behavioral, and Hindy's difficulties appeared primarily academic, Hindy's social development suffered too. She became withdrawn and self-conscious, terrified of having her inner world exposed.

"Hey Hindy," I'd see her classmate, Chana Leah, call to her as she walked past the neighboring driveway, "You want to join our Chinese jump rope game?"

I'd feel my heart expand. I knew Hindy was dreaming of Chana Leah's friendship. I held my breath.

"I can't," Hindy would mumble, breaking into a run. I recognized the cornered expression in her eyes. She was on her way to her tutor and couldn't risk being discovered. Not at any price, even if it meant giving up a coveted prospect of friendship.

From my vantage point on the front porch, I watched Chana Leah shrug, before she resumed the game. How could an 11-year-old realize that clumsiness and lack of courtesy were sometimes born of naked fear? I'd feel my heart contract with the unfairness of it. Another lost opportunity.

My insides ached for Hindy. She was such a delightful child at home, such a sensitive oldest daughter. She folded laundry like a pro, created the most artful craft projects, and kept the little ones enchanted with her stories. She'd leave me open mouthed with her analyses of the other kids' needs, or of my relationship with each of my siblings.

In school, however, she was a nonentity: a flower fated to wither in the harsh climate of the system, a song whose rhythm was not in sync with the beat determined by the board of education. And I was the mother watching that flower shrivel and wilt, listening to those notes fade out and die.

"How do you take the pain?" I asked my friend Shulamis. "How do you watch a kid wallow through the days, counting the hours until the next recess break, the next Chanukah vacation, the next summer reprieve? When I watch Hindy, something inside me crumbles. How many *adults* could stick to a job they were really miserable at, year after year, without breaking down?"

Shulamis was quiet. I heard the sadness in her silence, the silence of a mother suffering for her child. She knew, like I did, the pain of pushing time, of waiting for a kid's childhood to be up so he or she could really start living.

After a short lapse, though, Shulamis perked up. She was not one to lie flat for long.

"It isn't easy, it really isn't. I couldn't have gotten where I am without help, help from Above and practical help from right here below. I have a suggestion; how about consulting a social worker?"

My initial reaction was to flinch. Social workers were for people with problems, people who didn't have their lives together. I was a capable, intelligent mother with a handle on life. I'd been mature enough to own up to my children's problems. What did I need a social worker for?

"Think of her as any professional," Shulamis urged me. "You wouldn't attempt to close on a house without a lawyer, you wouldn't diagnose pneumonia without a doctor. Your kids' futures are at stake here; if a professional has the tools to help you, why should you attempt to tackle it on your own?"

I acquiesced to her logic. It was like removing a deeply embedded splinter from my own flesh. Every time I went near my old notions with the tweezers, I felt myself reflexively jumping back. How could I cut away those layers of resistance, of pride and self-sufficiency, of social anxieties? There were so many sensitive nerve endings there. I couldn't see myself doing it.

Inhaling deeply, I took the plunge. I punched the numbers on my phone and waited for a ring. *There*, I thought, trying to still my racing heart, *just another moment and the splinter will be out.*

The social worker, like the specialists preceding her, had no instant potion to offer, no magic formula that would turn things around so that they ended happily ever after. Still, from that first meeting on, she has given me a new lease on life. She has helped me see my challenges from a fresh perspective, has helped me listen to the innermost whispers of my soul, where my true calling lies.

Children, I've learned, aren't our own handiwork. They aren't a measure of our talent or success and they aren't subject to our personal preferences. They are gifts from Above, individually crafted and lovingly bestowed. They are born with a design imprinted on their souls, and the precise package of supplies they will need to complete that design.

We don't create our children's destiny; we follow it. We cannot preclude the challenges that make up their tapestries; we can only use our own set of provisions to help them embroider their lives.

I have had to tell myself these truths over and over again, have had to study them as I've watched my nieces bring home honor certificates, as I've heard my fellow teachers boast of their children's achievements. I've had to repeat them fervently as I've watched a neighbor stare at the logo on Sarah Baila's school bus, as I've braced myself for my colleagues to teach Hindy on her first day of ninth grade.

And I've learned, also, to redefine my definition of success. People hit roadblocks at different points in their lives. Some of us glide through our formative years, barely stopping for a red light. We sit back, score hundreds, receive honors, and land the most prestigious jobs. We get engaged to the catch of the yeshivah, and then, inevitably, we hit those roadblocks that slow us down.

They could be potholes dug by the abrasion of time, they could be the result of construction taking place, or an accident colliding with our fate. Or they could be the simple strains of making ends meet and caring for a family, struggles with which we were never properly outfitted to cope.

And right there, on the opposite lane, are those drivers who have been thrust against the swerves of life early on. They've gripped the steering wheel and bounced with the lurches along the road, sweating to master the most basic skills. They've learned to challenge the impossible, to cultivate sensitivity for others, to appreciate the value of something hard earned.

And just when the cars in our lane are grinding to a halt, those drivers on the other side pick up speed. They've emerged from their tunnel and are ready to sail ahead, ready to travel the road they have waited so long to conquer.

My Hindy may not drive the sleekest model, and Sarah Baila may have to wage a mighty struggle until she gets onto the thruway.

When they get there, however, they will be spared the painstaking plodding I have had to endure, the shock of the collision with the uphill side of life.

And until they get there, I'll be learning.

My children may not be star students, but they have been my most powerful teachers.

I feel it unfair to write this without mentioning the special teachers who have shown extraordinary sensitivity in dealing with Hindy. One particular teacher thought of a novel idea to spare Hindy the embarrassment of receiving a special test.

Instead of handing out the tests to be taken in the usual manner, she went through the pains of pre-labeling each test paper and handing them out in alphabetical order. That way no one would notice a girl who received a different test than her classmates. I was deeply touched by her ingenuity and have since adopted this practice in my own classroom. Isn't preserving a student's self-image worth a few minutes of time?

From the Depths

I was never naive. I knew all about mountain climbers from the stories. An avid reader, I read just about anything in print; books, pamphlets, solicitation letters, cereal boxes. And as a reflection of the turbulent times, I knew about childless couples and older singles, widows and orphans, single parents, sick children. In fact, as I got older, I almost wondered, with a faint tinge of apprehension, why my own life seemed so picture perfect.

As the sixth child of a large and happy family, I grew up with a fabulous support system; warm and loving parents who were living role models, siblings who had complete confidence in me, and friends who were there in need and in deed. My heart cried for those girls who came from dysfunctional homes, for the learning disabled and the socially inept.

I excelled in school, both socially and academically. I spoke at my eighth-grade graduation and then went on to high school. Those were some of the sweetest years in my life. Aside from the learning, which I loved, I formed close, lasting relationships and my class bonded in a special way.

We weren't the usual conglomeration of adolescent cliques and petty politics; our class fused as a rich and wholesome unit and we were held up as an example to the rest of the high school. I still feel a twinge of nostalgia when I think about it now, how we reveled in those deep friendships and the esteem in which the entire school held us.

Once again I was chosen to speak at graduation and then it was off to seminary. I had been accepted into the seminary of my choice, a prestigious one-year program in Eretz Yisrael. That year put a clasp on my high-school experience; it was a year full of learning and growth, a year that fine-tuned my sense of awareness and filled my spiritual oxygen tank for the pending journey called life.

I came back home, full of it all. Full of the *kedushah* of Eretz Yisrael, full of the idealistic breath of seminary, full of excitement and anticipation to put it all into practice. The chance came soon enough. I landed a good teaching job, and just before the year was over, I became engaged to a wonderful boy.

As soon as *sheva berachos* were over, we began our new life in Lakewood, New Jersey, where my husband was, and still continues to be, a full-time *talmid* of Beis Medrash Govoha. I loved Lakewood from the start, and though we were one of hundreds of *kollel* couples, I never felt like a nameless stereotype. I felt, and still feel, truly blessed, privileged to be able to support a husband whose primary preoccupation is Torah.

I took advantage of the spiritually fertile soil of Lakewood. I found a weekly *shiur*, which I attended faithfully and was offered a teaching position in one of the local Beis Yaakovs. Although I wasn't very experienced at the outset, the warm atmosphere in the school, and the encouragement of my principal and coworkers gave me the confidence to accept the position. I thank Hashem to this very day.

Within the first year of our marriage, I gave birth to a baby boy, followed in close succession by a girl and another boy. As I looked around the house at my little treasures, I felt so keenly aware of my blessings. What more could a girl ask for? A loving supportive, family, devoted husband, precious children. A close circle of friends and neighbors, a good job, and to top it all off, I was living in Lakewood, the *ir haTorah*.

There was not a cloud in the sky, not a wisp of foreshadowing on the horizon. I took walks with my children, told them stories, picked flowers. I rose above my almost constant state of exhaustion and baked and read and sat on the floor building Lego with my little ones.

Imbued with an upbeat nature, I tried to make my home the happiest place to be. Though babies and toddlers can try the most patient person at times, I made an effort to see the humor in their antics, to brush aside the slight annoyances and focus on enjoying my abundant gifts.

My efforts paid off. Hearing the oldest one's lilting *berachos,* the middle one's barely decipherable "*gam zu l'tovah*," and the baby's happy giggles infused me with the most gratifying sense of success. My home was, indeed, a lively little nest, a place where healthy children were blossoming and growing, learning to appreciate Hashem and to love *Yiddishkeit*.

I walked around, feeling accomplished. I was succeeding at my job, I drew inspiration from my weekly *shiur,* and I felt I was doing my best at being a kind and considerate wife.

Nu, you're thinking, *so get to the point already; what happened?*

As an introduction to a mountain climber's article, all this seems like almost superfluous preamble to the necessary climax of the story. In real life, I harbored not an inkling of suspense, not a clue that the life I was living was anything but the point. I was happy and content, working hard, reaping results. How was I to know that a heavy fog lay right ahead, thick and gray, obscuring the rest of the landscape?

Unlike staged drama, it happened slowly, almost imperceptibly. I never saw the impending fog, dark and dense in the distance. I only sensed it once I was in it, hazy and indefinable all around me.

Nothing had changed, but life seemed different, darker, as if a shadow had intercepted my sun-drenched existence. I felt heavy, unmotivated, drained of my enthusiasm and zest.

Initially, I thought it was just a fleeting bad mood, the kind we are all privy to at one point or another. Perhaps I hadn't slept enough, or eaten properly, perhaps I hadn't gotten enough recognition for something I had done, or had experienced an especially stressful day at school.

Trying to trace my feelings, however, I couldn't find a single reason for them. Not a physical reason, and not a biological reason, not an emotional reason and not an intellectual reason. Everything seemed to be in perfect order, yet I couldn't brush away the almost tangible gloominess weighing down on my heart.

The obvious D word, the dooming, daunting, debilitating word, depression, didn't even cross my thoughts. Not that I didn't know it existed. I had read all about depression in the past. Depression, though, was far away, somewhere in crazyland, in that place where emotionally unbalanced people had to go for therapy and take medication. Depression was a monster, black and scary.

I wasn't scared yet, and life wasn't black. I was just wondering what had come over me and when it would end, something like the edgy restlessness of a driver suddenly sucked into a long, low-ceilinged tunnel.

I remember sitting on the couch together with my children, reading them a bedtime story. Suddenly, about halfway through the book, I realized with a start that I didn't even know what I was reading. My lips had been enunciating the words, my fingers had been turning the pages, but my thoughts had been deep within myself, furrowing through my turmoiled mind.

I longed to go back in time, to return to those simple, happy evenings a few short months before, when reading a book to my children had been just that: reading a book to my children. I would delight in the pictures, smile at the author's choice of words, and stroke my children's shoulders as I read. The furthest my mind ever wandered was to the imminent challenge of preparing a bedtime strategy.

Those days, it seemed, were gone, elusively out of reach. Everything I did was fraught with the choking sensation of strangled tears. What was wrong with me?

I tried cultivating new interests, taking time out for myself. My husband bought me an inspirational *sefer* and we began to learn it together. Nothing, however, appeared potent enough to dispel my mood.

And then, suddenly, it was gone.

One day, just the way I had entered the impenetrable cloud, I simply came out of it, drove right out of the dismal mist into the clear, bright light of day. It was utter relief, myself once again, free of the horrible, clinging, doom of the past few months. I felt like singing. I felt like laughing. I recognized myself; it was good old me. Cheerful, positive, energetic.

Giddy with relief, I went about my work, attacking neglected chores with renewed gusto. "Whatever it was," I told my husband with a profound sense of gratitude, "it's completely gone, *Baruch Hashem*."

We discussed it for some time after, and then let it go. The ordeal was over.

Or so we thought.

A week or two later, one Friday night after the meal, I was relaxing on the couch with a book. My husband had gone upstairs to bed, the children were sleeping peacefully, and I had remained downstairs to savor the delicious tranquility of the moment. A notorious bookworm, there was nothing more relaxing to me than curling up on the couch and getting lost in a book.

The book I was reading, written by a *frum* psychologist, depicted several intriguing case studies and their resolutions. I devoured the pages in eager fascination, oblivious to my sleeping foot, unmindful of the ticking clock.

Suddenly, a feeling of absolute dread gripped me.

I felt an awful, sinking pit at the bottom of my stomach, that dizzying plummet one sometimes experienced midnightmare.

I looked up wildly, expecting to see something terrifying, something ghastly. My heart thudded loudly against my chest, my palms were cold and clammy. My eyes darted around, petrified of what I would see.

The contrast couldn't have been greater. The house was peaceful and cozy, bathed in the soft glow of the still-burning Shabbos candles. The tablecloth exuded snow-white purity in the tidy room. I could hear my husband and children's steady breathing from their rooms.

Still, the blood pounded through my arteries in frantic alarm. Something was terribly, terribly amiss! I dropped the book like a hot coal, jumped off the couch and dashed up the stairs, sensing the enemy hot on my heels.

I burst into my room, panting, and gripped my bed. As I lay there, the feeling of dread escalated until it became so intense, I felt as if I was going crazy.

This is it, I thought, my mind reeling, *I'm going off the deep end.*

Trying to grab control of myself, I woke my husband. He had always been the one to navigate me through my feelings, to say just the right thing at the right time. I needed him desperately now.

"Avigdor, I don't know what's the matter; I'm going crazy."

Rubbing his eyes, he tried to appraise the situation. What had happened, he wanted to know. I didn't know myself.

It sounded strange.

"Avigdor, tell me," I pleaded, "what's the matter with me?"

He looked at me helplessly.

"You think I should see a therapist?" I whispered, my heart still racing.

He looked at me, groping for the right words.

"Maybe," he said, finally, "but only if you want to."

Calmed by his presence and by the thought of therapy as a panacea, I slowly steadied my breathing and drifted off to sleep.

When I woke up the next morning, it all seemed so unreal, so far removed from the soothing reality of daytime. The kids were up, chattering gaily, and the sun was streaming through the windows. I started to dress the kids and prepare for the *seudah*, sure that the whole thing had been a terrible nightmare.

In the middle of the meal, that feeling of dread started inching its way up my chest again. I panicked. My whole body went into a frenzied state of terror, and the table spun around me wildly.

"It's that feeling again," I whispered to my husband, with the helplessness of a child about to vomit. "What should I do?"

My children were singing and laughing around the Shabbos table; the baby gurgling happily in his infant seat. I felt totally out of touch with the reality of what was happening. It was as if I was losing my mind.

So this is what it feels like, I thought dizzily, *to go crazy.*

Somehow, my husband managed to distract the kids, and sat at my side, talking, soothing, reassuring. It took two hours for me to get my emotions in check. Only temporarily, though.

Throughout the rest of the day, the wave of dread kept rolling back and then engulfing me, retreating, and then submerging me, until I felt I was suffocating. It was only a matter of time, I felt, before I would burst out of my house and run into the streets, screaming. And then everybody would know I was crazy.

As soon as Shabbos was over, my husband called ECHO and described my symptoms. I hovered nearby and listened anxiously. Would they know what I was talking about? We were put in touch with a therapist.

The next morning, we got a baby-sitter and drove to her office, which was situated in a densely populated area of Lakewood. I was beside myself with worry that no one should notice me going there. No one I knew had ever needed therapy, and to me, going for help instantly labeled me as a misfit.

I had no idea what to expect. I imagined that therapy was some kind of magic spell that was imposed on the patient, immediately solving his problem. I was quite disappointed, when after a few mundane introductory questions, she told us to book an appointment later that week.

What do you mean, later? I panicked. I wasn't cured yet.

"What if I have another attack?" I asked in alarm. "Can you promise me that it won't happen again?" my eyes pleaded for her reassurance.

The therapist smiled.

"I'm not a *navi*," she said. "I can't promise you that anything will or won't happen."

My heart sank.

"What I could promise you is that you will learn to handle what will or won't happen. That when another panic attack hits you, you will have the tools to deal with it."

I sighed in resignation, wishing I could forever hold on to the sense of sanity and serenity I felt at that moment. Couldn't I just learn some prevention tactic that would successfully ward off impending attacks?

My dreams were dashed soon enough. The attacks kept coming, invading my fortress of inner peace, making a wreck of my stability. The second time I spoke to the therapist, it was over the phone. She empathized with my vulnerable feelings, and then taught me a few breathing techniques to employ when I felt an attack coming on.

It was right before Pesach. We were going to divide Yom Tov between my parents and in-laws, and I found myself wondering frantically how I would handle the attacks in our families' presence.

Indeed, the attacks were impervious to the circumstances. As we sat around the *seder* table, reading the *Haggadah,* I suddenly felt that icy hand clutch my throat. My heart began to beat wildly as I tried desperately to steady my escalating dread. *This can't happen now,* I thought, *it just can't.* I felt myself hyperventilating as everyone around me calmly intoned the *Haggadah.*

Help, I thought, panicking. *I'm going crazy; I can't breathe.* My kids, the beautifully set table, the merry explosion of *v'hi she'amdah,* all receded into the distance as I struggled furiously to regain control. My temples were throbbing; I felt the blood pounding in my ears. *I'm fainting,* I thought, as I battled to slow the frenetic drumming inside my chest.

It took all my restraint not to signal to my husband, not to clutch my sister-in-law's arm in fright. Finally, after what seemed like an eternity, my breathing slowed, and I felt the terror slowly draining. Ah, to be normal again. I quickly turned the pages in my *Haggadah*, and tipped my *becher*, letting the customary wine drip down. Had anyone noticed my encounter? I wondered. I couldn't wait until the *seder* was over.

The rest of Pesach passed in a similar vein. The attacks came without rhyme or reason, hitting me at the most inopportune moments. I found myself either experiencing one, recovering from one, or praying in fear of the next one. It took superhuman control to try and maintain a normal facade. *They probably know anyway, I thought miserably; what else would they have made of my strange behavior?*

I felt vulnerable and afraid. I knew perfectly well that there was no justification at all for the panic, that my body was going into the fight of flight mode for no apparent reason in the world. I was experiencing all the symptoms people feel when faced with imminent danger; yet the threat was nonexistent.

I felt a sense of such utter loneliness; I thought I was losing my mind. Throughout the ordeal, my husband was incredible. He was my one-man support group. All I had to whisper was "It's happening" and he would immediately take charge. He'd discreetly take over with the kids, accompany me to my room or take me for a walk. If not for his support, I would not have pulled through that Pesach.

My husband reassured me over and over again that I was normal and that I would be normal, and that the attacks would subside. I don't know how he knew what to say; in his shoes, I don't think I would have possessed the understanding to react the way he did.

My suffering during those months was unimaginable. It's hard, almost impossible, to describe a panic attack to someone who has not experienced one. Picture yourself alone in your kitchen, at 2 o'clock in the morning. All the members of your household are asleep upstairs and you're quietly finishing up for Shabbos. All you hear is the hum of the refrigerator as you make a mental list of what has to be done the next day.

Suddenly, you hear the unmistakable sound of a key turning in the keyhole of your front door. You freeze in your tracks, suddenly sweating all over. The door opens almost silently and you hear someone breathing heavily in your front hall.

That is what a panic attack feels like.

Except of course, that there is no key and no keyhole to trigger the alarm. And nothing, not the presence of familiar people, nor the solid reality of daylight, can diffuse the fear. It is an all-engulfing panic, gripping, choking dread that sucks one into a quicksand of terror far away from the actuality of real life.

My torture was compounded by the fact that nobody aside from my husband knew what I was going through. It is impossible to graph *nisyonos,* to compare suffering. Every person has his own mountain to climb and some people are given especially steep cliffs to scale.

When someone is sick or single or childless, however, other people are aware of their pain. Neighbors offer assistance, family members try to extend themselves. With mental disorders, the anguish takes on a dimension of solitary confinement. One wonders what others would think if they knew; how one's own children will be affected; if one will ever pull out of the insanity and be normal.

My body had become a prison; several times each day I felt like I was being picked up by some huge monster and hurled down a sheer cliff. Down, down, down, I'd go, hurtling over and over again, gasping for breath, choking for air.

Even as I write this now, I cannot recapture the intensity of the dread. I felt as if all the joy in my life had been pumped out of me; I was eroded by the constant looming threat of an oncoming attack.

During that period, I remember hearing that someone I knew had lost a child in a tragic accident. Normally, my heart would have contracted in pain and any trials in my own life would have instantly shriveled in comparison. Indeed, my heart was torn for the mother. In my misery, however, I remember thinking, *At least she has a life; at least she isn't being blown apart by panic attacks.*

I felt like I was living a double life. I would schmooze on the phone, talking to my children in the background, and friends would commend me, "You're such a calm mother."

Calm, I would scoff inwardly. *You should have been here last night; you'd look at me a little differently.*

When people would comment that they were panicking because they hadn't started cleaning for Pesach, I would feel so aloof, so detached. *What do you know about panic?* I'd think. Had I also spoken like that only a few months ago?

I continued to talk to my therapist twice a week over the phone. She was my lifeline. She encouraged me to ease my burden by telling my parents. I followed her advice. My parents were warm and accepting; my mother had an intuitive knack for knowing just when and what to ask me, never prying, but always ready with support and encouragement.

My therapist advised that I read up on panic and anxiety. There were excellent books available with self-help techniques and phrases that could be used to decrease the intensity of the attacks. She also opened my eyes to my inner perfectionism.

I had never thought of myself as a perfectionist. Everyone, including myself, knew me as an easygoing, even-keeled person, who went along with the ebb and flow of life. My house was a comfortable place to be; my children were allowed to play and explore freely.

Inside, however, I demanded perfect performance. I wanted to be patient and calm, kind and loving all the time. I expected myself to be tolerant and forgiving, responsible and punctual. If I ever failed, I berated myself.

My therapist taught me to maintain my long-term goals, while lowering my short-term expectations. She taught me to appreciate my qualities and accept my weak points. No human being was perfect; every person had faults and vulnerabilities.

At the same time, she helped me deal with the attacks by minimizing the anxiety they generated. Instead of letting myself be paralyzed with fear the moment I sensed the panic creeping up on me, I could take the reins and try to ride the rocky terrain. I also stopped adding fuel to the panic by telling myself I'd be stuck in the rut forever, or that my children wouldn't have a normal mother.

Slowly, the attacks began to subside. They came less frequently and less intensely, and when they did, they didn't last as long. Slowly, ever so slowly, I felt the fragile peace of normalcy settling over my household again. I wasn't tiptoeing around anymore, afraid of my own shadow.

Still, I remained traumatized by my ordeal. I dreaded being alone and grabbed the phone any time my husband left the house. I remained on the line, chatting with friends until he was safely back home. On Shabbos, I made sure to go out and visit someone, anyone, but not to be alone with my thoughts. If I had too much time to think, my thoughts inadvertently turned to panic.

I remember Tishah b'Av evening that summer. I had always savored the time alone when my husband was in *shul,* to read the *kinnos* and privately mourn the *churban.* This time, however, I felt terrified of the quiet heaviness; I ran to the phone and dialed my mother, trying to quell the wave of panic that was quickly welling up inside me.

It took me many months to be able to talk about the harrowing experience. It was as if the monster was still lurking right behind me, impalpable, and if I gave him any validity, he would turn into a full-fledged entity once again. *Baruch Hashem,* I can finally dare to look down from the top of the mountain and relate it as a thing of the past.

Months have elapsed without a trace of an attack. It's so precious, so sweet, so indescribably dear, to able to live life with all its ups and downs, joys and frustrations, to feel normally happy and normally frustrated, free of the black shadow of panic. I have climbed a mountain, and I am not the same person who embarked at the bottom almost two years ago.

I have been humbled beyond words. I used to feel unwittingly superior to other people around me. *Why does she yell at her children?* I'd think, watching my neighbor disciplining her kids. Or, *I'd never wear that skirt; it's really tight.*

She's always borrowing things, I'd note, *Doesn't she have her act together?*

Well, if I thought I had my own act together, Hashem certainly showed me. Sanity and insanity, health and illness, peace and trauma — I had always believed that they were divided by an intraversable chasm. Suddenly, I knew that they were only an imperceptible hairsbreadth apart.

None of us have earned our stability, our health, our serenity. They are all gifts from *Hakadosh Baruch Hu,* precariously packaged in the illusion that they are ours. My ordeal has punctured that illusion, ripped the flimsy wrapping, revealing a sense of self sculpted by gratitude, acceptance, and faith.

I've been there, in the darkest place there is, and *Hakadosh Baruch Hu* has given me His Hand. I treasure my life today as I never have, grateful for every particle of my existence.

My marriage has been infinitely deepened, my motherhood enriched. I have learned to cope with obstacles, to see things from the perspective I've honed as I battled to survive each day.

I look at my five children, listen to their peals of laughter, their cries of rivalry and dismay. I observe the songs and snubs, kicks and kisses, smashed Cheerios and spilled milk. Our house today resounds with the normal sounds of doors slamming, music playing, bathtime, bedtime, and above all, the echoes of my silent prayer that things remain just the way they are.

Keeping Afloat

In the airport, on a recent trip to Eretz Yisrael, I hoisted my box onto the scale, when the customs officer frowned.

"That box's too big, ma'am," she said flatly. "It ain't gonna go through."

I tried arguing. "This is the size I always take; it never presented any problems."

"The box is too big, ma'am," she repeated, an edge of impatience in her voice. "These are the measurements."

She pointed a manicured nail to the figures plastered to the side of the scale. "No use fighting regulations."

"What do I do now?" I tried to appeal to her sympathy. "I don't have another suitcase on me."

The servicewoman seemed unimpressed.

"Sorry, ma'am; we gotta stick to regulations. Your box is *too big.*"

I could have pleaded with the scale, for her indifference. Luckily, another *frum Yid* on the line came to my rescue with an empty duffel bag.

Only later, when I'd had ample time to recover from the tension, did I have a chance to reflect on the irony of the encounter. It was like the story of my life in a nutshell.

I don't remember much about my formative years; I suppose I experienced as normal an early childhood as any. Preschool was fun. The youngest of older parents, I was thrilled for the chance to interact with other girls my age, to color and paint and play in a bright sunny classroom. I may not have been your most agile child, but I loved my teacher and I reveled in the happy atmosphere.

As soon as I passed through the school gates, however, my fate was sealed.

Sorry, ma'am, your box is too big.

Won't go through.

Not through our system, anyway.

No use fighting regulations.

I don't know if my box was too big or too small, too active or too unattractive, but it didn't fit the measurements. It didn't fit the criteria set by a reputable school that catered to bright, obedient, traditional students.

And there was nobody there to bail me out with a duffel bag.

The problems began in first grade. My teacher was a firm disciplinarian who expected us to sit like well-behaved dolls and raise our hands before we spoke. From the outset, I had difficulty with reading. If I had been slightly confused with the *aleph-beis*, the addition of *nekudos* really messed things up.

Frightened into compliance, I never challenged the teacher. I sat in my seat and fidgeted with my pencil case, fumbling my way through whenever it was my turn to read. We got our *siddurim* and I took part in the *siddur* play, although I wasn't given any solo or narration.

It was just as well. I couldn't read from my *siddur* anyway. I felt frustrated, afraid, undeserving. Even back then, I remember the paradoxical feelings. On one hand I dreaded being found out; I sat through the lessons taut with tension and sighed with relief when my teacher passed over me.

On the other hand, I fervently wished the teacher would realize I couldn't read; I almost hoped she would confront me so that I could grab her hand and climb out of the muddle in which I was mired.

It never happened. My teacher must have told my mother that I was having difficulty, because I have vague memories of my mother drilling my reading with me. It wasn't done, though, with the patience and understanding of an experienced remedial teacher. My mother would be almost as frustrated as I was as I repeatedly stumbled over the sounds, confusing letters and transposing vowels.

Second grade brought little relief. I was a labeled misfit, clumsy Kaila, who sat alternately at the back or the front of the classroom and wasn't expected to perform. I was almost never called on to read or to show my homework. My teacher would pay a perfunctory nod to the open notebook on my desk and continue down the aisle.

Look, I wanted to scream. *It's empty. There's nothing in here.* But my teacher was past my desk, pasting a gold star on the next notebook, frowning with disapproval at the next.

I didn't need a gold star. A frown would have done. Anything, but the complacent acceptance of me as a non-functional student. Many nights, I would wistfully envision the scenario of my teacher bending over my math book, carefully scrutinizing my work, while my heart pounded with apprehension.

Then she would patiently show me where I had gone wrong and review the process again one step at a time. Though I'd squirm in humiliation even thinking of the scene, I wished it would happen. Maybe then I would be able to catch up and become a regular participant in the classroom.

My dreams never came to be. While they went as far as my teacher discovering my poor work and demanding that I redo the assignment during recess time, it was never followed through to the end. My performance deteriorated, and my teacher stopped calling on me altogether. Perhaps she wished to spare me the embarrassment of exposing my ignorance.

I, however, felt abandoned and afraid.

My elevator was stuck somewhere between two floors, and all I could see was a concrete wall through the narrow window in the door. In the distance, I could hear the merry sounds of girls running ahead, tumbling, thriving, scurrying down the school hallways. No one, however, seemed to hear the muffled rapping coming from the trapped confines of my soul.

The rest of the girls would open their books enthusiastically, shout out answers, and read *pesukim*. I would stare out the window to the parking lot, watching packages being delivered to the office by Federal Express, observing the high-school teachers walking purposefully to and from their cars.

During recess time I'd perk up. I'd run around in the playground, join in the classroom games, and trade snacks with my classmates. Then, as the teacher's imposing figure reappeared, I'd mentally bid farewell to my friends as they settled into the lesson, and I reverted to the painstaking watch-watching until the elusive ring of the bell rescued me from my isolation.

I passed through the next few grades like a dummy on an escalator. I was promoted only because third grade necessarily followed second, and fourth succeeded third. Candidly, I had not mastered any of the requisite curriculum.

I learned how to kill time. I'd ask permission to go to the bathroom, which was readily granted, and I'd wander the halls, striking up chats with punished persons, or watching the preschoolers practice for their Chanukah play.

When I was satisfied that a sizable portion of the morning had passed, I would slip back into class, just in time for the redeeming bell. The second part of the morning was easier to handle, what with the smells wafting up from the lunchroom and the promise of a long break looming in the tolerable distance.

Sometime during fifth grade, someone, somewhere, remembered about me. I was pulled out of class one day and called into the resource room, where a nice-looking lady asked me some questions. I was given sheets to fill in, *pesukim* to read, problems to solve. It was like awaking someone from the Dark Ages to come operate a computer. I was clueless.

By that time, I had written myself off as a hopeless case, and indeed, I was desperately out of touch with anything that sounded like learning. I had also developed enough sensitivity to realize that the resource room was not considered a very respectable place. Though my self-esteem was seriously lacking, I had enough pride left to resent being tactlessly singled out in the middle of a lesson.

I resisted the efforts of the resource room teacher. There was no way I was going to be humiliated into practicing reading when my classmates were tackling *Navi* tests and social studies reports.

There. Everybody's suspicions were confirmed. Kaila was just a lazy, unmotivated student who wasn't interested in, or capable of, helping herself.

If my experience at school wasn't enough to erode my self-esteem, the constant criticism I received at home completed the job. Though my parents surely loved me, they didn't possess the tools to demonstrate their affection. To me, it seemed, I remained forever frozen in my position as the baby, inviting the skepticism and admonishments reserved for very young children.

"Why are you wearing that sweater? It's hot outside."

"Where are you going? What are you doing? You can't hold that; you'll break it."

All I heard all day were comments reinforcing the notion that I was incapable, unattractive, and unsuccessful. I was too young to hold my sister's baby, too scatter brained to run a daycamp, too clumsy to learn dancing. If my ego had ever boasted a sheen, it had been sanded down to a dull, matte finish.

I'm sure my parents didn't mean to destroy every shred of my confidence. Nobody willfully makes mistakes, especially with their own offspring. Intended or not, however, that's what happened. Scholastically, I knew I was a zero. I flunked my tests, if I ever took them, and I was a nonentity during the lessons.

Writing this, even in retrospect, pierces my soul. Looking at my childhood from an adult perspective, I know there must have been something I could have contributed in school. I may not have been the conventional student, but I definitely could have been made a part of discussions and debates.

If there had been an oasis at home, at least, to water my soul with the warmth and acceptance for which it thirsted, perhaps the flower inside me would have blossomed despite the arid conditions at school. If I could have been staunch with the belief that I was my parents' pride and that I was capable of many things outside the classroom, perhaps I wouldn't have felt so completely down trodden.

In reality, what I felt couldn't have been further from that rosy idyll. I wasn't trusted with the simplest of tasks; if my mother ever did ask me to do something, the request was accompanied by a million instructions and admonishments insinuating that I was bound to mess up.

"Remember to close the freezer door well. And don't bang it too hard, because then it'll open again. And just make sure the container of soup doesn't come falling out. That's all I need now, a big puddle of soup all over the floor. You know what, forget it, I'll get the vegetables myself."

By the time my mother came huffing upstairs with the bag of frozen vegetables, I almost felt as if I had, in fact, spilled the soup. No matter what I did, all I seemed to merit was criticism. If I chose an outfit, it didn't match; if I sang, I was making noise. It was an incessant litany, from the minute I came through the door until the time I went to sleep.

Another thing I resented terribly was my lack of space. The closer I came to being a teenager, the more I craved some privacy, some corner where I could say, write, and keep, my own personal things. My parents never saw any reason for this need. My mother regularly went through my drawers, reading my diary, perusing personal notes friends had written me.

Later, she would confront me with the evidence, asking me why I had written what I had, who a particular friend was, and where I had gotten the money to buy the birthday present mentioned in the letter. I would cringe, trying desperately to remember whether she had been privy to other information that was hidden in my drawer.

Harder to bear, though, than these invasions on my property, was my parents' violation of my self-respect. My mother wouldn't hesitate to criticize me while she was on the phone, or worse yet, to vent her frustrations and deliberations regarding me within my obvious earshot.

There was nothing in my life that I could call a secret, no failure or shortcoming, no plan or proposal, no rejection or disappointment. My weight, my scholastic issues, my choice of friends, everything was up for public discussion. If I ever voiced my objection, my mother would laugh with seeming disregard.

It hurt deeply, especially when I knew that my mother was talking to another classmate's mother, nonchalantly disclosing my most personal matters. I would go up to my bedroom, blushing with shame, feeling powerless to do anything.

All I could do then to soothe my fury was to stew in the fantasy that I would run away from home, leaving nothing but a note on the table. I tried to imagine my parents' consternation, the regret that would fill them when they realized the implications of their perpetual put-downs.

For a few minutes, I would revel in the sweetness of this drama, and then a sardonic voice would mercilessly burst my balloon. *Don't kid yourself, honey, nobody gonna miss you that much.*

That was all I needed for the tears to come, tears of humiliation and rejection, tears of anger and helplessness. I felt like an ant planning a revolution against an able-bodied homeowner. It was foolish to even think I could make a dent.

My frustration drove me to seek my identity somewhere, anywhere. I wasn't an A student, and I wasn't my parents' prize daughter. I wasn't Princess Charming, nor was I anybody's gifted artist or talented singer. There was only one place where I had carved myself some sort of a niche: the halls.

The halls were the place where latecomers congregated, where the violators of the law were exiled. I found myself attracted to these girls, girls who enjoyed my sharp wit and mischievous spunk, girls who respected my opinions and listened to my advice.

Though I never became a discipline problem myself, I forged comfortable companionships with the girls in the halls. I saw an ally in these friends who hadn't found their niche in the school system, who were struggling to assert their individuality in an establishment that suppressed their inner needs.

Understandably, these weren't your honor certificate holders. There were girls from homes whose values clashed with the school's, girls who were disruptive in the classroom or had a hard time sticking to the school's dress code.

We would air our indignities together, venting our bitterness, sharing our frustration. Of course, we wouldn't have been caught sounding vulnerable. We associated under the gallant veneer of cool rebellion.

By the time I hit high school, I was a wreck of a human being. My self-esteem was in shambles, my situation at home seemed unbearable. On the outside, I sported a self-assured swagger. My friends viewed me as the one with the wisecrack, the cool watch, the pulse on the politics. Inside, I was screaming in pain.

Somebody heard those screams.

She wasn't my *mechaneches*; she wasn't even my main teacher. She was a once-a-week *parashah* teacher who also ran the school *chessed* program.

It was common knowledge that Mrs. Mandel would call girls into her office to help her collate booklets or work on her upcoming *chessed* campaign. Less common was the knowledge that these *chessed* campaigns were often pretenses for the real *chessed*, the campaigns that went on right there in her office.

Almost for the first time since I had entered school, I was shown that five-letter word that my heart had almost despaired of: trust. Mrs. Mandel didn't give me pep talks or flowery speeches; she simply entrusted me with tasks that needed to be done, conveying her confidence that I would get them done to her satisfaction.

This trust was laced with caring. She would pour me a drink, offer me a chair, run to the other side of the school to find a scissors that would make the cutting easier for me. In the meantime, she shared some of her frustrations running the program, and asked me my opinion about different aspects of her job.

There was something so genuine about her demeanor. She wasn't artificially sweet or manipulatively probing. She simply appreciated me for who I was and valued my opinion, facts that weren't all that simple to me.

I found myself feeling a little more positive, about life, about school, about myself. One evening, spurred by these upbeat feelings, I decided to surprise my mother and make a really thorough cleanup of the kitchen. I cleared the table, and scrubbed it down. Then I stacked the dishes and pots neatly in the sink, scoured them, washed them, and dried them. Driven by my newfound motivation, I swept the floor, smiling in anticipation of my mother's delight.

It was not to be. My mother came in from shopping, sharply demanding to know why I was still up. I padded upstairs sheepishly, secretly gloating in the surprise that would meet her when she entered the kitchen. Craning intently at the top of the staircase, I listened for her reaction.

All I heard was the rustle of some papers, the creak of a drawer being opened and then banged shut.

"Where is that bill?" I heard her mutter with annoyance. "I should have known Kaila would throw it out. No matter how many times I tell that kid to leave the bills on the counter, she doesn't listen. It's like talking to a wall."

Well, the wall broke down.

Crumbled and shattered and collapsed into a million pieces of human rubble at the top of those steps. I sat there and sobbed, contractions of self-pity and anger and hurt clamping down on my heart. The pain was so intense, I felt as if my chest was going to split.

I didn't feel the carpet beneath me, or see the pale green wallpaper on the wall. All I was aware of was that deep, gagging sensation, that all-consuming vacuum of pain sucking me into my inner maelstrom.

I don't know how long I sat there heaving, matted hair nestled in my soaking sleeves, but all at once, I got up and went into my room. I tore a paper out of a spiral notebook on my desk and began to jot furiously. When my emotions were spent, I folded the paper, fished around for an envelope, and marked it in capital letters: for Mrs. Mandel.

That was the beginning of a long and cherished relationship. Mrs. Mandel listened to my pain, heard my despair, empathized with my suffering. Her eyes were a well of acceptance and understanding. I lack the verbal agility to paint the subtle nuances of her perception; all I could say is that she was a master of understanding.

She knew the fine line between condescension and compassion, between *mussar* and guidance, between glib talk and hope. It was she I turned to every time I thought I had reached the end, every time I considered leaving home, or even worse, the life for which my home and school stood.

She always heard me out, never dismissed my threats with a protest or a chuckle or even an indulgent pat. She looked at me seriously, her eyes intent on my face, her brow furrowed in concentration. And yet, her gaze communicated the belief that she knew I would pull through, that indeed, although I felt like I was drowning, she was sure I would take a fresh gulp of air and I would have the strength to go one more lap.

It was turbulent swimming, but I kept at it. Mrs. Mandel was like a lifeguard, walking steadily along the side of the pool holding a safety net. Just seeing that net was enough to reassure me whenever I floundered. I wouldn't drown. I would make it.

When Mrs. Mandel told me that she and her family would be moving to Eretz Yisrael, I felt my equilibrium faltering. I was in the middle of eleventh grade, just about hanging on, thanks to her comforting presence. How would I brave life on my own? Whom would I turn to when my situation at home reached breaking point?

Again, Mrs. Mandel wholeheartedly understood my feelings. She told me that the connection would never be severed and that I could call her at any time.

"But you know what, Kaila?" she winked, "You're not the same fragile kid you were two years ago. Separation hurts, there's no denying that, but I'm positive you're going to pull through with flying colors."

I don't know about the flying colors, but I pulled through. When the jobs for the play were announced in twelfth grade and my name didn't appear on the list, I felt a stab in my heart. I bit my bottom lip and walked away from the bulletin, fighting the tears.

"Mrs. Mandel," I felt like wailing, over and over like a toddler disconsolately crying for his mother. No one was there to hear my silent cries. All I beheld was an excited tangle of girls, pushing to find their names on the list. I was too distraught to ask anyone about the omission; I didn't want the tears spilling in public.

My sister had just given birth to her fifth child and needed help. I packed my bags and went to Monsey, grateful to have a haven for my wounded spirit. I don't think anybody even realized I was gone. If they did, they surely made no mention of it.

Two weeks later, I met the principal of my school in a store. I had changed out of my uniform and was wearing an outfit that didn't comply with school regulations.

My principal surveyed me and arched her eyebrows questioningly.

"What's this, Kaila?"

For a moment, the blood rushed furiously to my head, while I struggled to keep my cool.

Inside, every fiber of my being was screaming.

What's this?

This is a girl, a person, a human being with a heart, a very crushed heart. This is a student of your school who was absent for the past three weeks without anyone batting an eyelash. This is a child who has never gotten a hug from her mother or a compliment from her principal, who has never been spoken to or listened to with interest.

This is a child, a kid, a teenager, whose sole gratification in life is social acceptance, who could be dealing drugs and hanging out with gangsters, who, miraculously, has never acted out in the classroom, and conforms to the dress code in school.

I didn't say a word. Instead, I gave her a lingering glance, and left the store.

Twelfth grade passed. I dipped several times, almost drawn into the spiraling current beneath the surface. I had my contacts in the teenage netherworld. They beckoned me to leave school, leave home, and come live the good life. At certain points, I was almost swayed.

No one had ever sat with me, looked me in the eye, and explained the beauty of *Yiddishkeit*, the nobility of *tzeniyus*, the precious potential of every *neshamah*. Nobody had ever taken the time to frame the rules with a story, a smile, a personal pat of encouragement.

All I had ever encountered in school and at home was failure. Failure to read and failure to learn, failure to be understood and failure to be loved. Success winked temptingly from the other side of the fence.

Each time, however, I ended up spluttering to the surface. Even with miles between us, Mrs. Mandel continued to be my safety net. If logistics precluded me from talking to her, I envisioned her reaction, heard her oft-repeated encouragement ringing in my ears.

It's tough, Kaila, but you're tough, too. How else would you have gotten where you are?

I spent my seminary year in Eretz Yisrael. How my parents agreed to send me abroad is still a mystery. Intuition tells me that Rabbi and Mrs. Mandel must have pulled more than a few strings to help it happen.

The year was a boon for me. Obviously, I wasn't in one of your tight-laced, cream-of-the crop institutions. I was in a place where marks and honors had very little impact on one's acceptance, a place where every girl was welcomed with love and respect.

For the first time in my life, I really had a niche in the classroom. I listened and participated, asked and argued. I was Kaila Gordon, a student, a person, an individual whose feelings and opinions counted. I didn't have anyone going through my drawers or snooping under my pillow. My sense of self was slowly restored.

It would make a poignant ending if I could recount how I came back from seminary spiritually and emotionally uplifted, landed a job, found a *shidduch,* and went on to build a warm, loving, family.

Actuality, though, is not always poignant. At least not in the way that human beings can conceive.

I came home from seminary to the familiar challenges I had left behind. Although I felt rejuvenated, my parents had not changed their stance. The minute I came in from the airport, I was greeted with recriminations. I had gained weight, I had chosen the wrong thing to wear on the plane, and where was the change from the money they had sent for my trip?

I felt the wind going out of my sails. It would be a fight just to remain upbeat, to fortify myself with the strength of spirit to ward off these emotional attacks.

I am a respectable human being, I told myself over and over again. If my parents don't see it, that's their loss, not mine.

It wasn't all that easy to internalize. My parents constantly measured me up to my older siblings, discrediting my accomplishments, expressing their doubts that anybody would want to marry me.

When *shidduchim* entered the scene, it was a conflict of desires. My parents wanted someone just like my older siblings, while I had needs of my own. I *wasn't* just like my older siblings.

Though I wanted someone *frum* and committed, I didn't need the most serious learner in the yeshivah. I had been singed in the system, and I was happy I had come out stable and sane. I was looking for a spouse with a little broader experience of life, someone who would understand me and respect me for the person I am.

I presented my predicament to *daas Torah* and received strong backing for my position. Though I felt validated, it did little to relieve the friction. My parents had a hard time viewing me as an adult, an individual person with individual needs.

It's been tough, but, as Mrs. Mandel says, I'm tough too. I've learned to channel my energies, to turn sarcasm into humor, hurt into sensitivity for others. I've learned to walk away from insult, to cultivate my self-respect regardless of what others may say.

It isn't easy to face rejection time and again, to have your privacy intercepted, your judgment ridiculed. It isn't easy to be 26 and single, living under the eagle-eyed scrutiny of your parents. But I've learned to shrug, square my shoulders, and go on with life.

I've fooled around enough to know that the answers don't lie in the shallow thrills on the other side. Neither are they to be found in anger and revenge.

Bitterness is paying for one's past with one's future.

And I'm not ready to give up my future.

Not just yet.

Not when I know that just around the bend, just a little bit further up the path, there are delicate buds waiting for my sunshine.

*Although Kaila's account is the authentic tale of her struggles, challenges, and feelings the way she experienced them, it is important to note that this story took place 20 years ago when there was little awareness of the ramifications of letting an academically challenged (and challenging) child "drift" through the system.

Fortunately, and to the great credit of our extraordinary mechanchim and mechanchos, things have improved radically. Much physical, emotional, and financial energy is expended today to seek these children out, help them overcome their struggles, and allow them to shine.

וְחֶרְפָּה לֹא־נָשָׂא עַל־קְרֹבוֹ.

... nor cast disgrace upon his close one.

Different Languages of Love

"So you're coming for the second days," I checked, drawing my conversation with Zevy to a close.

There was an awkward silence at the other end of the line instead of the automatic confirmation I had been expecting.

"Um, do you think you can get a separate apartment for us? Sarah Leah really wants her privacy."

"A separate apartment?" I held the potato peeler steady, suddenly drained of my ambition to start making blintzes. "I guess I can try. It isn't that easy Yom Tov time."

Zevy, my oldest son, was married only two months. I had been so eagerly looking forward to hosting him and Sarah Leah in the beautiful new addition we had built only last year. And now she wanted a separate apartment.

I hung up feeling a vague sense of déjà vu. I had been in this scene once before, played the part, seen the script. Only there was a curtain a quarter of a century thick separating me from that vision, splitting the stage juxtaposing the two settings. Fortunately, I was looking down from near the top of a mountain. I'd need all my climbing gear to hoist myself up the next incline.

I was the youngest of five siblings, six years my youngest brother's junior. The sister above me was 14 years old at the time of my birth, making me into a double celebrity: a baby, and a girl to boot. The baby paraphernalia had been battered by the boys preceding me, and I merited all the indulgences of a first baby.

Swathed in a brand-new bunting, I came home to a beautiful white crib, a state-of-the-art carriage, and a crew of older siblings who were only too happy to be at my beck and call. My earliest memories are of my older sister taking me along to her friends on Shabbos afternoon, making me repeat over and over the songs I'd learned in kindergarten. For my part, I was happy to oblige. I would sit in the company of my sister's teenage friends, swinging my patent leather shoes importantly, as I took in their admiring comments.

My mother was of Hungarian background. A perfect *balabusta* and fabulous cook, she took pleasure in playing her role to perfection. Our linen closets were trimmed with lace and perfumed with pastel-colored, sweet-smelling soaps. The dining-room buffet was a polished mahogany buffed to a high shine, adorned with cream-colored doilies that matched the heavily starched lace tablecloth. Though my father earned a modest income, our home was a palace, always tidy and welcoming, furnished and maintained in good taste.

Stronger than any of her other housekeeping hobbies, however, was my mother's penchant for cooking and baking. She was a queen in her kitchen, and I, being the recipient of all her culinary stints, was certainly a princess. It was ordinary for me to come home to blintzes and knishes, pudding, strudel, stuffed cabbage. Every meal started with an appetizer, was followed by a rich soup, and then a savory main course. Disposable dishes were unheard of in our house; my mother delighted in serving on her good china.

Despite all this indulgence, though, I must say, I was an obedient little girl. I did well in school, got along beautifully with my friends, and never gave my parents much trouble. As the youngest, I didn't bear much of a burden in the house, but I was happy to run an errand for my mother when she needed it.

I was The Baby of the house until I reached about age 6 or 7. Suddenly, with the marriage of my siblings, babies once again frequented our home in the form of adorable grandchildren. It was an adjustment on my part, expanding the spotlight to include my new nieces and nephews, but I loved them just the same.

My mother was the proverbial doting grandmother, keeping pictures of her *einiklach* in her purse and forever pulling chocolate bars from the recesses of her leather bag. Whenever the married children came, and they came pretty often, she'd bustle around serving, plying them with containers and foil-wrapped parcels. It was as if her refrigerator and freezer sprouted these packages. My father would joke that she stuffed all her mother's love into the delicacies she doled out.

Though I wasn't an only child, as a teenager, I usually felt pretty much like one. The last one of my siblings was married by the time I was 14, and though I pitched in on *erev Yom Tov*, when there was plenty to be done, the house was usually serene and orderly. My friends loved coming to the house, where they were always treated to *rugelach* and cheese danishes, courtesy of my mother.

"It's a shame you aren't a chef, Mrs. Berkowitz," my friends used to say, and my mother would feign insult.

"What do you mean? I *am* a chef," she would protest, "I cater to my sons and daughters; what could be a better job?"

And she sincerely believed it. While my brothers were in yeshivah, she took every opportunity to show her appreciation of their learning by sending them her baked goods. Later, when they set up homes of their own, she continued to send care packages, making no differentiation between her daughter and daughters-in-law.

When I got engaged, it was hard for my parents to believe it. No matter that I was nearly 20; to them I was still little Ricky, the baby of the family. My *chassan* was from out of town and was the oldest of 11 children, the youngest of whom was barely 2 years old. It was an entire new world for me.

I smiled as my *chassan's* mother introduced me to her children. They stood back smiling, eager to meet their brother's new *kallah,* yet too shy to make conversation. It was overwhelming just trying to catch each of their names as they bashfully identified themselves one at a time. My mother, as usual, was a wonderful hostess, serving and making conversation, introducing the new *mechutanim* to family and friends,

At the *vort,* numerous people came to tell me what an impact my future in-laws had had on their lives. My father-in-law was involved in a worldwide *kiruv* organization and my mother-in-law was a renowned high-school teacher. They were both active in the local community, and were respected and well liked. I was proud to be engaged to a boy from such a special family.

Though I knew marriage would be an adjustment, I thought I was fairly well prepared. I had five happily married siblings, and my parents enjoyed a wonderful relationship. My mother was of the old school; she served my father like a king, careful not to burden him with household duties, and my father, in turn, valued my mother's opinion and showed appreciation for her unswerving devotion.

What I didn't realize at the time was that marriage wasn't comprised solely of husband and wife. No individual exists in a vacuum; every spouse was the product of parents, a home, an upbringing. True harmony was hinged on accepting that reality. Accepting and respecting it. I was too young and immature then, to realize that.

Hearing about 11 children, *kiruv,* and teaching was one thing. A very respectable thing at that. Stepping headlong into it was quite another. Especially for the pampered youngest of a smaller family.

Coming in after the long ride that first *erev Shabbos*, we were almost assaulted by a bunch of eager youngsters. My mother-in-law greeted us warmly and showed us to our room, while the kids relieved us of the *sheitel* box and garment bag. My mother-in-law quickly retreated to the kitchen, while the younger children followed us right into our room.

If I was annoyed by the intrusion on our privacy, I didn't say anything. Kids were kids; it was hard to quell their curiosity. They

Different Languages of Love / 281

watched in open fascination as I unzipped the hand luggage and unpacked our belongings.

After a few minutes, I heard my mother-in-law call in a slightly exasperated tone.

"Tzirel, Yanky, it's *erev Shabbos*! Please come finish your jobs right now!"

The kids reluctantly left us to our own devices, and my husband helped me put our things into place.

When we were settled, I saw my husband check his watch.

"Do you want me to stick around now, or do you think you'll manage on your own?" he asked as he calmly took his brushed hat.

Like a newborn's eyes, our relationship was still shy of showing its true colors. Though I was apprehensive about being left alone in my in-laws' home, I knew my husband would appreciate being able to learn before Minchah and *Kabbalas Shabbos*. I smiled my bravest smile.

"I'll be fine."

Frankly, I was starved. In our haste to leave the house, I hadn't eaten much more than a bowl of cereal and milk. I felt awkward, however, leaving the room, almost as if I'd be intruding. My mother-in-law was bustling around the house, cooking, answering the phone, issuing instructions. She seemed to have totally forgotten that I'd just come in from a long trip. What did she expect me to do, walk into the kitchen and open her fridge on my first visit?

Without malice aforethought, I automatically envisioned my mother, place sparkling, table spread with drinks, fruit and cake. Her potato *kugel* would be hot and sizzling on the counter, waiting to be served, and my mother would be waiting, just as graciously, to do the serving.

It wasn't as if we were coming unannounced. My mother-in-law had had all week to prepare for her young couple's first appearance. Feeling resentful, I took a book down from the bookshelf and halfheartedly perused the pages.

Our first visit was the precursor of many visits to come. I felt unwelcome and unappreciated in my in-laws' home. The house was small and crowded; it was a miracle we even got our own room. My mother-in-law was nice, but she was always involved in a million projects. There were her students on the phone and *baalei teshuvah* couples at the table. This besides all her little ones who made for a lively household on their own.

"We make you feel very at home here, Ricky," my mother-in-law often chuckled. I was hard pressed to get the joke. If at home meant all this noise and ruckus and activity, then, yes, I guess you could say they made me feel very at home. For my part, I'd pass up on the pleasure. My own parents were ready to have us at any time, and treated us like visiting royalty.

I just couldn't get used to my in-laws' mentality. When my own married brothers came for a Shabbos, my mother waited on them, hand and foot. She'd prepare the delicacies that they especially liked and went out of her way to make my sisters-in-law comfortable. The conversations at the Shabbos *seudah* centered around the guests, and once the couple became a family, the grandchildren became the center of attention too.

At my in-laws, we were hardly noticed. If my mother-in-law wasn't in the middle of some important phone call when we came, she gave us a spontaneous greeting, after which she went right back to her kitchen duty. As she spiced the chicken and added water to the *cholent,* she'd ask us if we wanted to eat something.

Each time this scene repeated itself, my mother's motto came to mind. "*A kranker fregt men; a gezunter gebt men.*" (An infirm person should be asked; a well person should be served.) Even if I was starving, which I often was after the trip, I wasn't about to answer in the affirmative to these offhand offers. If my mother-in-law hadn't thought it important enough to set out food, then I wasn't going to inconvenience her in the middle of her myriad tasks.

The Shabbos table was very different from the one I was used to. There were usually several guests besides us, and there were always a few simultaneous discussions in process. The food was served family-style in the center of the table. It took me a while to realize that if I wasn't going to serve myself, I would remain hungry all Shabbos.

There were no elegant settings, either. The little kids were served on paper, and plastic cups took the place of glassware for everyone. The only really expensive serving piece displayed with pride was a crystal wine bottle in the center of the table. It almost seemed out of line with the rest of the decor.

When I once commented, my mother-in-law explained that the bottle had tremendous sentimental value to her. It was an heirloom from her mother who had received it as a wedding gift from a great-aunt and uncle. "It makes the whole Shabbos *tisch*," my mother-in-law proudly remarked. For once, we concurred on something.

I tried to pitch in with the serving and cleaning up. With a family that size plus company, there was always an overwhelming amount to be done. My efforts never generated too much response. Whereas my mother would express appreciation if my sisters-in-law as much as picked up after their own kids, my mother-in-law seemed to take my help for granted. She would push in the chairs after I had swept, and then sit down on the recliner with her *Chumash,* bringing out a bingo game to keep the little ones busy.

While I acted like a polite guest in front of my in-laws, I always ended up airing my grievances with my husband. I knew that it had nothing to do with him, but after a whole Shabbos of feeling like a fifth wheel, I always felt belligerent and resentful when we got home. My husband tried to get me to see the other side. He explained how busy his mother was running a large family, how involved she was with so many different *chassadim.*

To me, all these explanations seemed like a flimsy rationale. Everybody knew that charity began at home. What good were dedicated *kiruv* efforts and captivating *yahadus* lessons if one didn't take the time and effort to make one's own children feel at home?

Our first anniversary passed. Little Zevy joined the scene. If I had thought a baby would improve matters, the birth of our first child did little to relieve my feelings. While our little prince was smothered with attention by my parents, my mother-in-law was hardly swept off her feet by the novelty of a grandchild. She sufficed with buying Zevy a cute outfit and booties when he was born, and admiring the pretty things my mother had gotten.

When he started to crawl, she offered me outgrown stretchies from her own infants.

"These aren't in great shape," she said as she handed me the gray-tinged pile, "but they're perfect for crawling around the house."

I tried not to show my contempt. I didn't expect my mother-in-law to ply my baby with all the expensive apparel my mother had supplied. I knew she had never dressed her own children in anything more than the local outlet-stores' best. The idea of proposing shabby hand-me-downs for a first baby, though, was taking it a bit far. I accepted her offer politely, adding another offense to my mental list.

It wasn't that I was being uppity or ungrateful. I would have gladly taken something in good condition from one of my older sisters. It was my mother-in-law's insensitivity that irked me. She seemed so oblivious to accepted proprieties, so out of touch with my taste and preferences.

The only thing that ever seemed to interest her was whether or not I had found a teaching position in the local school. As if teaching was the only worthwhile pastime with which a wife and married woman could be preoccupied.

Whoever coined the adage, "You don't marry your in-laws," was missing some very basic perception of human relations. While no one marries his or her in-laws, one certainly marries their child. And no matter how different a child is from his upbringing, the cord that binds parents to their children is spun of familiarity, love, and a strong dose of loyalty. Qualities that grow especially taut when that cord is tugged by a spouse.

Though I did a pretty good job of acting diplomatic in my in-laws' presence, my husband got the brunt of my ill feelings. Our discussions were always the same, my offenses, his defenses, winding around and around both of our hurt feelings without getting anywhere. My attitude toward my in-laws was putting a strain on our relationship. Though my husband felt almost obligated to justify his parents to me, I could see that my incriminations bothered him deeply.

Fateful moments come in many different forms. Sometimes they are accompanied by the shrieks of a siren or the flash of a camera. Sometimes they are permanently etched in one's memory by the sharp stylus of terror or relief. And sometimes, they are simple moments, unremarkable to any onlooker, startling only in the way they open a window to some still undiscovered territory in the privacy of one's own heart.

That's the way it was with the wine bottle.

One minute I was sitting, calmly serving Zevy *cholent,* and the next minute the crystal bottle was shattered in smithereens, rivulets of dark burgundy liquid spilling along the folds of the plastic tablecloth. I looked on in horror. It was any daughter-in-law's worst nightmare.

My mother-in-law's cherished heirloom, the irreplaceable antique that had graced her table since her mother's passing, was smashed to pieces. It had happened so quickly. Zevy had scrambled off my lap, catching the edge of the plastic tablecloth in his shoe. In my haste to untangle the mess, I had risen, unwittingly pulling the plastic together with me. Before I knew it, I had a crying Zevy, a growing puddle, and a heart pounding in alarm.

My mother-in-law didn't lose her composure. She picked Zevy up out of the mess and carefully checked his legs for splinters of glass. Then, as if nothing extraordinary had happened, she asked one of the girls to bring a dustpan and gloves.

"Don't worry, Ricky," she reassured me. "Nothing lasts forever. Not in this house, anyway." She chuckled with simple resignation, not a thread of pretense in her laugh. It was the same chuckle that ordinarily grated on my nerves.

I took the dustpan from my sister-in-law's hand, desperate to do something constructive. My mother-in-law sat down serenely and dished out some salad from the middle of the table. She turned to my father-in-law and asked a question about his exposition on the *parashah*. Her expression wasn't strained or drained; she appeared completely composed. I cleaned up the shards, thankful for the practical activity.

All through *bentching,* my mind tumbled around as my lips unconsciously mouthed the words. How would I compensate for the damage? Would my mother-in-law talk to my husband about it? Should I apologize now or later?

I kept stealing sidelong glances at my mother-in-law, trying to detect the inner distress she had done a valiant job of concealing.

I couldn't find it. Not a trace of conflict or aggravation. She was *bentching* with her usual fervor.

All at once, I was flooded with admiration. It wasn't esteem born of intellect or reason. It was that sort of unbidden feeling that comes in a wave at an unexpected moment and washes away the debris from the shore.

I don't remember much of anything about the rest of that Shabbos, except that there was nothing much to remember. There were the usual *zemiros,* storytime with the children, cleanup after the *z'man.* When I mustered the courage to apologize before we left, I remember catching a glimpse of genuine surprise in my mother-in-law's eyes.

"I thought you knew me better than that, Ricky. It's forgiven and forgotten. It could have easily been me or anyone else. Objects are transient. Other things are forever."

I was overcome. Not as much by the simple profundity of her statement, as by the sudden realization that her words totally resonated with her inner being, with her outer reality. It wasn't the revelation of seeing a new dimension in a personality; it was the clarity of seeing the same dimension in a totally different light.

My mother-in-law would never be my mother. She would never be me. She wasn't a master of culinary arts or aesthetic design. She wasn't a gushing parent or a hovering hostess.

And by the same token, she was an easygoing, accepting person who valued eternal ideals over anything material. She was a non-pressuring, even-keeled individual who didn't attach particular importance to outer demonstrations of love or beauty. She wasn't missing respect or sensitivity; she expressed them in a completely different way.

If my insight sounds elementary, perhaps your mountain is not on my path. Or perhaps, more likely, you have yet to experience that bolt of illumination ripping straight through the darkest crevices of your heart, transforming all the festering negativity in that split-second, blue-white flash of truth.

Lightning strikes in a fleeting instant. Transformations take time. Time and hard work. I can't say it was love at first oversight. My mother-in-law was of a very different makeup than I was, a fact that wasn't altered by my awareness. Certain things she did or didn't do still rankled.

Over time, though, I learned to appreciate the beautiful facets of her personality. I learned to enjoy her undemanding nature, her tolerance of children, her lighthearted acceptance of external limitations. Slowly, painstakingly, like a foreigner picking up the native tongue, I learned the nuances of my mother-in-law's language.

Every family speaks its own language, and every dialect has its own set of rules. Its own grammar and its own structure, its own pronunciation and its own inferences.

Some families speak with humor, some speak with exactitude; some speak with indulgence, some speak with pride. Some demonstrate closeness through invitations, some through understanding. Some express respect with formality, some with food. Some with clinging togetherness, others with independence.

No one language is perfect, or universal or absolute. Like a leveler, we each have a bubble of imperfections that inevitably surfaces in one area or another, depending at what angle our mind-set is tilted. And no two people are tilted on the same slant.

A fact that, when realized in time, can set a lot of things straight.

Like any other mountain climbing, it took a constant conscious effort to keep going upward. Many times I was weighed down by feelings of insult and negativity, by unconscious comparisons and contrasts. Each time, though, I tried to recapture that initial streak of inspiration and continue my ascent in the ebbing shaft of its afterglow.

My husband and children, my life and my circumstances have mellowed me dramatically. I am not the same person who married at 20 with expectations and standards of precisely how things (and people) should be. I am grateful that I have gotten this far.

This past winter, I've reached a milestone. We've married off our eldest son, welcoming a new daughter-in-law into our family. And as I held my daughter-in-law in my embrace, I remembered my mother-in-laws' words, the words that have far outlasted any wine bottle.

Objects are transient. Other things are forever.

Stepping Upward

Ask anyone who knew me when I was little if they remember Brochy Weissfish. Chances are, you'll get a faint smile, the kind that comes with a fond wisp of a memory. "Oh sure I remember her; you mean that girl with the blond braids and dimples? The one with the perpetual smile?"

Like I said, you'll get the same reply from anyone.

Other than me.

Oh yes, I was a happy, sweet-natured child. I had blond braids and dimples that flashed with disarming appeal every time I smiled. Smiles can be deceiving, though. The happy face I put on for the world did not have its roots in my heart. There, deep inside, was a reservoir of turmoil and confusion.

My parents married late in life. Of divergent backgrounds and upbringing, the one thing they had in common was rock-hard strength woven with optimism. It was a strength borne of character, of *emunah*, and of having endured no small measure of life's hurdles. When *Hashgachah* brought them together in the most fascinating way, they fused this dimension with their deepest longings to build a Jewish family. Nothing short of a small miracle, my twin brother and I were born several years later.

Nothing about our childhood fit the austere image of children born to older parents. If I had to size up our home in a word, the word would undoubtedly be happiness. True inner happiness.

My mother was the epitome of this joy. It shone from her eyes and danced off her forehead. She never spoke about it. She lived it.

My mother's happiness wasn't only about inner serenity and peace. It was more of a tingling thrill, a barely suppressed giggle, a sweeping, swelling, soaring passion with everything life had to offer.

She loved music and she loved art; she loved reading and she loved socializing, she loved order and she loved tumult. She loved people and she loved children. And she loved prayer.

Did she love prayer!

I remember her sitting in her favorite armchair chanting from her *Tehillim* with an expression I cannot contain in words. It had something of the affection with which one would greet a dear friend; something of the calmness with which a baby would gurgle in contentment. And something else, something otherworldly that I can only fumble to describe. It was a comfortable, trusting, intimacy, effortless and animated at the same time.

I would catch her in this pose with unswerving predictability every morning at 7 o'clock. This was after she had already completed Shacharis and prepared breakfast for my father. Her eyes would slide back and forth, riveted to the text, while her mouth intoned the words with the ease of utter familiarity. It was a spellbinding sight.

In all the years of my childhood, I cannot recall ever waking my mother. She was never torn out of her sleep, never shaken out of sweet dreams to the harshness of life's demands. She entered each day like a queen, embroidering the sweetness of her dreams into the intricate brocade of her prayer. And she was ready to start her day by the time the last strokes of sunrise had painted the sky a pale yellow.

She wasn't of the "early to bed, early to rise" population, either. The telephone in our house would ring without any compunctions at almost any hour. There were my mother's overseas friends and her married seminary students calling for advice. For her, there were too few hours in the day for everything that had to be accomplished.

How she never lost it the next day is something I'll never understand. Along with the many other paradoxes in her personality, such as how she combined her spontaneous sense of adventure with her extreme efficiency. Or how she could sit and play with a child while tackling the most intense existential questions thrust at her by adults.

As children, though, we never pondered the complexity of these apparent incongruities. She was our mother, and we were glad to bask in the naive bliss of childhood. Even when she was intermittently hospitalized for a few days here and there, we took it in stride. One day she was in the hospital, the next day she was home again, full of life and vigor, listening to our lively interaction. It was perfectly acceptable to us, perfectly viable. There were no questions. If she did it, then apparently, it was part of the superhuman reality called motherhood.

Somewhere along the way, I absorbed the notion that my mother was ill, or sick, in my lexicon. I had no other experience to compare with, and accepted this fact of life with trusting simplicity. In fact, I remember my brother and I sitting on the couch innocently discussing the facts. Children were sometimes sick with a strep throat or the flu, wherefore they went to the doctor, and mothers were sometimes sick with whatever it was that mothers got sick with, and consequently went to the hospital. We sensed nothing frightening or unusual.

Later, I learned the facts. My mother was diagnosed when we were only 2 years old. The doctors gave her six weeks to live. She refused to accept the sentence.

She simply attacked life with her characteristic gusto, loving with all the love she had, giving with all the time she had, listening, sharing, laughing, with all the intensity in her soul. She passed the six-week ultimatum and continued to forge ahead.

There was too much for her to do, to keep peering over her shoulder in fear. She had my father to care for, her twins to raise, and scores of students to nurture and inspire. She would schedule her chemotherapy around my class plays, and my brother's *siyumim*. She was the first to volunteer to bake a cake for a *siyum* or to chaperone a class trip. We were deceived by her almost conspiratorial optimism. Never once did we sense death hovering over her head.

Even later on, when my mother was considerably weaker, the house continued to run on par with her standards. There was always cake in the freezer, and the Shabbos table was set on Thursday nights. Her high-school and seminary students were only too thrilled to come over and help with the housework, and my mother wasn't too proud to accept their offers.

I loved having the girls around. It gave me a sense of status, having high-school girls lavish me with attention, and I loved the noise they brought along with them. They cleaned, folded laundry, and even baked, while my mother helped them sort through their personal issues with sensitivity and perception. The atmosphere was never heavy. She was always ready with a wise quip, a cute joke, a reassuring chuckle to disperse the clouds when they settled.

When I turned 8, my mother was hospitalized for a longer stretch of time. Nobody told us she would be away for longer, or that her situation had worsened. Actually, nobody had ever told us a thing. My mother's illness was an almost abstract actuality; we knew it existed and yet, if we wanted to, we could almost make believe it didn't. Only now, when my brother and I had to be separated and sent away from home until my mother would return, did we sense a tug of anxiety pulling at our tranquil existence.

Even with my mother in the hospital, I continued to take refuge in my rosy oblivion. My father took us a lot to visit her, and if she ever came home for a short reprieve, she'd take us home and try to be everything a mother could be. She succeeded with flying colors. We had no inkling that she was holding on to life by a hair.

The truth is, I don't think she did either. Not that she was in denial. She was very much aware of her prognosis, and was fully in tune with her *neshamah's* calling. She had outrun the enemy so many times, though, I think she almost believed the chase would go on forever.

And then she was gone.

Just like that. With no warning and no parting, she was gone.

We had visited her on *Erev Shabbos*, and we spoke about her coming home. I showed her the picture I had drawn for her and she listened proudly as my brother recited his *mishnayos*.. She embraced us both in her delicious embrace.

And we went home.

And we never saw her again.

On Shabbos morning, the Baumgarten girls, our neighbors, came to pick me up. By the time late Shabbos afternoon came around, I had the gut feeling that something was amiss. My father's *talmidim* kept coming and going; now I know they were taking shifts as *shomrim* until the *levayah*; and there was a lot of grave murmuring among the adults. My heart was heavy with anxiety.

I didn't have long to wait. As soon as *Havdalah* was over, my father came in, somberly holding my brother's hand, and broke the news to me.

Mommy was *niftar*.

Niftar. The melodramatic word of books and plays. It was something eerie and mystifying, almost sensational. I had just seen my mother, just talked to her and touched her. I don't know what I had thought was on the verge of happening, but it definitely hadn't been this.

Crazily, my anxiety was suddenly gone, dissolved, replaced by a queer surge of excitement. I shot out of the house to tell my neighborhood friends what had happened. At 9 years old, I was too young to grasp the ramifications of the tragedy. I didn't realize that the life I knew and loved had ceased to exist and that my dear mother would never be back.

For the moment, I had earth-shattering news, and I savored the element of drama. I would be a heroine, the talk of my class, of my neighborhood and friends. And if I ran around on a mission, telling everybody, I wouldn't have to think; wouldn't have to cry. It certainly was a lot less frightening than staying in the house, traumatized by the stifled sobs.

The rest of the night is a blur to me. My father took me home. I remember feeling secure in the solid grip of his hand. He didn't talk much. My brother, too, was strangely silent, staring numbly into space. There were *rabbanim* in the house, and a whole warren of women who all seemed intent on serving as my mother. I was told to change, given a sweater I didn't like, and explained that it didn't matter because it would soon be slashed. I felt violated. Shoved around and bossed. I was handed my mother's *siddur* and *Tehillim*. I didn't know what I was expected to do with them. Mrs. Baumgarten came to pack up my clothes. My father said if I wanted, I could stay home for the week. I wanted to.

At the *levayah*, I suddenly panicked. This was the end. The end of my mother. They were taking her away. I wouldn't be going home. Ever. I felt numb and dizzy, as if I was someone else, watching the slow moving procession and listening to the long drawn-out speeches. Several women took care to make sure I was okay, but I felt vulnerable and alone.

Indeed, loneliness is the feeling that stands out most prominently when I relive that miserable day. On the men's side, my brother had my father's hand to hold onto. I had no sisters and no aunts to cling to; no one who could whisper to me in shared confusion, who could clutch my hand or hug me intimately. No one who could protect me, and no one whom I felt a need to shield, in turn. I was like an unanchored soul trying to find my grief among a sea of strange, albeit caring faces.

Perhaps it was this aching isolation that prodded me to choose to go to school the next day, when my father asked me whether or not I wanted to stay home for the week of *shivah*. The house, with its sad shadows and solemn visitors, scared me. At least in school, I would be surrounded by my friends and teachers, by the colorful bulletin boards, by the boisterous activity of a fourth-grade classroom.

It was a mistake, the precursor of many other mistaken choices that cost me years of pain.

As a teacher myself now, I can imagine the shock that must have registered when my teachers saw me sitting in my seat the next morning as if nothing had occurred. They had probably just barely digested the news and figured they had a few days to think about what they would say to me. There I was, sitting upright in my seat with unnerving regularity. Wisely, they chose the path of prudent men: silence.

I, however, sitting there in casual compliance, was silently screaming for words. Words of understanding, words of empathy and encouragement, words of love, anything. I needed someone to help me defrost the freezer of my heart, to unpack the emotions one by one, discard the extraneous ones, label the rest, and put them all back in some semblance of order.

Nobody around me, though, had been endowed with the ability to hear inaudible pleas. Nobody had learned to decode the complex emotions that hid behind innocent, almost angelic smiles. And so nobody said a word. Not the teachers and certainly not the students. Leave well enough alone, they must have reasoned. She seems so herself, so normal; why open a can of worms?

As an adult still carrying around a fragile 9-year-old girl in her heart, I have one message to convey to parents and teachers facing similar challenges. Little children are little human beings. They may not know what or why they are feeling, but the feelings are there, thick and strong. If you think you see a serene little suffering child, it's either a sham or a mirage, but it is not a child who has escaped the blows dealt to him by the rude shifts in his life.

Granted, we are all busy tackling our own portions. And yes, there is no one universal combination that will ease open the lock to any individual heart. But every child needs that someone who will plunge in and help him weather the storm.

I was a dream of a child. Not too loud and not too quiet, not too social and not too shy. I participated in class and jumped around during recess time: the epitome of a healthy, well-adjusted child. Nobody would have dreamed that underneath my guise of happy obedience was a mess, a mess so forbidding that I myself stayed as far away from it as I could.

All through that winter of fourth grade, I stayed with the Baumgartens. My twin brother was placed with a second cousin and occasionally, he and my father would join me at the Baumgartens for Shabbos. Although my brother and I had always been close, our personalities were very different. My brother was a straightforward, mind-over-matter type, who had never enjoyed delving beneath the surface. His pragmatic, logical nature was in stark contrast to my intensely emotional, dramatic makeup. Although I'm sure the loss was just as devastating for him as it was for me, he wasn't mired in the swirling maelstrom of feelings that were sucking me under.

Chavi Baumgarten, my classmate and friend, served as my confidante. We shared a room and often spoke late into the night. Although she chided us to stop talking and go to sleep, Mrs. Baumgarten was understanding of my needs. If I wasn't home, it was the best place I could be. I had a built-in friend and homework partner, and the lively pace of the Baumgartens' large family suited me.

My father came to visit me every single night. Though he never shared his innermost emotions with me, those visits gave me the feeling that I was still someone's little girl, special and meaningful in a unique way. Without any deep discussions, those nightly reunions were a catharsis for me. In no way was I ready for the dizzying plummet awaiting me just at the top of the hill in the roller coaster of my life.

Right before Shavuos, when the lawns were beginning to don their summer frills, when jump rope games sprouted like dandelions all over the courtyards and my heart was filled with dreams of swimming pools and daycamps, my father slung his shot. He was seriously thinking of becoming engaged, and he wanted me to meet his prospective *kallah*.

I was speechless. I had just been releasing my white-knuckled grip from the roller coaster seat, just about getting lulled into the routine of the slow, rattling, uphill climb along the tracks life had laid down for me. I had a bed I finally felt comfortable in, a drawer where I could store all my personal mementos, a place where I felt accepted and even loved. And now this. The pause before the plunge that would send me hurtling once again into the unknown.

We met shortly thereafter, but it was nothing short of a formality. Though my father had sincerely assured me that he would only go ahead if I felt perfectly comfortable with the decision, I knew that my fate had been sealed. Sensitive by nature, I would never be able to shame someone with rejection, or to foil my father's plans for happiness. In any case, I had no reason to. My prospective stepmother seemed nice enough, though my immediate impression of her was light-years away from the mother I had loved so fiercely. I knew my father sincerely wanted me to be happy; that was one of his chief motives for remarrying.

And so I did what I had grown so accustomed to doing; I swallowed the lump in my throat and flashed my most endearing smile.

Then I went home to the Baumgartens, paid Mrs. Baumgarten a hurried greeting, and sprinted off to get into pajamas. I downed the cookie and glass of milk she had set out for me, almost choking on my tears, and bid her a polite good night. Then I tiptoed into the bedroom where Chavi was fast asleep, closed the door behind me and flung myself into bed, where I gave vent to long-wrenching sobs that came from somewhere deep inside my wounded heart.

My father remarried in the summer, and I remained with the Baumgartens until after Succos. My brother and I would join my father and his new wife for Shabbos meals, an arrangement that was fair enough. The meals were not that long and they were geared solely toward us.

Then one Shabbos, while we were sitting together after the *seudah*, enjoying each other's company, they broke the news that they thought we were ready for the next step. We would be moving in with them to stay the very next day.

Shocked and unprepared, I felt my stomach turn inside out. I looked helplessly at my brother, wondering if he was feeling as fear stricken as I was. Then a huge bubble rose to the center of my throat and grew until it burst. The tears were splashing down my face before I knew what was happening.

I was mortified. I kept wiping my eyes with my sleeve, trying to procure a reassuring smile from beneath my tears. I desperately wanted to avoid hurting them, especially my father. My efforts to stanch my emotions, though, were as futile as a pair of windshield wipers in a downpour. I was terrified of the change.

Despite my misgivings, my stuff was transported the next day. I'm sure it wasn't done rashly or callously. The transition was inevitable, and I guess the experts assumed it was a good time as any to take the plunge. Once again, I was marooned on an isolated island of silence.

Theoretically, I had my father at my side and my brother who was experiencing the transition along with me. I should have been thrilled at the thought of finally going home and being reunited as a family. In reality, I felt like I was losing my emotional foothold. I had come to feel so secure at the Baumgartens; all I wanted was to leave things the way they were. Home? I would have given everything to return to my previous existence. This new setup, though, with a stranger as a mother in an unfamiliar new apartment, made me shudder with apprehension.

I was consumed by anxiety, yet had no one to whom I could unleash my fears. Mrs. Baumgarten, who had never probed where my feelings were concerned, wasn't the person to turn to. My teachers didn't suspect that anything was roiling under the surface, and my father, with whom I was close, was much too involved to serve as my confidante. Even at the tender age of 9, I sensed the delicate nature of his new relationship. I wasn't going to burden him with my fears.

Although my brother felt sorry that I was so distraught, he couldn't relate to my feelings. Mommy, he reasoned, couldn't come back, and living together as a family, in his opinion, was a lot better than staying at a second cousin's house. Besides, he shrugged, he spent most of his day in *cheder* and still had my father to accompany him to *shul* and review his work with him. Of course it wouldn't be the same, but he would make the best of it.

And so I started the painstaking climb up the next incline.

Ironically, the only ones to understand my emotional turmoil were the Baumgarten kids. On a zealous mission to protect me, they kept calling the house to check on my welfare. Chavi came over with some stuff I had inadvertently left behind, and we spoke in hushed whispers on the couch in the little apartment. She brought along a bag of her mother's cookies that she knew were my favorite.

My stepmother took an immediate dislike to Chavi. She perceived her as an interloper who was deliberately trying to undermine her efforts to form a relationship with me. As long as I was emotionally bound to the Baumgartens, she reasoned, I would be unable to form a close relationship with her. She told Chavi in no uncertain terms that she didn't want her calling or coming without permission.

For me, that was a devastating blow. Chavi was my close friend and confidante, almost like a sister. We had shared a room, a bedtime, and all our secrets over the past couple of months. Now, more than ever, I needed her support. I needed a palm my own size to grasp as I crossed the bridge to a new unknown. The wisest parent couldn't have given me what a friend my own age could provide.

Never mind a stepparent.

Not that a stepparent is any less able or any less wise. The fairy-tale profile of the wicked stepmother is as unfair a portrait as the proverbial, meddlesome mother-in-law. There are certain dynamics, however, that come into play to make the relationship a lot more fragile than a biological parent-child relationship. And it isn't a fault or a virtue. It is a fact.

When she curtailed my friendship with Chavi, my new mother was unwittingly setting the stage for battle. Children are fiercely loyal. If my stepmother was Chavi's enemy, then that put me in the rival camp together with my friend. Though I was outwardly polite, I resisted her attempts to form a close bond. I had nothing against her per se, but if she had made it into a choice, I wasn't about to opt for an imposing new woman over a good old friend.

Relationships are like plants. They cannot be forced to grow, and they bloom very gradually. Even with the noblest intentions, unnatural doses of water or sunshine don't expedite the process; on the contrary, all they do is cause the leaves to shrivel and die. And every plant needs roots in order to grow.

My stepmother wanted me to make a sterile start, to sever my bonds, junk my past, and begin all over again. There was a new house, a new room, new kitchen utensils, and new menus. She was so determined to see it work, so set on giving me the mother I didn't have.

I was almost 11 years old at the time, and I did have a past. I did have a mother and I did have memories. There were foods I was used to, habits I'd engrained, liberties I'd been given. When saplings are transplanted, utter care is taken to preserve their roots. Otherwise, they cannot possibly take to their new soil. Many adults, in their urgency to see the tree grow, forget this little bit of logic.

I tried to be compliant. I listened obediently and thanked her politely for the efforts she made on my behalf. Inside, however, I felt distrustful and rebellious. If this new mother was so bent on taking the place of my real one, then she would have to measure up. And though she was clever and talented and special in her very own way, she most certainly was not the graven image of my mother *a"h*.

Where my mother had been efficient and organized, housekeeping was not my stepmother's primary forte. She was often late with meals and became flustered when company showed up unexpectedly. This usually didn't bother me, when the ramifications didn't spill over to her demands on my father. Overprotective, as I was, I bristled with indignity when he was subject to her frustrations.

Today, as a married adult, I can appreciate the multiple difficulties of my stepmother's challenge. Not a youngster, she was suddenly faced with the dual roles of wifehood and motherhood. This, added to the fact that both the husband and the children were coming with a preconceived notion, and a very real image, of how an ideal home should operate.

As a child, though, all I knew was that I had lost a mother whom I had loved very much. I had barely dealt with that crushing loss, when a strange woman stepped into my life and presumed she could take my mother's place. It was a tremendous strain on a child who had no support system in her life.

I longed to air my struggles, to discuss my difficulties, and receive validation for what I was going through. The world then, however, was not what it is today. Going through the school system, I was the only one in the grade, if not the whole elementary-school wing, grappling with the adjustment to a parent's second marriage. I passed through junior high school, swept along on my personal tidal wave with no help or guidance.

When I reached high school, my fort was tottering, threatening to give way. I was living a double existence, docile and submissive on the outside, resentful and insecure on the inside. As far as anyone was concerned, I was a popular, spunky kid who perpetually sported a sunny smile. Only I knew that my insides were crumbling with tension and conflict, that I was alternately plagued by pangs of guilt and of longing for my dear mother whom I had never bidden a proper farewell.

In 10th grade, I finally made the decision to drop my defense, to shed my cool exterior and call out for help. Anyone who knows what it means to be a teenager can appreciate what an enormous amount of courage that required.

I did it, though. I put my social footing on the line and took the plunge. I approached my teacher in private.

Despite the fact that I was desperate, I was proud enough to conceal my plea under the veneer of a casual query connected to the day's lesson. Fortunately, my teacher was clever enough to take the bait.

She looked straight into my eyes and told me she would think about my question. And if I wanted to discuss anything else, then she was there for me.

Discuss? I knitted my brows in feigned puzzlement.

The next day, though, I was back.

And the day after.

I'd love to say that my life just leveled off into a pleasant sort of plateau, but it didn't. It was a constant struggle, learning to respect my stepmother for what she was, to let go of my defenses, and understand where she was coming from. Sometimes I wanted to give up; I wanted to leave go and crumple to the ground and roll down the side of the mountain all the way to the bottom.

Sometimes I felt like screaming in frustration and insult. Why was *I* always expected to iron things out? Wasn't my stepmother supposed to be older and wiser than I was? During times like those, I had to strain every sinew to overcome my hurt, to rebuild my respect, to accept rather than resist, to empathize rather than resent.

It wasn't an easy feat, but fortunately, I didn't climb the mountain alone. I was lucky enough to reach out just in the nick of time and I was tossed a rope by an astute rescuer to whom I am eternally grateful. I'd take refuge in my teacher's home (allegedly, I was studying with a friend) and I'd spend time talking to her, helping her around the house, cuddling and playing with her little ones. Often, our discussions revolved around my questions and conflicts, but just as frequently, we simply spent time together, letting my hurt heal in the natural warmth of her happy home.

Slowly, I learned to relate to my new stepmother, to see her as a person in her own right, completely separate from my cherished memories of my departed mother. I learned to validate my emotions, to let myself grieve when I needed to, to be candid with myself about what I was feeling. I visited my memories often, but

I stopped measuring and comparing, stopped consciously resisting my stepmother's efforts to win my love.

Losing a parent is not something one gets over. One learns to go on, to close the doors to one's past and open new ones to the future, but the scrapes and scars accompany one into adulthood, shaping one's fears and joys, subtly honing one's feelings and sensitivities. The wife, the mother, the teacher that I am today were all born of the frightened little daughter who climbed the rocky mountain of loss and confusion to reach the liberating plateau of acceptance.

And I like to think that it was my mother, sitting on high with her *Tehillim* in hand, just the way I remember her, who gave me the fortitude to reach that plateau.

Give-and-Take

I grew up in Dayton, Ohio, the typical Jewish dayschool kid, proud of my heritage and my homeland. I was almost 20 when I made *aliyah*, and settled in Yerushalayim, eagerly looking forward to building a family on the holy soil of Eretz Yisrael.

When I became engaged to Avner at 26, it was all a rosy dream. All except for one thorn, that is, that pricked me each time I brushed my cheek against the velvety petals of bliss. The name of that thorn was Tamar.

Not that I had a rational explanation for my feelings about Tamar. She was my mother-in-law's niece, only a year older than Avner. Coming from a small *yishuv* some distance from Yerushalayim, she had boarded with my in-laws for high school. She was sweet, sociable, and had never harmed me in any way.

Perhaps, though, that was just it. Tamar was too sweet and too sociable for my liking. She was totally at home in my in-laws' house, and acted like a daughter. Just the confidence and ease with which she fit into the family made me feel like an outsider by contrast.

Tamar wasn't just a cousin. Tamar was a year older than Avner and had grown up with him since babyhood. Though he'd already been out of the house when she'd actually lived with them, she was annoyingly familiar with his hang-ups and idiosyncrasies and was privy to a trove of shared memories to which I had no access.

Then there was the mentality factor. Avner came from an Israeli family, while my mind-set and mentality were purely American. Tamar's quick Hebrew and sharp Israeli wit had a ring of condescension to me. Whatever it was, her presence irked me right from the start. As soon as Tamar entered the room, I'd feel myself stiffen involuntarily.

Though she always took care to greet me warmly and inquire about my welfare, I found myself resisting her overtures. If she ignored me, I fumed in insult; if she addressed me, I would misconstrue her friendly gestures as being manipulative.

"Oh hi, Barbara," she would exclaim, "how are you?" And before I could even consider answering her in kind, the unreasonable child within me took the floor.

"Fine," I would reply, in a tone that clearly conveyed my disinterest in her or the conversation. Then I would shift my weight impatiently, waiting for her to leave the room. When she didn't, I would feel my insides tightening with resentment. *Get out of here already*, I would hiss inaudibly, as she made some remark to Avner. *Get out and stay out.* As if to irritate me purposely, though, she never seemed to pick up the vibes.

She didn't even have to talk about anything personal to chafe my sensitivities. It was enough for her to settle comfortably into one of the living-room armchairs and ask him his opinion on the news, or to comment that the Elazaris from the second floor were moving out, to make me feel like she was encroaching on our private time together.

Though I tried to paste a polite smile on my face, it didn't quell the anger rising inside me. Will as I might, I couldn't bring myself to carry on a gracious conversation with Tamar in the room.

Give it time, I told myself. *You're still new in the family and insecure with your relationship. You'll see,* I reassured myself. *As soon as you'll be married for a while, Tamar will be nothing but an insignificant detail in your life.*

I was wrong. Avner and I were happily married; Tamar was engaged and married, and still, I could not get myself to change my attitude toward her. She and her new husband were frequent Shabbos guests at my in-laws' home, always there to greet us, always there to bid us farewell, and always there to bring out the nastiest side of me, the side I had never known existed until our destinies had crossed.

Just let go, I chided myself; *you're a grown adult. Tamar isn't taking anything away from you. She has her own life and so do you.* Much as I spoke to myself, however, I couldn't find it within my heart to relax my defensive attitude. Tamar would sit around the table, freely contributing to the family chitchat, serving and clearing off like an old hand, and I would seethe inside. *Who needs you here,* I would silently sneer, *who needs you here to ruin our visits every time?*

When I voiced these thoughts to my husband when we got home, he always looked perplexed. "I can't understand what Tamar did to ruin your visit. Didn't she keep Eli occupied the whole time we were there?"

That clinched it. Husbands. They had an uncanny way of toppling the tallest tower with simplicity that made you look foolish, but left you feeling frustrated. Avner's innocent question only served to add fuel to the fire.

No, thank you. I didn't *need* Tamar to occupy Eli. Didn't he see that she had only been trying to outdo me, to imply that I didn't give 2 year-old Eli enough attention? He was my son and I was perfectly capable of playing with him. I did it all the time.

Avner was stunned by my reaction. "If you ask me, you're really distorting things way out of proportion. Why do you take a negative magnifying glass to anything that Tamar does?"

Why? It was a question that plagued me too. I was generally good natured and easy to get along with; aside from an occasional argument, I had always enjoyed only peaceful relationships with the people around me.

What was it about Tamar that provoked me? Try as I might, I couldn't rid myself of my resentment toward her. Whatever she said, rankled; whatever she did, rubbed me the wrong way. It was as if, where Tamar was concerned, there was some inner bow perpetually arched taut, strained to the limit, just waiting for one flick to send an arrow flying her way.

Negativity doesn't exist in a vacuum. Jealousy breeds resentment; resentment breeds anger; anger breeds hostility. My hostility wasn't lost on Tamar. She began to deliberately dodge me whenever we visited, and directed her comments to little Eli. I felt like the comical monkey in the middle, pouting belligerently as the two volleyed over my head.

Shani was born, and then Michael. I was busier than ever before trying to juggle the various responsibilities of motherhood. Apparently, I had everything going for me. I had a wonderful, supportive husband and three adorable, healthy children. Yet *Chazal* knew what they were saying when they described envy as the "decay of (one's) bones."

As long as Tamar was on the scene, I never felt completely at peace. Something about her presence made me feel like my whole identity was being undermined, as if my worth as a person was being threatened. I started to pray earnestly that Hashem remove these baseless feelings from my heart; that he cleanse my soul of every last vestige of animosity. I wracked my brain for an idea, something, anything, that could peel off the layers of negativity and plant a seed of love.

Giving, I had learned, awakened love. Tamar was going through a failed marriage and needed help financially. When my husband had mentioned that perhaps we could help her, my initial reaction had been to object. Thinking things over, I reconsidered his proposal. Perhaps, giving, indeed, would promote closeness.

Reality disappointed me. Though we overextended ourselves, both financially and physically, to assist Tamar, I didn't feel that surge of love that was supposed to accompany an act of giving. Quite the contrary; I was only feeling more and more distanced, enmeshed in my self-constructed net of bitterness and resentment. The more I sacrificed, the more I seemed to resent Tamar. I couldn't get myself to break the cycle.

Then one Shabbos morning, before the birth of my fourth child, the truth suddenly hit me the way an elusive fact sometimes dawns in a moment of distraction. As we sat around the *seudah*, me bristling, as usual, at Tamar's comments, the solution came to me, clear as day. I had been working in the wrong direction. I didn't have to *give* Tamar; I needed to *take* from her.

The rest of the meal passed over me in a blur, as I worked through my thoughts. Giving Tamar, though it had lent me the illusion of feeling like a saint, had not humbled me into a position of mutual friendship. Benevolence was sometimes a cleverly camouflaged form of control; it put one into a temporary position of superiority, which inevitably crashed into resentment just as soon as the recipient didn't bow down out of utter indebtedness.

If I were to really put my ego aside, which, frankly, was the issue between Tamar and me, I would have to be the recipient of her kindness in a real and meaningful way. And I knew just what that way would be, though I wasn't ready to face it yet.

When the kids were settled in bed that night, my husband broached the topic of the upcoming birth. I was ready. I sat up straight and dropped the bombshell.

"I'm planning to call Tamar to be with me during the birth."

"What?"

If I had said that I wanted to move back to the States, I don't think Avner would have been more shocked.

"I've thought about it carefully, and I'm calling Tamar to come along."

I knew it was what I wanted to do. Though it meant shedding every last bit of pride, scrapping every last drop of anger, I had my mind made up that that was what I wanted to do.

Tamar was as shocked as my husband had been.

"You're sure?" she asked slowly, her voice quivering with unconcealed excitement.

"As sure as could be. I need someone I feel comfortable with and someone who could be available at any time. My mother couldn't make it this time and I thought of you."

"You did!" Tamar sounded downright flattered. After an excited pause, she shifted into high gear. "You have my cell number, right? Don't hesitate to call me at any hour. There's no one to wake up in my house, besides for me," she giggled. "In fact, I'm on my way to the *Kosel* right now. I'll be having you in mind for an easy time."

I hung up, feeling the elation of a hard-won victory. Step one was behind me. Now I would have to pray that I didn't regret my decision when the time came. After all, I could think of some better places to have one's adversary present. I hoped that my decision alone would affect the change I had been praying for; the change that would turn her from foe to friend.

Nadav was born on a gorgeous, summer day in Elul in the holy city of Yerushalayim. The recollection I have of his birth is not of myself, or of Avner, or even of Nadav's newborn cry. It is a picture of Tamar, her face bathed in sunlight, holding my swaddled little newborn son. It is one of the most precious pictures I have in my memory bank, a picture that brings tears to my eyes each time anew. If I had to give it a caption, it would be "birth and rebirth."

The human heart is so complex. Giving, taking, both can be either, and either can be both. If the act is fueled by rivalry and insecurity, it will only broaden the chasm between two human beings; if it is inspired by humility and acceptance, then it will foster love. For the first time since I had become engaged, I was able to view Tamar at eye level, not from either the top or the bottom of the see saw. And what I saw was a human heart like my own, a giving, taking, loving human heart.

That winter, for the first time since my marriage, I really knew peace. I had taken the plunge and I had clutched Tamar's arm during my most vulnerable hour. Now, my defenses were permanently down. My heart felt clean and light, and I no longer felt threatened by her presence.

Not that we became the closest of friends; we still had our differences, both of culture and character. We were bound by having shared. Our hearts now beat in synchrony and we enjoyed the comfort of belonging to the same family. I laughed at her jokes, listened to her advice, and offered some of my own. Without all the envy and resentment clogging my heart, I was able to make some room within for Tamar's personal plight.

Life hadn't dealt her such an easy share. She was desperate to get married again and build a family of her own. Though there wasn't much I could do on a practical level, I prayed for her to meet her prospective husband soon. Often, I found myself daydreaming about her wedding, the way I would glide across the wedding floor to a glowing Tamar, pump her warm hand, and embrace her with all my heart and soul. I could almost feel the pulsing intensity of that embrace against my heart, and I knew that when that moment arrived, the circle would be complete.

Indeed, very soon after, I got the call. Tamar was engaged again. She sounded thrilled when she filled me in on the details and told me they would be getting married in the spring. I shared her ecstasy, and told her I couldn't wait to dance at her wedding. In the meantime, I wished her *hatzlachah* with the upcoming preparations and offered my help with whatever she needed.

Tamar got busy and so did I. Pesach was fast approaching, and after that came a very hectic season. The Women's Auxilary in Shani's school was putting on their annual production, and I had been chosen to play the lead role. The timetable was tough, and I had to reschedule my agenda around practice sessions. It was a lot of pressure, but I loved it. Drama had always been my field and my part in the production gave me the creative outlet I so craved. My husband and children put up with my stiff schedule and cheered me on.

I'll never forget the phone call. We'd been out of touch for a while, Tamar and I, when she called me one day from work. That's how it was with us those days; my existence was no longer measured as being one up or one down to Tamar; we could both be sailing along pleasantly on our own parallel routes without being so keenly aware of each other.

I was genuinely pleased to hear her voice.

"How are things coming along, Tamar?" I inquired.

"Oh great! Just great!" she gushed, "The date is set, and things are starting to fall into place. The wedding is going to be in Atzulat

Yerushalayim and we even booked Yaakovi Photographers for the night."

"When's the big night?" I asked.

"It's the second of Sivan."

"Uh oh."

Snag.

"What's the matter?"

"Well," I said slowly, "Avner's going to be there, my in-laws will be there, the kids'll be there. But I'm not going to be there."

If it had been a line in my script, I would have gotten the pitch just right. Real life that it was, I felt tears forming at the corners of my eyes.

"Wwwhat do you mean?" stammered Tamar. "What's the problem with the date?"

"You know about my play, right?" For some reason I heard myself sounding annoyed. "The first performance is scheduled for the second of Sivan."

"And there's no way to change it?" Her voice treaded the tightrope between resignation and hope.

"Are you kidding?" again the annoyance. Anger is always easier to vent than disappointment. "These dates are booked since last June."

"I can't believe it. And you say you're playing the lead role."

There was silence on the line, as we each mentally circled the dead end. No way out. I felt myself choking on a growing lump. I wouldn't be at Tamar's wedding after all. Never mind that nobody from the family would be there to see me starring in the play. That was trivial.

Suddenly, I found a window.

"What about you? No way to change it anymore? Maybe the hall had some last-minute cancellation or something."

"I don't think it's an option," Tamar replied. "It isn't just the hall. It's the photographer, the band, everything. It's late already, you know." Now Tamar sounded irritated.

My hands felt clammy. I switched the receiver to my other ear. Gridlock. There was nothing more to say. Besides, the tears were already gargling at the dam, trembling right beneath my voice.

"Okay then, Tamar," I sighed, trying mightily to keep the tears down. "I guess you'll be getting married without me."

Then, the dam broke. Tamar listened uncomfortably as I tried to regain control. It was no use.

"I'm sorry, Barbara," she said, almost inaudibly. "I didn't mean it this way."

Long after she hung up, I found myself sitting in one place, mindlessly running my finger over and over the touch pad of the telephone. So I wouldn't be at Tamar's wedding. After all I had invested to come around and save our relationship, her wedding had to coincide with the evening of my performance. The pure, hurting irony of it.

Shaking myself out of my stupor, I forced myself to do some shopping and prepare supper. I went through the motions of baths and bedtime. I had practice at 9 o'clock. I couldn't see myself going in my miserably dispirited state.

The phone rang.

It was Tamar on the line.

"Oh hi, Tamar," I said limply. I knew I was being unfair, but I just couldn't seem to swallow the disappointment.

Tamar ignored my tepid greeting and got straight to the point, like a kid bursting in from school, too excited to hang up her coat.

"You're not going to believe it, Barbara, but I changed the date."

"You what?"

I stopped in my tracks. I had underestimated Tamar.

"Moshe thought I was a little crazy, but he was willing to go along with it if I worked out all the arrangements."

"I can't believe it, Tamar. I really can't believe it. You actually switched the date. You don't know what it means to me."

"I sure do," chuckled Tamar, pleased with my reaction, "If I didn't, I never would have considered taking such a rash step. The caterer literally snickered when I asked him about switching the date.

"'Are you kidding, Giveret? You're talking about another eight weeks. This is our busiest season; you think the dates just sit around waiting?' I told him it was crucial that he find a date, and by some miracle he had an opening on the Monday before the original date. It's Yom Yerushalayim, and the traffic is terribly heavy then. I guess that's why nobody took it."

"Wow, you mean it! And you managed to work it all out with the photographer and musician?"

"I still have to get back to the musician; he had a tentative booking for that date, but he said he would try to figure it out. Moshe's parents were really upset when they heard about the change. I know the play means so much to you, Barbara, and there's no way you could possibly back out, but to other people, it just doesn't seem like a good enough reason to toy with a wedding date. Never mind, though, everybody's happy now, and I'm the happiest of all."

"No, *I'm* the happiest of all," I amended. "I know what it took on your part, and I can't tell you how much I appreciate it." My heart swelled as my deflated dream began to balloon once again.

"Well, let me circle Monday on my calendar. Monday, the 28th of Iyar, Tamar and Moshe! I want you to know, Tamar, that I am deeply touched that you did this for me."

When I walked through the glass doors of Atzulat Yerushalayim to the strains of wedding music, I felt my heart do a somersault. Ten months before, I wouldn't have given a hoot to miss this wedding. Now, I felt the deepest stirrings of emotion as the music strummed at my heartstrings. "You're the catalyst for all of this," I whispered to little Nadav, beautiful in his starched light blue outfit, as we entered the air-conditioned main hall.

As I approached the white wicker chair, I overheard some loud whispers, "That's her; she's the one they switched the date for." The words felt like silken flutters in my heart.

Tamar looked up and a broad smile lit up her face.

"Barbara!"

We fell into each other's arms, and once again, I was engulfed in that feeling I had felt at Nadav's birth. It was more than love. It was the elation of victory, of having conquered pettiness and animosity for the sake of *shalom*.

I stayed until the very end of the wedding, dancing as I hadn't danced in ages. When I hit the pillow late that night, it was a sweet sleep that overtook me. *Metukah shnat ha'oveid.*

I didn't have too much time to savor the festivities. Thursday was my big day, and with the pressures of dress rehearsals and last-minute adjustments, I was barely even home. For the second time that week, I savored the experience of actualizing a long anticipated dream. I had celebrated Tamar's wedding, and now I was to appear under the public spotlight on stage.

The play far surpassed our expectations. The wild clapping reverberated long after the curtain had been drawn on the final scene. Flushed with euphoria and drained from the exertion of performing, I retreated to my private dressing room backstage where my close friends and family awaited me.

I basked in their raving compliments as I got my stuff together and waited for my husband to come pick us up. As we walked out into the cool Yerushalayim evening, we were greeted by the unmistakable wailing of sirens; not one and not two, but a whole cacophony of shrieking sirens faded in and out of the crisp night air.

Terror attack. That's the first thing that crossed our minds, as our excited chatter died on our lips. More sirens. An unending tumult of racing sirens crisscrossing each other. My cell phone rang. I picked it up, anxious to hear some news.

"Barbara?"

It took me a moment to identify Tamar's hysterical voice.

"What happened, Tamar?" I shouted, my world going black.

"Oh Barbara," she sobbed, barely getting out the syllables, "Thank you. Thank you. Thank you for saving our lives."

Tamar's voice sounded surreal. The whole scene felt like an appendage of the drama I'd just been through. But this wasn't part of the script.

"What in the world are you talking about, Tamar?" I demanded. "Are you okay?"

"Atzulat Yerushalayim is gone, Barbara. The dance floor of the hall on top of it, the Versailles, caved in."

"Whaaaat?" Again, I had the feeling of acting in a play. What was Tamar talking about? Who ever heard of a floor caving in?

"There are dozens of casualties, and they haven't finished counting yet. Barbara," again the hysterical sobbing crackling over the static of the cell phone. "If not for you, we all would have been dancing there tonight."

Somewhere, in the midst of her hysteria and my horrified numbness, the connection was severed. Avner showed up, white as a sheet, shaking with the latest news report.

The floor of the "Versailles" had collapsed at the height of a wedding celebration, instantly killing tens of celebrants, injuring scores more. The hall beneath it, Atzulat Yerushalayim, was completely demolished, though by an incredible stroke of fortune, there had been no affair taking place there at the time. Investigations were still under way.

Incredible? Indeed. Stroke of fortune? Not in the least. The details of the script had been written and orchestrated by a Force incomprehensibly larger than fortune. The drama had been staged over the course of many months, long months of supreme effort for the sake of harmony and love. And, now, I had been privileged, for the second time in one night, to witness the unfolding of my role leading up to a grand finale.

Keeping the Vessel Intact

I've never really shared my story with anyone. Perhaps I just wanted to get my past behind me and slurp the refreshing reality of the present. Perhaps I still felt precarious, ungrounded, as if telling my tale would somehow shake the foundation of my existence. And then, maybe I simply felt that I couldn't tell a story that didn't yet have an ending.

My earliest memory is a painful flashback to the day of my 3rd birthday. I remember going to sleep the night before, jittery with anticipation, my velvet *yarmulke* proudly perched atop a crisp pair of *tzitzis,* laid neatly on the dresser.

I had been waiting impatiently for this special day, and I knew just what awaited me. I would accompany my father to his Rebbe after *davening* and the Rebbe would give me a *berachah*. After that, we would travel together to Miron to the *kever* of Rabbi Shimon bar Yochai, where I would receive my first haircut. Instead of a ponytail, I would boast two flowing *peyos,* and my head would finally be adorned with the *yarmulke* that I had dreamed of for so many months.

Morning dawned and I was up long before either of my parents. I eyed the special outfit that had been reserved for the occasion, and wondered when my mother would come dress me. Instead, it was my father who tiptoed into my room, and then broke in a beaming grin when he saw that I was sitting up in bed, waiting.

He quickly helped me get dressed, and I set out with him into the cool morning air, my little hand linked in his, bobbing up and down with excitement as we got near the *shul*. When we came home from the Rebbe, I was bubbling with enthusiasm, eager to tell my mother about the *berachah* I had received.

I found my mother still in her morning robe, preparing herself a cup of coffee. She gave me a wan smile, but her eyes seemed a million miles away.

"Mommy, quick," I barged breathlessly into the kitchen, "you have to get ready, we're almost leaving to Miron!"

"No, sweetheart, I'm not coming," my mother replied, stirring her coffee. She didn't look up at me.

I was shocked. Why wasn't my mother coming? Did that mean that our plans were canceled?

"You'll go with Tatty, and Zeidy and Bubby. I have a bad headache today."

A bad headache? I was taken aback and very puzzled. I kept silent, though. I could sense that my mother didn't want me to press her with questions.

All the while, my father kept busy in his study. He made a few phone calls in hushed tones, and then silently entered the kitchen. He opened the refrigerator, put a few bottles of water into an insulated bag, and then scavenged around the kitchen for some cookies and crackers. It was strange, my mother silently sipping her coffee at the table, my father tapping around the kitchen, soundlessly filling a bag. Even at 3 years old, I felt the heaviness in the air, the unnatural quiet preceding what should have been a lively trip.

Instinctively, I found myself walking on tiptoes so as not to disturb the awkward silence pervading the house. My usual chatter died on my lips, and I hung obediently near the couch waiting until my father would be ready to leave. This was not the way I had envisioned my *chalakah* at all.

I don't remember much about the actual trip. I vaguely recall being lifted atop my father's shoulders, surrounded by my grandparents. Years later, my grandfather told me that I had been unusually pensive during the proceedings. "*Daven* for Mommy's headache to go away," I had requested earnestly when the dancing died down. Little did I know then that my mother wasn't suffering from a headache; what she was suffering from was called heartache.

When we returned home, my father instructed me to go up to the apartment by myself and wave to him from the window. "Aren't you coming home?" I asked, bewildered.

"No, I have to take care of something. I'll be at Zeidy and Bubby's house," he replied offhandedly. I shrugged, sensing something strange in the making. First my mother's headache, and then this. And all on my long-awaited day.

I scrambled up the steps and waved goodbye to my father. I didn't dream that he would never be coming home again to our cozy little apartment.

I was 3 years old, just out of babyhood. It wasn't that long ago that I had uttered my very first words: Mommy, shortly followed by Tatty. That's the way I had perceived reality, Mommy, always followed by Tatty; Tatty, always followed by Mommy. I didn't conceive that the two could ever be separated.

I was generally a well-behaved child. I obeyed my mother and tried to make her proud of me. I never asked her why my father had left, why we weren't like a normal family. I intuited that these questions were treading on painful territory.

During the nights, however, the questions plagued me. Why did my father prefer Bubby and Zeidy to my mother and me? How come all fathers came home every night and took their *yingelach* to *shul* on Shabbos, and only my Tatty didn't live with us?

Once, when I was over at my grandparents to spend Shabbos with my father, I dared to voice my confusion.

"Tatty, was I a very bad baby?"

"Babies aren't bad," my grandmother lovingly patted me on my cheek. "Some babies cry a lot, and people call them hard. But they aren't bad, *chalilah*."

"So was I hard?" I persisted, "Did I cry a lot?"

"Not at all," my father replied. "In fact you were a little angel." He looked at me proudly.

"Oh," I said, disconcerted, "I thought maybe I cried too much, and you decided to leave."

An uncomfortable silence settled on the table, as my grandmother quickly collected the empty fish plates, and my grandfather cleared his throat to begin *zemiros*. My father looked unmistakably upset. If I had been hoping for reassurance, for a plausible explanation that would dispel my guilt, I was disappointed. I picked up the unspoken cue and didn't bring up the subject again.

I was only 5 years old at the time, but I was old enough to sense the invisible tension, to feel the intangible pain. I would hear my grandparents conferring with my father in whispers, I would see my mother wiping tears when she thought I wasn't around. No one thought of taking the time to clarify the situation to me, to explain to me in simple terms, if there was such a thing, what was going on.

I guess they thought that as long as I didn't openly challenge them, it was better not to broach the subject. Why rock a boat that seemed to be sailing just fine?

As an adult with a window to my painful childhood, I know that there is no such thing. Children, no matter how carefree they appear, aren't impervious to the upheavals in their lives. Even if they seem obedient and well adjusted, even if they never express anxiety, fear and guilt are tearing at their souls. A heart-to-heart talk never rocks the boat; it only provides the life jacket of which a brave little sailor may be in desperate need of.

Kids can be ruthless. Without realizing the pain they were inflicting, boys in my class would whisper behind my back or ask me personal questions. I was very sensitive about my position. No one else I knew had divorced parents; no one else in my class went to visit his father at his grandparents' house. I was very careful, though, not to share my social embarrassment with my mother. I knew she was trying her best, and that it was difficult for her too.

I also learned very quickly what to tell each of my parents so as not to put them on the spot. I would never tell my mother about the gifts that my father bought me during my visitations with him; I refrained from telling my father about my mother's tears. I became a little diplomat, carefully steering between the tangled branches of hurt and resentment and pain.

When the solid foundations of a child's life crumble beneath his feet, when the invincible fortress of his life collapses and the bond between his parents is severed, his concept of absolute security is put on the line. He is no longer sure that anything in this world is stable, that his parents' love is unconditional, that their loyalty and faithfulness will forever accompany him, regardless of the way he behaves.

Some children react to this insecurity with violence and hostility, testing the threshold of their caretakers' forbearance. Other children, like me, become overly mature and sensitive in a frightened effort to sustain their parents' love and approval. Looking back, I was an unnaturally good child. I suppressed my feelings and behaved like a model student, keeping all my turbulence bottled up inside.

Just recently, as I passed a public telephone booth, I overheard a young boy of 9 or 10 pleading on the telephone.

"Don't be upset, Tatty, I'll make sure to come another day; it just doesn't work out today because of my dentist appointment. I promise you; I really wanted to come today. So you're not upset?"

My heart contracted for this little boy whom I didn't know, yet whose conflict I understood so well: always torn, always appeasing, always trying to smooth out the creases that obstinately appeared in the fabric of his life through no fault of his own.

My yeshivah years were a relative island of peace. For once, I was a *bachur* like every other *bachur,* learning three *sedarim* a day and sleeping in the dormitory. My visitations weren't as frequent or as obtrusive, and I had a chance to throw myself wholeheartedly into my learning. In the interim, my father had remarried and was now preoccupied with his new budding family. He still took interest in me, but with not a fraction of the intensity he had shown before.

When my friends began to get engaged, I was thrust once again into the reality of my situation. While I excelled in my learning and had a sterling reputation, I knew my stigma would follow me into the arena of *shidduchim*. I tried not to concentrate on my apprehension and doubled my efforts in the realm of my studies. I also invested a lot in my *tefillah*, entreating Hashem that He send me a worthy partner in spite of my rough background.

"*Ein tefillah shechozeres reikah.*" (There is no prayer that is returned empty-handed.) That's what I remember thinking when the cries of *Mazel Tov* rang out around me, and I was none other than the celebrated *chassan*. My mother had repaid me for all the years I had so carefully protected her, and had constantly reassured me that a good *shidduch* would come up, despite the fact that I came from a broken home.

"Every person has his destined mate," she'd encourage me, "and no one can take yours away from you. You keep learning and *davening*, and Hashem will take care of the rest."

I kept my end of the deal, and my mother screened the suggestions that came her way. If she harbored her own anxieties, she never let on. After several months, an incredibly promising proposition came up. I was afraid to ask the unspoken question: Why was the other side interested? Instead, I held my breath, waiting for rejection.

It never came. I was engaged to Henny three weeks later, a radiant *chassan* brimming with joyful hopes and idealistic dreams. I wasn't inflated with the empty thrill of the fanfare and festivities. I was filled with a deep sense of peace and anticipation.

I had had such a precarious childhood, always tiptoeing over a fissure of uncertainty, always paying double doses of loyalty. Now I would finally have the chance to lay the groundwork for a solid foundation, to build a warm and secure nest for the next generation. If anyone knew the importance of the task that lay ahead, I certainly did.

What I didn't know was how difficult that task would prove to be.

My wife was the eldest of a large family who lived in the center of Yerushalayim. My in-laws were especially devoted parents, who, in typical Israeli tradition, graciously invited us to eat our main meal with them every day. Naturally, I appreciated their offer, and was happy to oblige. After all, our apartment was only two buildings away from theirs, and Henny seemed thrilled to revel in the familiar warmth of her family's dinnertime.

Soon enough, however, I began to feel uncomfortable with this daily setup. My in-laws' house was small and crowded and mealtime was especially hectic. There was no official time for dinner; the shifts ran into each other as the various members of the household returned home from school, *cheder,* and work.

Henny saw no problem with this. She was used to the homey atmosphere, the loud chatter and elbow rubbing that provided the background for spilled soup and cutlery clattering to the floor.

I, on the other hand, had grown up in a quiet, almost austere home. Though I appreciated the congenial atmosphere, I was more than a little overwhelmed by the explosion of noise around one little crowded table. Besides, I desperately craved a little private time with my new wife. Though my mother-in-law tried to shoo away

Keeping the Vessel Intact / 319

the little ones while we ate, I could barely get a word in edgewise over their constant interruptions.

I had enrolled in an intense *kollel*, and dinnertime was the only real break in my schedule. I sincerely wished we could spend that hour or two in the privacy of our own little abode. Our relationship was still stiff and polished, like a pair of brand-new shoes. We needed time and togetherness to break into marriage, so that it would afford the comfort of a pair of familiar, well-worn shoes. The way it was, I found myself hurriedly finishing my portion and retreating into some quieter corner while Henny helped her mother with the dishes. This was not the way I had envisioned marriage, becoming the 12th member of a lively family.

Mealtime was only one illustration of a much larger picture. As time passed, I came to realize that Henny was still very much attached to her mother's apron strings. She instinctively consulted with her on every big and little matter, and wouldn't make a purchase without having her mother accompany her. It went without saying that most Shabbosos and Yamim Tovim were spent at her parents' home.

My in-laws, in turn, were unusually generous and went all out to provide us with our every need. Every need, that is, besides for the most essential prerequisite: some privacy and independence to build our own home.

When I tried gently broaching the subject, Henny seemed to have no clue as to what my problem was. She couldn't understand my distress over the fact that we weren't getting to build our own separate unit, apart from her parents' home. Why sweat to cement our own flimsy twigs, she reasoned, when we could lean on the sturdy edifice of her parents' experience and expertise?

I felt a helpless passivity crawl over me. I couldn't find the words to express my frustration, to justify the urgency of my dissatisfaction with the way things were going. My garbled explanations sounded lame even to my own ears; I seemed selfish and ungrateful for the bounty that was being handed to us on a silver platter.

Deep down, I felt my old vulnerability coming to the fore. I had a deeply ingrained aversion to confrontation and didn't want to say anything that would upset the equilibrium, even if that stability was nothing more than a superficial illusion of harmony. When I saw that Henny was becoming agitated by our discussion, I immediately folded and tried to appease her.

I also felt intimidated by my in-laws who were so much older and more experienced than I was. No matter what a competent husband I knew I could be, I had an inferiority complex talking about marriage and relationships. Who was I, who had never seen a model marriage, to suggest that my in-laws were stifling our chance to develop a healthy relationship?

My oldest son was born, had a *bris* and *pidyon haben*, and I hung at the edge of the celebrations like a guest at my own *simchah*. Understandably, my wife now needed her mother's help and support more than ever. She was weak and emotionally fragile and automatically turned to her mother for guidance. My in-laws set up all the paraphernalia and hovered over the new mother and baby, while I felt like an outsider, whose assistance was unsolicited and unnecessary. I almost felt as if I had to ask permission before I was allowed to hold my newborn son.

I went to *kollel* every morning, aching to feel the harried irregularity most new fathers experienced after the birth of their first child. I listened with envy as I heard two of my friends sharing their frustration with colic and the unpredictable whims of a fatigued new mother. If only those were my concerns. I yearned to be involved in the beautiful fusing of my own little family. It seemed that I had been locked out of the circle.

Late in the middle of the night, while my wife shuffled to the kitchen where her mother was warming a bottle for the baby, I found hot tears trickling onto the side of my face, soaking pools of disappointment and self-pity into my pillowcase. I felt so disconnected, so estranged. I should have been the happiest man in the world, yet I was sick with misery.

I had waited so long for this; I had dreamed and prayed and pinned all my hopes on the time when I would be able to give a wife and child everything I had never had. And here I was, apparently witnessing the unfolding of my dreams, yet so far from experiencing the rosy utopia.

In the dark of those nights, I contemplated the option of separation. It was the last thought I had ever dreamed of entertaining, yet somehow, my desperation drove me to the edge of my rational sensibilities. No one would sense my absence anyway, I reasoned bitterly. And I was so lonely already, it couldn't get too much worse.

Though I had tried to be actively involved at the outset, I slowly withdrew. Henny was wrapped up in her own cocoon, with her mother flapping nearby like an overprotective butterfly. She courteously served me my meals and smilingly told me that Henny had gone to nap. It was all I could do to try and smile back. Inside, my heart was screaming in pain.

Obviously, it was screaming loud enough for someone to hear.

One morning, as I zipped my *tallis* bag after *davening,* thinking despondently of my shattered dreams, I noticed an old man near me slowly finishing *Aleinu*. For some reason, I was mesmerized by his unhurried manner, by the deliberate way he pronounced every syllable. I felt my eyes unabashedly following his lips, riveted to his radiant countenance.

He must have felt my eyes on him, must have sensed the pools of sadness within those eyes.

"*Shalom aleichem*," he smiled warmly to me when he had finished *davening*. "Might you perhaps be going in my direction? Would you care to accompany me home?"

I nodded, eager to clear my head before I started my day. "The direction doesn't matter," I responded apathetically. "It's all the same to me."

He arched his eyebrows questioningly, but didn't say a word. The single gesture of interest was all I needed in order to rupture the thin membrane that had been valiantly holding back an ocean of tears.

I hadn't had a shoulder to cry on for so long. I had always tried to paint a rosy picture for my mother; my father was so busy with his family, he barely even inquired about my welfare. My wife and in-laws were completely oblivious to my pain. The old man's compassionate eyes and gentle gaze were all I needed to spill my soul.

Like a faucet sputtering water after a long shutoff spell, my words first came out stilted and faltering, and then suddenly gushed forth in a torrent of unchecked emotion. All my loneliness and rejection, all my dashed hopes and stifled dreams, the home I craved, the closeness for which I yearned. I was so swept away by my emotions, I didn't even realize that we had been circling the same street for about an hour, and had passed the old man's house many times over.

"Why don't you come up for tea?" the man suggested, and I readily took him up on his offer. I knew I couldn't learn in this agitated state. Perhaps this anonymous benefactor could help me sort through my feelings.

Once we were upstairs and had comfortably settled with two glasses of piping hot tea and a dish of cinnamon cookies, the elderly man looked into my eyes.

"You've got to turn to the One Who put you into the situation," he said softly. "I know right now you're so desperate, even separation seems like a viable option. It's not what you really want, though. Who, like you, knows the agony of breaking apart a Jewish home?"

"What should I do then?" I asked helplessly. "I can't see myself continuing this way. I feel myself getting more depressed every day."

"Only Hashem really feels the extent of your pain. He knows what you went through as a child, and how badly you long to build a warm, loving family. We don't know His calculations, but one thing is sure; there is a reason for every bit of your ordeal. Every drop of hardship is measured and will be rewarded from Above.

"As for you, as long as your wife is integrally a good person, and is not suffering from a real disorder, you have my reassurance that things will turn around. It might take a lot of effort on your part, but there is no way that your investment won't affect a change."

"You've got to make a deal with the *Ribono shel Olam*. Tell Him that you'll do anything in your power to keep the vessel intact, and in turn, you would like Him to pour his blessings inside."

I listened to him in silence, like a little child pacified after a crying spell. Just listening to his calm tone of voice had sort of lulled me into a detached state of serenity. It was reassuring to have someone take the reins, to have someone older and wiser take my hand and show me where to go. Suddenly, the import of his words penetrated my consciousness.

"You think that'll help?" I asked skeptically.

"*That* won't help," He answered firmly. "Hashem will help."

The old man went on to outline some practical advice; some steps I could take to make things better, some measures I shouldn't take no matter what things came to. I listened to his suggestions with half a heart, too dispirited to really believe anything could change the situation.

Suddenly the old man got up and brought two *Gemaras* to the table.

"Now let's see what you know," he challenged, his eyes sparkling with excitement. He proceeded to pose a question related to the *sugya* I was learning. Reluctantly, I sat up and shook myself out of my lethargy. Before long, I found myself being plunged into the waters of the *Gemara*, animatedly debating a *sevara* the old man had presented.

At first the waves lapped shyly at my heart, but slowly, I became submerged in the current. We sat at the table, the old man and I, oblivious to the passing of time, lost in the steady back and forth of the complicated *sugya*. When he suggested that we break for lunch, I was shocked that three hours had elapsed. Why, it had been ages since I had gotten so carried away with my learning.

My newfound mentor suggested that we form a steady *chavrusa* in the evenings.

"No problem," I responded, rejuvenated by our refreshing session. "I know where you live. Just tell me a time."

"No," the old man smiled, "We'll have the *chavrusa* in *your* house. Is 8 o'clock all right with you?"

I was only too happy to oblige. Our dining room chairs would finally come to some use.

In the meantime, I tried to implement some of the old man's suggestions. I poured my heart into my *davening*, begging the *Ribono shel Olam* to bring about some change, and to give me the stamina to hold out until I saw it coming.

At the same time, I tried to exude a positive attitude, genuinely inquiring about my wife's day and the baby's progress. It took all my determination not to retreat into a protective shell when I felt so totally ignored and excluded. The old man's words are what kept me going. I had made a bargain with Hashem, and I was resolved to keep my end of the deal.

One day, I told Henny that I preferred to be home during my lunch breaks. I had a lot of material to study for a new learning commitment I had undertaken and found it a lot easier to concentrate in the solitude of our apartment. She understood. I didn't need any fancy meals, I assured her; a sandwich and a salad would be just fine. And if she didn't feel up to preparing once in a while, I could fix myself something quick.

The transformation wasn't instant or magical. My wife had only recently gone back to work, and my mother-in-law felt it was unfair to saddle her with the additional burden of meal preparation just then. I tried to swallow my resentment, while firmly sticking to my stand. It was important for me to spend my lunch break at home, I politely maintained, even if it meant eating cold food.

I also offered to pick up the baby from the baby-sitter and take care of him until I was ready to go back to *kollel*. Until then, one of my teenaged sisters-in-law had been picking him up and taking him to my in-laws until my wife arrived home from work. At least, I comforted myself, if I didn't have a wife home to serve me, or a warm meal to lift my spirits, I had my adorable son gurgling in the infant seat beside me.

This setup went on for months. I would eat my sandwich and then spend time playing with my son before I took him to my in-laws. My wife would arrive from work straight to her mother's house, where she would eat a warm meal. I felt the optimism draining from my soul. What kind of way was this for a family to exist?

My new *chavrusa*, the old man, frowned at my discouragement. Trust me, he said, the *Aibeshter* will come through with His side of the bargain. You keep the vessel whole, and you'll see, He'll fill it to overflowing.

Several months passed with no apparent change, The only thing that kept me going was my nightly *chavrusa* with my elderly mentor. During those sessions, the spark of Torah kindled a light that spread a tangible halo of warmth around our little apartment.

I found real pleasure in our vibrant arguments, in pounding my fist on the dining-room table and bringing out *sefer* after *sefer* to support my arguments.

My wife usually spent the evenings at her mother's house, and only returned home after we had finished learning. Once, when the baby had a slight cough, she decided to stay home. I saw my *chavrusa's* face register surprise when my wife opened the door for him at 8 o'clock. He nodded a greeting and we sat down to learn. Soon the sounds of our learning filled the little dining room, as we sparred noisily, each defending his position.

Going to the *sefarim shrank,* I sensed a shadow hovering near the entrance. My wife was standing there, smiling faintly, drinking in the scene.

"Do you want me to prepare a tea?" she asked, when my gaze met hers.

I almost dissolved in the sheer rapture of the moment. Such a simple request, yet so laden with meaning for me. It was like the first tentative ray of dawn, like the baby's first faltering step, like the first shaky letter in a little girl's notebook.

Slowly, our personal dawn broke. My wife began staying home in the evenings, reveling in the warmth and sweetness of our learning as she saw to some things in the house. My *chavrusa* always thanked her warmly for the refreshments she served, and blessed us that we see only *berachah* in our home. I fervently answered *Amen*, appreciating the depth of his blessings.

A few months later, my brother-in-law got married. The spotlight of my in-laws' attention swiveled to the new couple, and my wife instinctively gravitated more toward our own home. She cut her hours at work and began to prepare dinner for both of us at home.

The first time I smelled soup simmering in our very own kitchen, I thought my heart would burst out in song. I had been eating sandwiches for several months, alone with my little infant son in our cold kitchen. Suddenly the house felt so warm, so whole, so full of the *Ribono shel Olam's* abundant blessings I had been desperately awaiting.

Baruch Hashem, I've merited to partake of many bowls of soup since, but I have never yet recaptured the taste of that first steaming bowl. In it, I'm sure, was a little of the taste of *Gan Eden,* the flavor of sweat and toil, of persistence and *emunah* and *tefillah.* In it was the taste of *shalom,* so painstakingly achieved, so patiently cultivated.

We've been married for 17 years now, and have, *bli ayin hara,* a family of eight lovely children. We live in one of the blossoming new neighborhoods about an hour's drive from Yerushalayim, where we were able to afford a bigger apartment for our growing family.

When we speak about the early days, my wife cringes. "I can't believe I was that callous," she says, "What gave you the strength to persevere?"

And in my mind's eye, I see an elderly man with compassionate eyes, standing right beside me, prodding me to go on.

Not every vessel can remain whole. Sometimes there is an intrinsic flaw, a serious chink that necessitates its dissolution; often what appears to be a jagged crack is in fact an integral part of the design. The design fashioned by our Creator to help us strengthen the vessel so He can fill it with His infinite blessings.

The Labor of Love

I walked into the house, unzipped the baby's snowsuit, and ran to start the washing machine. As I got into a comfortable pair of slippers, I casually checked my messages on the answering machine. The guy from the heating company calling back; Chany Buxbaum asking me if I could switch car pools; my mother, if I had gotten her message yesterday. Nothing prepared me for the sudden lurch in my stomach, the intense rush of blood to my temples brought on by the next message.

"Hi, it's Tehilla Wagner, Morgenstern. Remember me? I thought you might want to know that I had a baby girl. I guess I'll try another time."

Beep.

Time stood still.

The washing machine, the car pool, the heating company; I was oblivious to all of it.

Tehilla Morgenstern.

Tehilla.

Did I remember her?

When I opted to spend the last summer before my wedding, in camp, I joked to my friends about my decision.

"I'm going to spend the rest of my life being a wife; this is my last chance for some single-minded fun."

Little did I know.

The summer started innocently enough. I reveled in the distinct smell of damp grass and wood, and stayed up late nights planning *shiurim,* preparing for activities and helping revise the script for the major play.

Knowing that my destiny would be taking me to unknown vistas in the very near future turned the simple notion of camp life into a sentimental experience. I'd spent the past five summers as a staff member and nearly half of the girls on grounds had been my campers at some point.

I was excited for the opportunity to exchange a few words with them whenever we met in the dining room or in between activities. Being mainly involved behind the scenes, however, I didn't have much actual contact with them.

So I was surprised when I collapsed into bed one night, close to dawn, and a little pink memo note fluttered off my pillow. I switched on the night-light and scraped the note off the weathered wooden floor.

"Dear Tzivy,

I don't know if you even remember me, but I definitely remember you. I need to speak to someone and I think you're the right person. I know you're crazy busy and don't need another pest on your head, but I'm going NUTS ... I'll be waiting for you behind the red shed during rest hour. Thanks a million, Tehilla (Morgenstern)"

My eyes gobbled the lines curiously and then slowed down to read each word. Though the note was signed at the bottom, I instinctively turned it over to check for another lead. Blank. I read the note again, and then tucked it under my pillow.

Tehilla Morgenstern had been a camper of mine three years earlier. She was slight, cute looking, and had an endearing sense of humor. We had never had any major personal connection, but I definitely remembered her. She had played the main lead in the play two years before, and I had spent many hours perfecting her performance with her.

Tehilla was a J.C. now herself. She was right; I *was* crazy busy. I certainly had enough to do during rest hour. The nurturer inside me, however, had been nudged. If Tehilla had sought me out, she was probably desperate. I was filled with a sense of mission as I flicked off the night-light and drifted off to sleep.

All through the next day I couldn't get my mind off Tehilla. After *davening*, I read the note again, trying to pick up a clue. Was something going on in her personal life? Was it a problem with one of her campers? Perhaps it was just a bad case of politics. There was no use guessing, I chided myself. Whatever it was, it was important

The Labor of Love / 329

enough to have made Tehilla call out for help. I would be there for her.

Behind the red shed, I found a very different Tehilla from the fun-loving camper I remembered. The three years had done their job and she looked taller and more sophisticated than when I'd been her counselor. Though her face still sported a charming smile, something had changed in her eyes. Was it maturity? Sadness? Worry?

"Thanks a million, Tzivy," she started hesitantly, as she pulled a leaf off a nearby bush and nervously ripped it apart.

"It's fine, Tehilla." I was careful to convey candid concern without sounding too eager to help.

Tehilla shot a furtive glance around the empty field.

"First of all, you have to promise me that not a word of this goes anywhere. I know how it is; I have my own issues with campers. You think you can help and you start getting people involved. Tzivy, I chose you because, of this whole staff, I think I can trust you."

I nodded solemnly. I didn't know what had prompted Tehilla's decision, but I would certainly do my utmost to respect it.

Tehilla sighed, crumbling another leaf into tiny shreds.

Campers and politics off the list, I thought. Tehilla obviously had some internal conflict pressing heavily on her. I looked at her expectantly, waiting for her to gather the courage to spill the beans.

She gave me another lingering glance, her eyes on me, her thoughts deep within herself. Then she plunged ahead.

Tehilla's father, it seemed, had been seriously involved in some shady business, of which the family had had no inkling. Someone, allegedly a close business colleague, had reported him to the authorities and the police had come for him in the middle of the night.

Tehilla had already been in camp. She had gotten an emergency phone call from her younger sister, Chana Rochel, the next morning. Chana Rochel had sounded traumatized. Tehilla's own voice faltered as she described the scene.

It had been late Thursday night; her father had already gone to sleep and she had been finishing up in the kitchen together with her mother. They were to be leaving with the family for the mountains the following morning.

The knocking had begun civilly. When Tehilla's mother had checked the peephole in alarm to see who it could be at this late hour, she had nearly passed out. Four grim-faced police officers in uniform were standing at her doorstep.

When she didn't answer right away, the knocking turned into ringing and violent kicking. Several of the children woke up and stumbled out of bed. It was a spectacle out of a medieval scene.

The officers broke into the house, gravely read the charges, and dragged Tehilla's father down the stairs. There was no time to negotiate, to pack up respectably, to part in privacy. Two of the officers gruffly escorted her father to the waiting car; the other two flashed a search warrant and proceeded to recklessly pull apart the cartons they had just spent hours packing.

Tehilla was the oldest of 10 children; the youngest a 5-week-old baby. Her mother was lost now. Out of the blue, she had been left with a tiny baby and a family of children, the whole burden of her husband and her household on her shoulders. She had no clue regarding legal procedures, and even less of an idea of how she would finance them.

I listened intently. The grassy fields, the warm breeze, the strains of lively music coming from the bunkhouses, all seemed miles away. Tehilla had dropped her casual veneer. She was crying freely, continuously removing wet strands of hair from her face.

"What's going to happen now, Tzivy? I'm afraid my mother is going to fall apart."

There was some cheery announcement over the loudspeaker. Rest hour was over. Tehilla couldn't go to her bunk this way. I told her I'd arrange for someone else to take the activity, and that if she wanted, we could meet again after night activity. As an older staff member, I had my own "bedroom," if it could be called that. It was a tiny cubicle, but at least it afforded some privacy. After some lame protest that she would be fine, Tehillah acquiesced. I hurried to the office to take care of finding a stand-in for her.

After night activity, Tehilla was there again, waiting.

"I don't even know what I want from you, Tzivy," she said apologetically.

"My mother would faint if she knew I was telling someone all

The Labor of Love / 331

of this, but I have to get it off my chest. I feel like I'm going off the deep end. I haven't slept one decent night since last Friday. My hands are trembling and I am literally gagging on my food."

Someone burst into the room.

" Tzivy, here you — Oh, you're in the middle of talking to someone?"

Tehilla blushed furiously, shifting her weight from one foot to the other as she fumbled with my pillowcase. I tried to sound casual.

"We're just trying to straighten out a little hitch. Anything important you wanted?"

"Never mind. I just wanted to know if Shany Mashitz was available to give a double *shiur* tomorrow. I'll figure it out already. Sorry for intruding."

"Some little hitch," Tehilla smiled wryly, as the screen door slammed shut. "I'm only having a mini nervous breakdown."

I laughed despite myself. Tehilla had always had a flair for drama.

We spoke until the wee hours of the morning. Actually, Tehilla did most of the talking. I listened quietly as she vented a torrent of feelings. It seemed things were a lot more complicated than they appeared on the surface.

Though her father's sudden arrest had brought everything to the fore, there was a lot of baggage that Tehilla had been carrying around with her for a long time. Her mother was a high-strung perfectionist who demanded an awful lot of her children. She ran a tight ship and expected things to be in perfect order all the time. Their relationship was very strained.

Tehilla's younger sister, Chana Rochel, had always borne the brunt of her mother's expectations. She played the perfect martyr, never going on class trips, always staying home from *chagigahs* and parties in order to baby-sit. While Tehilla did her share of work, she was a social butterfly who thrived on school and camp functions. Next to Chana Rochel, she was made to feel like a selfish, lazy, good-for-nothing.

"It's bad enough to be measured up," Tehilla chuckled sadly. "It's pathetic when it's your younger sister and you're always being measured *down*."

Tehilla didn't even know what her father's job entailed. All she had ever heard was something vague about real estate, and all she knew was that he was almost never home. He compensated for his absences by footing the bills his wife rang up. They were a large family and had always lived in style.

"On the outside, we look like the most put-together family," Tehilla whispered. "But it's a major mess on the inside." She was talking quickly, almost afraid that she would regret having spoken.

"I feel like the biggest traitor telling you all of this. My mother's the most secretive person. Where she shops is a secret; how much she paid is a secret; everything is top secret. Having her whole life exposed now must be the worst torture, even worse than the actual thing."

We sat together on the bed talking until the cacophony of crickets chorusing outside was drowned out by the shrill chirping of birds. A truck lumbered down the cobbled path to the camp kitchen, and Tehilla looked at her watch.

"*Raboseinu, higia z'man Kerias Shema shel Shacharis!* (Oops! It's almost time to daven.) There I go again, selfish brat. You can't even spend your morning sleeping. How are you going to manage?"

"Leave my problems to me, Tehilla. And by the way, I don't go for name-calling. You're not selfish and you're not a brat."

The light of dawn was quickly infiltrating, parting the dusky curtains around our private perch. The chill of the dew fresh on the grass and the sound of screen doors slamming was the cue for Tehilla to get up.

"I don't know how to thank you," she said, her eyes misting over again. Her pale face looked so fragile in the early-morning light. An almost imperceptible ripple of tenderness fluttered inside me.

"I can't even tell you not to lose too much sleep over me. You already did."

"Cut it out, Tehilla," I whispered, putting my arm around her shoulder. "It's not the first all-nighter I've ever pulled. You go to sleep now. And if you need me later, just leave a message for me in the office."

Relationships are an interesting phenomenon. Some bonds are welded slowly and laboriously, following the tedious, traditional,

The Labor of Love / 333

stitch-by-stitch rhythm before they are knitted into the hardy weave of loyalty and love. There are those exceptions, however; alliances cemented by the whispered baring of souls in the stillness of night, by the dire despair of one heart finding refuge in another, that gives vent to a fierce gush of faithfulness, an almost heady sense of intimacy.

Just the night before, the name Tehilla Morgenstern had been nothing more than a curious scrawl at the bottom of a pink memo note. As I brushed my teeth now and washed my face some 29 hours later, an all-consuming concern for her welfare tugged at my heart.

When I think back to that last summer in camp, I don't think of the theme song, the activities, or the play, though my heart and soul were invested in them. I don't think of the dreams and aspirations of a girl engaged to be married, though they must have been playing with my thoughts. All I can recapture, as vividly as if it were today, is my intense preoccupation with alleviating Tehilla's misery.

Torn between my pledge to keep her disclosure in confidence, and by my sense of inadequacy to handle the crisis by myself, I spent my days and nights agonizing over what to do. I knew I'd lose Tehilla's trust if I approached anyone on the staff, and yet I couldn't bear to see her suffering. Though there were rumors circulating, no one besides for me knew the extent of her emotional turmoil.

I spent hours combing through *sefarim,* listening to tapes, jotting down any encouraging thoughts I came across, any source of inspiration that could be of help to Tehilla.

Aside from her deep inner pain, Tehilla had a practical dilemma to deal with. She knew her family needed her; her sister, Chana Rochel, was taking care of all the children in the mountains, while her mother was in the city with the newborn baby trying to sort things out. Whenever her mother did join them, she was tense and critical. Chana Rochel was collapsing.

On the other hand, Tehilla didn't feel right dropping her job as a counselor, cold turkey. The last thing she wanted was to be the talk of the entire camp. We spent long hours discussing the options. With Tehilla's permission, I got in touch with a professional and presented the predicament, carefully disguising the particulars, of course.

In the end, Tehilla decided she would finish the first half and then go home. There was another week and a half left. When I went off campgrounds that week, I searched for something special to bring back for Tehilla, a parting gift of sorts. I found a poignant card in a Hallmark store expressing just what I wanted to convey.

Adding a few personal lines of my own, I wrapped my own copy of a beautiful *sefer* I had introduced to Tehilla, and taped the card to the gift. The next few days passed quickly. Tehilla was petrified of going home. She was afraid of facing reality, of feeling her mother's rejection again, of dealing with her younger siblings' questions. I tried to coach her, to give her some tools to be able to handle the multiple challenges ahead.

When Tehilla came to bid her final goodbye, I discreetly slipped the package into her handbag. I walked her to the gate and squeezed her hand. The tumult of luggage scraping against tar and the shrill drama of teenage departures snuffed out the privacy of the moment. I swallowed hard as the car pulled away. She was gone.

I remember feeling a vague sense of emptiness as I trudged back up to the bunkhouses. My thoughts had been so centrally focused on Tehilla for such a concentrated period of time. I had spent the last few weeks in and out of crises with her, talking, listening, advising on an almost hour-to-hour basis. I suddenly felt strangely purposeless, though I had a million issues begging for my attention.

This is what mothers must feel like when they marry off their children, the thought crossed my mind. I knew it was presumptuous to make the comparison, but something of the hollow ache, the itching worry, something of the piece of my heart that had left the camp gates with Tehilla evoked the association.

I continued to participate in staff meetings and offer my critique of the play practice. Something inside me, however, always had one eye on the watch, one ear cocked in anticipation of a telephone call, one finger on Tehilla's emotional pulse.

I never initiated the calls; I didn't want to force myself on her. Besides, I never knew when her mother would be home and didn't want to risk getting Tehilla into trouble. Most mothers didn't fancy their teenagers confiding in some 21-year old mentor, let alone when the subject of the disclosures were that mother's darkest secrets.

Tehilla, though, called me often enough. Her mother was hardly ever in the mountains and in between her duties, she found time to closet herself away with the phone. From mundane questions about getting stains out of laundry to her innermost anxieties and difficulties, she knew I was always there for her.

The summer drew to a close and I bid emotional farewells to the people and the place I'd known since I'd been 11 years old. I came home to my family, my job, and my wedding day almost upon me.

"Last licks over," my mother joked affectionately. "Now it's for real, Tzivy. Hope you're ready to jump right in, because there's a lot to be done."

There was. I had new classes of students, tons of material to cover before Yom Tov, and lists of shopping to see to. Invitations had to be ordered, an apartment found, and myriad other little things to arrange. Still, Tehilla was at the forefront of my mind all the time. Her life was in shambles and she needed my support.

Tehilla's father had been released on bail. Tehilla claimed he was a broken man. He couldn't get out of bed in the morning and had no desire to do anything. It was demoralizing to watch her father slumped in the recliner for hours, moaning and staring into space. Her mother was stressed beyond words, and the children were terribly affected.

I knew the circumstances called for professional intervention, but my hands were tied. Tehilla claimed that her mother had severely admonished them not to reveal what was going on. The only person her mother ever spoke to herself was a brother-in-law who had became involved.

The only thing I was able to do was apply first aid to a wounded soul. I listened and empathized, cried along with Tehilla and tried to lift her spirits. When her mother flew to Canada for a few days, I dropped by with freshly baked cookies and helped her with the household chores. I knew my own neglected responsibilities would wait.

Tehilla sent me a moving card on *erev Rosh Hashanah*. All throughout Yom Tov, as I davened for myself and my *chassan*, I implored Hashem to bring relief to Tehilla and her family soon. I begged Him to grant me continued *sechel* to guide her, and the emotional resources to be there for her when she needed me.

Yamim Tovim passed. There were new crises every day. I tried all my powers of persuasion to get Tehilla to speak with someone older and wiser. I mentioned the name of a respected Rebbetzin who had a wealth of experience dealing with traumatic situations. Tehilla scrapped the idea.

Things couldn't continue the way they were going. Tehilla sounded so bad, I was sometimes afraid for her emotional welfare. She looked pale as a ghost and had lost a considerable amount of weight. In my desperation to do something, I presented my dilemma to a wise Rebbetzin whose counsel I had sought on several occasions.

"This is a question for *daas Torah*," Rebbetzin Goldstein stated unequivocally after listening to the quandary I was in. " Involving a third party in these instances can be complicated and tricky. Only a rav can determine if the severity of the situation overrides your commitment to keep things confidential."

Giving me the name and number of a respected Rav who had experience in these matters, she assured me that if outside intervention was indeed indicated, she would be glad to be of assistance.

I hung up the phone feeling a little lighter. The responsibility for Tehilla and her family wasn't resting solely on me. I would follow the advice of *daas Torah*, secure in the knowledge that I was doing the right thing.

Two days later, I was sitting in the Rav's study, not believing my own gumption. My concern for Tehilla was driving me to do things I would have shied away from doing under any other circumstances.

The Rav was quick to dispel my discomfort with his patience and understanding. He listened carefully to my detailed account, occasionally interjecting with a question. After hearing me out and summing up the facts to make sure he had gotten them right, he clearly ruled that a competent and wise person needed to be drawn into the picture. I mentioned Rbebetzin Goldstein and his eyes lit up.

"Yes, she's definitely the right person," he confirmed, "I trust her 100 percent to handle the situation with sensitivity and tact. Tell her that I told you to fill her in on the details."

Mission accomplished. I felt a huge stone roll off my chest.

The weeks went by. Tehilla was trying to make a decision about the upcoming seminary year. Her heart was split between her obligations to her family and her dream of attending a seminary in Eretz Yisrael. I helped her sort through her thoughts and advised her to present the question to an understanding Rav. I did a lot of legwork, calling friends who had connections in various seminaries, writing recommendation letters and helping Tehilla find the right person to whom to pose her predicament.

Those were the days when I'd finish preparing at 1 o'clock in the morning and then sit on the phone with Tehilla until some unearthly hour, trying to smooth out her present and map out her future. Then, of course, I'd pretend to be perfectly well rested the next morning, not wanting to aggravate my parents in those tense weeks before my wedding.

My invitations arrived and we sat down to stamp and address them. I felt my hand tremble as I wrote out Tehilla's envelope, felt my heart surge with a well of hopes and prayers for her. I took my pen and let my heart spill onto the back of the invitation. I described how much she occupied my thoughts all the time and how especially at my own *simchah*, during those elevated moments under the *chuppah*, I would be entreating for her and her family. I signed off warmly, stressing that I wanted to see her there until the very end. Then, not trusting the conventional postal service, I slipped the invitation into an opaque bag and gave it to a trusted colleague of mine to deliver to Tehilla in school.

When I didn't get any response, I felt a faint sense of unrest. Though I had a million and one things crowding my schedule in those hectic, pre-wedding weeks, I was still troubled by the absence of Tehilla's phone call. Had she perhaps not received the invitation?

Come to think of it, she actually hadn't called for some time, even before I had sent the invitation. I picked up the phone without too much thought. As soon as she answered, I detected a subtle change in her voice. I couldn't put my finger on it.

"How are things, Tehilla?" I greeted her with genuine concern.

"*Baruch Hashem*, much better really."

Oh?

"Someone finally stepped in and things are really falling into place, *Baruch Hashem*."

"Really?"

I was taken aback. It seemed like a very dramatic turnabout since the last time I had spoken to her.

What about her father's depression? The tension in the house? Her complex relationship with her mother? Who? What? When?

If I had expected to elicit details, though, Tehilla wasn't very forthcoming.

"I got your invitation."

Oh, so she *had* received it.

Why the dispassionate tone? I suddenly felt like blushing, thinking of the warm inscription I'd penned. What had happened? Was she angry with me for having involved someone?

"I didn't think I'd have to wait for your response card," I tried sounding cool. It came out rather lukewarm.

"Sorry, I was just so busy with everything; I didn't get a chance to call you."

Sorry?

Oh.

She hadn't had a chance to call me. I had the queer sensation of having slept through something. When had I turned into her duty phone call?

Suddenly, there was nothing to say. Everything was "*Baruch Hashem*, really okay" and "*Baruch Hashem*, really under control."

May all of Klal Yisrael's problems be so speedily solved, I thought sardonically.

Somehow, we wound up the awkward conversation. I hung up feeling strange. More than strange. Baffled, stung, used. My mind was reeling. What had effected this sudden shift in attitude?

I tried to replay our last conversation. Tehilla had called me some time after midnight. I distinctly remembered that, because my

The Labor of Love / 339

father had been displeased, to say the least. She had sounded terribly agitated. I had implored her to seek out Rebbbetzin Goldstein and she had refused. She'd insisted that she wouldn't feel comfortable and that her mother would be furious.

After that phone call, I had indeed contacted Rebbetzin Goldstein. She had said she would pursue the matter if she got a go-ahead from a rav, and she had assured me that no one would know I had been the catalyst.

And now Tehilla was saying that "someone had stepped in and things were really much better." What did that mean? They certainly hadn't gotten her father off the hook; the trial wasn't scheduled for another few months. Was her mother speaking to someone? What about the kids?

I had a bunch of question marks and not one decent answer. Blank. It was one big blank. All I knew was that somewhere, somehow, the tables had turned on me. From the sought-out mentor, I was suddenly the nag. From the 24-hour crisis hotline, I'd become a wrong number. Currently out of service.

It was painful. Unbearably painful.

I thought of the invitation, the cards, the *sefer* I'd given her. I thought of the hours and hours of precious time, the sleepless nights, the *tefillos* on her behalf. Even if I had to, it would be impossible to describe the weight of her emotional load, the strain of guarding her secret, the heavy burden of knowing I was her sole support system.

What had I done to deserve this sudden stab in the heart?

I was suddenly fuming. What did Tehilla think, that she could take anybody for an emotional ride and then just leave them stranded in no-man's-land without ever planning to come back? It was a good thing I had called her; she hadn't sounded as if it had been on her agenda to phone me at all. And I, like a fool, had been standing and waiting, consumed with worry about her welfare.

Who was the "someone" who had stepped in? Did she have any inkling that it most likely had been my doing, that I had spent hours trying to get through to Rebbetzin Goldstein and talking to her?

I was sweating profusely. I wanted to pretend I didn't care. I had been there for Tehilla; Heaven knew I had been. If she didn't need me anymore, I wanted to say, then I certainly didn't need her.

The words stuck in my throat, though. Stuck in my throat, and caught my ego, snagging it right across the center.

I *did* care. And I *did* need her. I needed her trust and I needed her recognition. In a distorted twist of irony, I almost needed her dependence. Tehilla had been such an integral part of the last few months of my life. I hadn't *davened* without mentioning her name, I hadn't prepared a lesson without thinking of her.

I had grown so accustomed to giving intensely; I had become almost addicted to the fulfillment that comes with this kind of beneficence. Without realizing it, I had become reliant on the gratification of feeling so totally indispensable.

My mind slowed down. Tehilla had sought me out when she had needed me. I had given her everything I could give her and now she had decided that she wanted to try and walk on her own. Was I going to insist that she hold my hand?

I spent the next few days engaged in constant inner dialogue. One moment, I was smoldering with hurt, too injured to reason, the next moment I was taking a tour of my mental archives, analyzing incident after incident, trying to come up with a clue, a trace, some shred of a reason to explain Tehilla's abrupt change of heart. I wavered unsteadily between curiosity and coldness, between wonder and worry, rationalization and resentment.

Tehilla called once in between to ask me for a number of a mutual acquaintance. She appeared to be back to her breezy old self, talking about school and camp as if nothing had ever happened. *Do I know you from somewhere?* I was tempted to ask, but I swallowed the impulse.

Give her what she needs, my intellect dictated. *She needs to feel strong, independent, self-sufficient; give her the feeling.*

But it's only a sham, my feelings shot back. *Who knows what's really going on; maybe she needs help.*

Maybe. My intellect acceded. *But right now she doesn't need your help.*

Why?

The Labor of Love / 341

I don't know.
It hurts.
Giving hurts sometimes.

I never did find out exactly what had triggered the switch. Perhaps Tehilla felt smothered by our relationship. Perhaps she couldn't take the tension of concealing it from her mother. Or maybe things were indeed looking up and she regretted having revealed all her vulnerabilities in the heat of her hysteria.

Whatever her rationale was, it hurt deeply. I felt an almost physical throbbing sensation where the bud of Tehilla's trust had been torn out of my life. If she had only been open about her feelings; if she had only told me she needed some space instead of slamming the door on my outstretched arm. She had, after all, been the one to reach out, to grab that arm when things had been at their worst.

I wasn't waiting for a thank-you, for an expensive gift or a fanciful poem. I had given Tehilla out of honest concern; her relief alone was enough of a reward. If she felt ready to pick up the pieces of her own life, I respected that. All I would have asked for was a heartfelt goodbye, a personal, candid, explanation, instead of the cold stone flung in my face. Was that too much to expect?

Tehilla came to my wedding, but it was a mere charade. Instead of that intense moment I'd envisioned, that deep embrace of two hearts that have scaled adversity together, she flashed a charming smile and pecked me formally on the cheek. Then she was lost in the circle of my friends and acquaintances from camp, laughing and dancing like one of them.

The only thought that kept me smiling, despite the enormous lump in my throat, was the knowledge that true selflessness was the kind that went uncelebrated down below and waited to be reaped, intact, up on High. Watching Tehilla's receding profile, I could almost smell the sweet promise of Heavenly rewards undiminished by earthly indulgences of recognition and gratification.

It took a long time for the hurt to heal, for the pain to go away. It was a relentless process, an *avodah,* an ongoing haul up the steepest mountain there is, the rugged path that traverses the distance between heart and mind.

In those early days, I used to find comfort in dreaming of a happy ending where Tehilla would grow up and realize the extent of her debt, perhaps even apologize for the magnitude of the pain she had inflicted on me. I've come, since, to acknowledge that neither the ending nor my happiness is contingent upon Tehilla.

It is about *my* growth, *my* realization, *my* understanding that the reward for giving is not meted out in earthly returns. That credit and recognition, even gratitude, do not exist in the ledger of the true giver.

Selflessness is not the swirl of tenderness that almost compels one to reach out and nurture. It is the ability to extend oneself and give on someone else's terms, and then to retreat when one is no longer needed. It is the policy that characterizes any giveaway sale and eternalizes the business of true *chessed*: no credit, returns or exchanges.

עֹשֵׂה אֵלֶּה לֹא יִמּוֹט לְעוֹלָם.

The doer of these shall not falter forever.

Afterword

I saw a scene,
'Twas so pristine,
A thousand angels all in white,
All pure and clean,
And so serene,
I wanted to ascend in flight.

I gazed in awe,
At what I saw,
Transfixed by tunes too sweet to pen,
And felt so light,
And filled with might,
By words beyond the sphere of men.

I bowed in shame,
And asked the name,
Of one small angel enveloped in fire,
On wings of flame,
They looked the same,
Each crowned and clad in royal attire.

I wished to know,
From whence the glow,
I dared to mouth the words and ask,
What lends the force,
What ethereal source,
To these angels in whose blaze I bask.

And eager to learn,
To whom they would turn,
Which Heavenly servant would they anoint,
To whom did they owe,
Their fiery glow,
I looked to the angels and watched them all point.

To me. To me?!
I twisted to see,
But there they stood nodding, those thousands of scores,
I said, "'Tis all wrong,"
I cannot belong!"
But, lo, they embraced me, and sang, "We are yours."

Those moments you fought,
Those seconds you sought,
Those were the pangs of our Heavenly birth,
Those struggles you thought,
Were surely for naught,
Those were the garments you sent us from earth.

I saw them advance,
They raised me in dance,
And told me, remember, once you return there,
You'll wake from this trance,
Forget not your chance,
And we will protect you and stand ever near.

I felt my heart swell,
They bade me farewell,
Those thousands and thousands of angels in line,
And went on to face,
New trials with grace,
To nurture those thousands of angels of mine.

Glossary

a"h — acronym for *alav hashalom* — peace be upon him. Used in reference to a deceased person.
ahavas Hashem — love of G-d
Aibeshter — (Yid.) The One Above, i.e., the Almighty
Aleinu — concluding prayer of each of the daily services
aleph-beis — the Hebrew alphabet
Aleph Binah — primer used to teach Hebrew alphabet
aliyah — (1) being called to recite a blessing at the public reading of the Torah; (2) immigration to Eretz Yisrael
almanah — widow
ameilim baTorah — those who toil in Torah
ameilus b'Torah — toiling in the study of Torah
arichas yamim — length of days; a long life
Asarah b'Teves — lit. the tenth day of Teves; a fast day of national mourning.
Aseres HaDibros — Ten Commandments
Asher yatzar — blessing recited after using the bathroom
askanus — communal involvement
aveilus — mourning; mourning period
Avinu Av Harachamim — Our Father, Merciful Father
avodah — service of G-d, through self-sacrifice, prayer or self-refinement
avodas Hashem — service of G-d, esp. through prayer
Avos — Forefathers
bachur [pl. *bachurim*] — unmarried young men, generally yeshivah students
b'ezras Hashem — with G-d's help
b'seder — O.K.
baal tokei'a — one who blows the shofar
baalei teshuvah [sing., *baal teshuvah*] — a penitent
balabus — Yiddish for *baal habayis* — head of the household
balabusta — (Yid.) exemplary wife and homemaker
Baruch Hashem — Blessed is G-d

Bas kol — a voice that emanates from Heaven
bas Yisrael — a Jewish girl
Batya — In England, young girls' groups that have social gatherings on the Sabbath
bayis ne'eman b'Yisrael — a faithful Jewish home
bayis shel Torah — a Torah home
bechor — firstborn son
bedikas chametz — search for leaven on the night preceding the eve of Passover
becher [pl. *bechers*] — (Yid.) cup used for wine when reciting Kiddush
bein adam laMakom — between man and his Maker
bein hazmanim — intersession
beis hamidrash — study hall
Beis HaMikdash — Holy Temple
bekelach — (Yid.) cheeks
ben Torah [pl., *bnei Torah*] — observant Jew; a yeshivah student
ben zachar — a male child
bentching — reciting Grace after Meals
berachah [pl., *berachos*] — (1) blessing; (2) an invocation of Divine favor
berachah v'hatzlachah —blessing and success
beriah — creation
bikur cholim — (1) visiting the sick; (2) u.c. organization that coordinates programs for the welfare of the sick
bitachon — trust in G-d
bli ayin hara — lit., without a bad eye; traditional expression to forestall the negative impact of possible jealousy
Borei olam — Creator of the universe
bris — circumcision or the celebration thereof
Bubby — (Yid.) grandmother
bulkelach — (Yid.) challah rolls
chaburos [sing. *chaburah*] — learning groups whose members aspire to explore a given area of study
chagigahs — celebrations, festivities
Chagim U'zmanim — school subject
chalakah — boy's first haircut, usually at the age of 3

chalilah — Heaven forbid

Chanukah — Festival of Lights commemorating the Maccabee's rededication of the Temple

charatah — regret

chasdei Shamayim — Heaven's kindness

chassan — bridegroom

chassidim [sing., *chassid*] — (1) followers of a chassidic leader (2) pious individuals

chasunah — wedding

chatzos — midday or midnight

chaveirim — friends, fellow students

chavrusa — learning partnership, study partner

Chazal — acronym for *chachameinu zichronim livrachah* — our Sages of blessed memory — refers to Torah Sages

cheder — elementary school

cheder yingelach — (Yid.) schoolboys

chelek — share

cheshbon — reckoning, accounting

chessed [pl. *chassadim*] — act(s) of lovingkindness

chinuch — education, upbringing

chinuch habanim — children's [proper] upbringing

chizuk — encouragement

chodesh — month

cholent — (Yid.) stew that simmers from the onset of Shabbos until it is eaten at the Shabbos day meal

chovos hahishtadlus — obligatory effort

Chumash — Five Books of Moses

chuppah — (1) marriage canopy; (2) marriage ceremony

churban — destruction, specifically of the First and Second Temples

daas — wisdom

daas Torah — Torah viewpoint and perspective

daven — (Yid.) pray

derashah — sermon or discourse

derech halimud — study plan

din — strict justice

ehrlicher Yid — (Yid.) upright Jew

einikel [pl., *einiklach*] — (Yid.) grandchild

eishes chayil — a woman of valor; a dedicated wife

eitzah [pl., *eitzos*] — advice

emes — truth

emunah — faith, belief in G-d

emunah peshutah — a simple, basic faith

erev Shabbos — the eve of the Sabbath

frum — (Yid.) religious, Torah observant

gabbai — (Yid.) synagogue sexton; attendant of a Chassidic rebbe

Gadol [pl., *Gedolim*] — eminent Torah scholar

gam zu l'tovah — This, too, is for the good

Gan Eden — Garden of Eden; Paradise

gedank — (Yid.) thought

Gemara — Talmud

geshmak — (Yid.) sweet, enjoyable

geulah — redemption

gezel — theft

Giveret — Miss. / Mrs.

grammen — (Yid.) rhymes, generally humorous and clever

hachnassas orchim — hospitality

Haggadah — the story of the Exodus related at the Pesach seder

Hakadosh Baruch Hu — the Holy One, Blessed is He

hakaros hatov — appreciation, gratitude

halachah [pl., *halachos*] — a Torah law; the body of Torah law

Hallel — Psalms 113-118; recited on Rosh Chodesh and festivals

Hallelukahs — part of Shacharis prayer service

Hashgachah — refers to Divine Providence on a personal level

hashkafah — Jewish ideology

hatzlachah — success

Havdalah — ritual ceremony marking the end of the Sabbath or holidays

hechsherim [sing., *hechsher*] — Rabbinic certification, generally on food

hefker — ownerless

hentelach — (Yid.) small hands

Hilchos Shabbos — laws of the Sabbath

hishtadlus — effort

hotzaos Shabbos — Sabbath expenses

illui — genius

in gutte veggen — (Yid.) on the proper path

ir haTorah — city of Torah

Ivris — Hebrew language

kabbalah [pl., *kabbalos*] — to accept upon oneself a stringency in the desire to become spiritually elevated

Kabbalas Shabbos — Friday-eve prayers welcoming the Sabbath

Kaddish — prayer recited by mourners

kallah — bride
kapitel — (Yid.) chapter
kashrus — Jewish dietary laws
kavannah [pl. *kavannos*] — concentration, intent; specifically, intentions during prayer or religious observance
kavod — honor, esteem
kavod haTorah — give honor to the Torah
kedushah — (1) holiness, sanctity; (2) u.c., prayer recited during the repetition of *Shemoneh Esrei*
Kerias Shema — three paragraphs of the Torah recited twice daily, beginning with the words *Shema Yisrael*
kesher — bond
kever [pl., *kevarim*] — gravesite
kezayis — halachic unit of measure equal to the volume of an olive
kibbud av va'em — respect one's parents
kiddush — festive gathering following the Sabbath or festival prayer service
Kiddush Shem Shamayim — sanctifying G-d's Name
kinnos — poems of lament and mourning recited on *Tishah b'Av*
kippot [sing., *kippah*] — skullcaps
kiruv — outreach
kishronos — skills, aptitudes, talents
klal — group, community
klapped — (Yid.) banged on the lectern to silence the congregation
kneidlach — (Yid.) matzah balls
kochos — strengths
Kollel — learning program — generally for married men
korban [pl., *korbanos*] — sacrificial offering
Kosel — Western Wall, remnant of the Second Temple
koslei beis hamidrash — within the walls of the study hall
kugel — (Yid.) pudding; a delicacy prepared in honor of the Sabbath
kugelach — (Yid.) a children's game similar to Jacks
kumzitz — (Yid.) lit., come sit; a gathering usually devoted to group singing
l'Chaim — lit., to life! (1) traditional toast; (2) gathering to celebrate an engagement
lamdan — learned individual; Talmudic scholar
latkes — (Yid.) pancakes

lehavdil — to differentiate
levayah — funeral
maamarei Chazal — sayings of the Sages
maasim tovim — good deeds
machnis orach — extend hospitality
machsan — storage room
machsom l'fi — to be careful with everyday speech as a merit for one in need
machul — forgiven
mafteiach — key
maggid shiur — Torah lecturer
maidelach — (Yid.) young girls
makpid — stringent, particular
mashal — parable, analogy
mashgiach [pl., *mashgichim*] — dean of students in a yeshivah who fills the role of adviser and guidance counselor
mashkon — security deposit; pledge
mashpia ruchani — one who exerts a spiritual influence
masmid — diligent student; exceptional Torah scholar
Me'aras HaMachpelah — The Tomb of the Patriarchs
mechanchim — educators
mechanech — (n) educator, (v.) educate
mechaneches [f.][pl., *mechanchos*] — educator, teacher
mechilah — forgiveness
mechilah gemurah — total forgiveness
mechitzah — a partition
mechutanim — parents-in-law of one's child
Medrash — in school, the study of the Sages' homiletical teachings
mehadrin min hamehadrin — extreme stringency in mitzvah observance
meila — never mind; so be it
mein kind — (Yid.) my child
melaveh malkah — meal eaten on *Motza'ei Shabbos* in honor of the departed Sabbath Queen
menahel [f., *menahelet*] — principal
mesiras nefesh — spiritual or physical self-sacrifice; unusual effort or devotion
mesivta — yeshivah high school
metukah shnat ha'oveid — sweet is the sleep of the laborer
mezakeh — to give others merit
mezhinka — (Yid.) last child to be married

Mi shebeirach — prayer recited in the synagogue for the welfare of a particular person or persons

middah [pl., *middos*] — character trait

midrash — the body of the Sages' teachings

mikdash me'at — mini-Sanctuary — a Jewish home where the *Shechinah* resides.

mikveh — pool for ritual immersion

Minchah — afternoon prayer service

minyan — quorum of 10 men needed for conducting a prayer service

mishloach manos — gifts of food sent on Purim

Mishnayos — part of the Talmud based on the teachings of the *Tannaim*

Misrad Hapnim — Ministry of the Interior

mitzvah [pl., *mitzvos*] — a good deed; one of the 613 commandments

mizbei'ach — altar

morah — teacher

moreh derech — mentor

Motza'ei Shabbos — Saturday night

muktzah — items forbidden to be moved on the Sabbath or the festivals

Mussaf — prayer added after Shacharis on the Sabbath, the festivals, and on Rosh Chodesh

mussar — Torah teachings of spiritual and ethical self-improvement; rebuke

nachas — satisfaction, usually from offspring

navi — prophet; (u.c.) in school, subject that studies the Books of the Prophets

neder — promise; oath

negel vasser — (Yid.) ritual washing of the hands upon arising

neis [pl., *nissim*] — miracle

nekudos — vowels of the Hebrew alphabet

neshamah [pl. *neshamos*] — soul

niftar — (1) a deceased individual (2) to pass away

nisayon — challenge, test; connotes a situation that challenge one's faith in G-d

nissim giluyim — outright miracles

ozeret — helper; term for a household cleaning woman in Eretz Yisrael

parashah — weekly portion of the Torah read each Shabbos

parnassah — livelihood

paskened — (Yid.) ruled; rendered a halachic decision

pasuk [pl., *pesukim*] — Scriptural verse

peyos — earlocks

pidyon haben — ritual ceremony of the Redemption of the Firstborn son

pirkei [sing., *perek*] — chapters of

Pirkei Avos — Ethics of The Fathers; section of the *Mishnah*

pirsumei nissa — publicizing a miracle

rabbanim — rabbis

rachamim — mercy, compassion

Rashi — pre-eminent Torah commentary

ratzon Hashem — will of G-d

Rebbe — Chassidic leader who serves as mentor to a following of *chassidim*

rebbetzin — rabbi's wife

rebbi [pl., *rebbeim*] — teacher of Torah subjects

refuah sheleimah b'karov — a complete recovery, speedily

retzonos — desires

Ribono shel Olam — Master of the World — i.e. G-d

rosh hachaburah — head of a group formed to study a specific Torah topic

Rosh Chodesh — the beginning of the new month

Rosh Yeshivah — dean of a Torah institution

ruchniyus — spirituality

salatim — salads

sechel — intellect; good sense

seder [pl. *sedarim*] — (1) study period (2) festive Passover meal replete with rituals, including the reading of the *Haggadah*

sefarim shrank — book case

sefer, [pl. *sefarim*] — book(s)

seudah — meal; esp. a festive meal

sevara — theory, reasoning

Shaarei Shamayim — the Gates of Heaven

Shabbos Kodesh — the Holy Sabbath

shadchan [pl., *shadchanim*] — matchmaker(s)

shalom — peace

Shalom Aleichem — lit., peace be with you. (1) traditional greeting; (2) song of welcome sung on Friday evening prior to the Sabbath meal

shalom bayis — matrimonial harmony

shalom zachar — festive gathering on Friday evening following the birth of a boy

Shechinah — Divine Presence

sheitel — wig

sheitel macher — (Yid.) wig maker or stylist

sheloshim — the 30-day mourning period observed for a deceased relative
shemiras halashon — lit., guarding the tongue. Being careful not to gossip or speak negatively
shemiras hamitzvos — mitzvah observance
Shemoneh Esrei — silent standing prayer that is the main feature of the daily prayer services.
sheva berachos — (1) seven blessings recited at a wedding and during the following week; (2) festive meals honoring the newlywed couple during the week after their wedding
shidduch [pl., *shidduchim*] — marriage match
shiur [pl. *shiurim*] — lecture or discourse
shivah — mourning period
shofar — ram's horn blown on Rosh Hashanah
shomrim — those who guard a corpse until the funeral
shtender — (Yid.) lectern
shuk — market place
shul — (Yid.) synagogue
siddur [pl., *siddurim*]— prayer book
sifrei Torah — Torah scrolls
simchah — joy
simchas hachaim — joy in living
simchos — joyous occasions
siyata diShmaya — the help of Heaven; providential aid from G-d
siyum — (1) conclusion of a portion of Torah or Talmud; (2) celebration marking the completion of a course of study
sponga — method utilizing a stick and a rag used for washing stone floors in Eretz Yisrael
succah [pl., *succos*] — booth in which Jews are commanded to dwell during Succos
sugya — topic in Talmud
tachshit — gem; colloquial word of praise as in a "jewel of a person"
tafkid — purpose in life
tallis — prayer shawl
tallis katan — *tzitzis*
talmid [pl., *talmidim*] — student
talmid chacham [pl., *talmidei chachamim*] — student
Tatty — (Yid.) father
tefillah [pl., *tefillos*]— prayer
tefillin — phylacteries
Tehillim — Book of Psalms
tekias shofar —the blowing of the shofar on Rosh Hashanah
tenaim — betrothal agreement
teva — nature
tisch — (Yid.) lit., table. Gathering at a chassidic Rebbe's Sabbath or festival table
Tishah b'Av — the ninth of *Av* — day of mourning and fasting for the destruction of the First and Second Temples
tzaddik [pl. *tzaddikim*] — righteous individual(s)
tzaros — problems, trials and tribulations
tzeddakah — charity; charitable deeds
tzeniyus — modesty
tzevaah — last Will and Testament
tzibbur — community
tzintzenes haMahn — the jar of manna kept in the *Beis Hamikdash*
tzitzis — (1) fringed garment worn by Jewish men and boys; (2) fringes on the four corners of a *tallis*
vatranus — the act of being acquiescent and yielding
vort — (Yid.) a festive gathering in celebration of the engagement
yahadus — Judaism, Jewishness
Yamim Noraim — High Holy Days: Rosh Hashanah and Yom Kippur
yarmulke [pl., *yarmulkes*]— (Yid.) skullcap
yemei ratzon — times especially conducive to having one's prayer accepted
yeshuos — salvations, redemptions
yetzer hara — evil inclination
yingelach — (Yid.) young boys
yiras Shamayim — fear of Hashem
yishuv — settlement, esp. in Eretz Yisrael
yishuv hadaas — peace of mind
Yom Tov [pl., *Yomim Tovim*] — festival
yungerleit — (Yid.) young married men
yungerman'chik — (Yid.) young man
z"l — acronym for zecher l'vrachah — may his memory be a blessing. Generally refers to a deceased righteous individual
z'man — time; semester; appointed time
zechus — the merit of a good deed
Zeidy — Grandfather
zemiros — songs of praise sung at Sabbath or Yom Tov meals
zisse — (Yid.) sweet
zivug sheni — second marriage
zocheh — worthy, meritorious